Post-Politics in Context

'A very forceful and compelling argument as to the post-political nature of neoliberal societies.'
Julian Reid, *University of Lapland, Finland*

'In this theoretically sophisticated and wide-ranging book, Taskale shows how regimes of power are consolidated and work through affective logics. With a historically informed analysis and rich illustrative examples, he explores contemporary politics and shows why it fails to deliver.'
Mustafa Dikeç, *Ecole d'Urbanisme de Paris and LATTS*

As disciplines, Politics and International Relations remain dominated by ideas drawn from traditions of liberal internationalism and political realism in which political imagination is preoccupied with command and order, rather than with disruption and emancipation. Yet, they have failed to offer adequate answers to why political action is foreclosed in contemporary times.

Proposed through a historically informed engagement with seminal thinkers, including Walter Benjamin, Friedrich Nietzsche, Gilles Deleuze, and Michel Foucault, and examples from films and contemporary events, Ali Rıza Taşkale presents an original and much needed new perspective to interpret politics in our contemporary societies. He argues that post-politics is a counterrevolutionary logic which aims to create a society without conflict, struggle and radical systemic change.

Post-Politics in Context serves as seminal intervention upon the debate over the depoliticised conditions of contemporary neoliberal society as well as functioning as an introduction to the core theoretical frameworks of alternative tradition of social and political thought in a manner that is lacking in current debates about Politics and International Relations.

Ali Rıza Taşkale is currently an assistant professor of social and political sciences at Hacettepe University, Turkey. His research fields are social and political theory, political philosophy, cinema and political theology. His articles have been published in *Society & Space*, *Theory, Culture & Society* and *Journal for Cultural Research*, along with a number of book chapters in edited volumes.

Routledge Innovations in Political Theory

For a full list of titles in this series, please visit http://www.routledge.com

59 Time, Memory, and the Politics of Contingency
   Smita A. Rahman

60 Michael A. Weinstein
   Action, Contemplation, Vitalism
   Edited by Robert L. Oprisko and Diane Rubenstein

61 Deep Cosmopolis
   Rethinking World Politics and Globalisation
   Edited by Adam K. Webb

62 Political Philosophy, Empathy and Political Justice
   Matt Edge

63 The Politics of Economic Life
   Martin Beckstein

64 The Temporality of Political Obligation
   Justin C. Mueller

65 Epistemic Liberalism
   A Defence
   Adam James Tebble

66 Hegel, Marx, and 21st Century Social Movements
   Democracy, Dialectics, and Difference
   Brian Lovato

67 Ideologies of Experience
   Trauma, Failure, and the Abandonment of the Self
   Matthew H. Bowker

68 Post-Politics in Context
   Ali Rıza Taşkale

Post-Politics in Context

Ali Rıza Taşkale

Routledge
Taylor & Francis Group
NEW YORK AND LONDON

First published 2016
by Routledge
711 Third Avenue, New York, NY 10017

and by Routledge
2 Park Square, Milton Park, Abingdon, Oxon, OX14 4RN

First issued in paperback 2018

Routledge is an imprint of the Taylor & Francis Group, an informa business

© 2016 Taylor & Francis

The right of Ali Rıza Taşkale to be identified as author of this work has been asserted by him in accordance with sections 77 and 78 of the Copyright, Designs and Patents Act 1988.

All rights reserved. No part of this book may be reprinted or reproduced or utilised in any form or by any electronic, mechanical, or other means, now known or hereafter invented, including photocopying and recording, or in any information storage or retrieval system, without permission in writing from the publishers.

Trademark notice: Product or corporate names may be trademarks or registered trademarks, and are used only for identification and explanation without intent to infringe.

Library of Congress Cataloging-in-Publication Data
A catalog record for this book has been requested

ISBN 13: 978-1-138-54347-8 (pbk)
ISBN 13: 978-1-138-18851-8 (hbk)

Typeset in Sabon
by Apex Covantage, LLC

This book is dedicated to my parents,
Yeter and Ali Asker Taşkale.

Contents

Foreword by Julian Reid		ix
Acknowledgements		xi
	Introduction	1
1	Post-Politics: A Theoretical Intervention	21
2	Sovereignty	48
3	Discipline and the Birth of Neoliberal Governmentality	67
4	Societies of Neoliberal Control	94
5	Age of Spite	120
6	Post-Politics to Political Spirituality	138
	Afterword	145
	References	149
	Index	163

Foreword

In the time when philosophers were heroes, the task of philosophy was to recall to presence someone who once existed but who has long since passed away, and yet whose memory serves to inspire those who, captured in the present, are suffering from the declines and degradations which life has undergone. Sadly, philosophy rarely if at all bequeaths us heroes, anymore. And in being shorn of heroes, it is likewise shorn of that political capacity for recollection by which heroic philosophy was defined. To read philosophy today, or to be addressed by philosophers, is, by and large, to encounter the same enfeeblements and degradations encountered in any other kind of subject that we come across or find ourselves unfortunate enough to be assailed by. Philosophers and their academic cronies write and speak with a view to shoring up the crippled styles of existence that define neoliberal time. Philosophy remains, but its heroes have gone.

Fortunately, in Taşkale, we have someone who can help us see and understand the full nature of this problem, for his book makes a very forceful and compelling argument as to the post-political nature of neoliberal time, being very persuasive as to the extent to which the political itself requires saving, in the context of regimes which govern by preventing politics from taking place. It argues this by problematising the ways in which neoliberal regimes govern, focusing specifically on the affective aspects of their strategies, exploring how they produce subjects amenable to their sway—subjects which are incapable of political thought and action.

In other words, Taşkale is writing in the tradition of the very style of philosophy which neoliberalism has sought, successfully, to snuff out. For what his book does, besides condemning this stultified present, is to recall images from the past, not simply of this or that someone, but of the political itself, when the political was still known, and witnessed, seen, and encountered, as the revolutionary event it once was. Taşkale theorises the political, in essence, as the event of revolution, and shows how neoliberalism functions and preserves itself through the prevention of the event of revolutionary thought and action taking place. The post-political, as

Taşkale masterfully shows, refers not simply to the absence of politics but to a condition maintained through the exercise of sovereignty, discipline, government, and control. Preventing the event of revolutionary thought and action is thus strategically managed by neoliberal regimes, and the means to liberate the event of revolutionary thought lies in the revelation of that strategy—the very work which this book performs.

To do this Taşkale builds on and draws from a rich tradition of social and political thought, largely by Foucault and Deleuze, to examine neoliberalism as a regime founded on sovereignty, discipline, government, and control, and he provides a lucid analyses of the ways in which these foundations are organised today. Doing so, his book goes some way beyond the historical analyses provided by Foucault and Deleuze. It also contributes an original account of the way in which a further foundation of neoliberalism is to be found in terrorism and its associated affect of spite.

Taşkale's fundamental purpose is best understood, then, as that of liberating the possibility of the political, conceived as revolutionary thought and action, by utilising the past, just as heroic philosophy once did. Taşkale seeks to draw from the past record of counterrevolutionary events, a memory of the trauma of the failure of revolutions historically, to illuminate the present post-political condition. This way of conceiving the relation between history and politics owes much, as Taşkale makes clear, to perhaps, the work of the very last heroic philosopher, Walter Benjamin, and Taşkale provides a compelling account of the importance of Benjamin for theorising the post-political today.

In every instance of revolt there lives an element that is profoundly spiritual, unnamable, inexplicable, that cannot be reduced to the order of economy, and which has no raison d'etre other than a pure refusal. Yet, at the same time, it invites a naming, an act of fabulation, out of which it can give expression to a people which is simultaneously new in a qualitative sense, no longer bearing the hallmarks of peoples old and buried, but also real and powerful, in a constitutive sense. The task of the storyteller, he or she concerned with the narration of revolt, is to give voice to that spiritual element, to name it, create for it a memory, a myth, out of which it can emerge and declare its truth, however violent and animalistic it may be; each of which are, of course, qualities, fundamentally, of truth, politically speaking. In Taşkale we encounter a writer and thinker from the same spiritual family as those storytellers of times past but not yet forgotten. In the book which follows, he beckons us to join and make ourselves at home in the cellars and attics of their shelters.

Julian Reid

Acknowledgements

Special thanks are due here to Eric Olund for his guidance as well as constant encouragement and support through the travails of writing and completing the book. Thanks are also due to Jessica Dubow for her exemplary readings and invaluable comments on the chapters which now make up this book.

A special mention goes to Julian Reid and Mustafa Dikeç for their continued guidance and inspiration. They offered excellent commentary and valuable feedback on chapters.

I am very grateful to Bülent Diken. Without creative, 'disruptive' ideas he taught me this book would doubtless have assumed a different and more limited form. He remains a most inspiring figure, as a man and as a thinker.

I would also like to thank the group of friends who helped and supported me throughout this whole process: Ersin Vedat Elgür, Nick Piper, Hakkı Kurtuluş, Güncem Gültekin, Tomas Marttila, Deniz Çizmeci, Reşat Volkan Günel, Can Kaya and Esra İşgüzar.

Last but not the least, I would like to thank everyone and everything who has shaped my life and made it a story worth (I hope) telling.

December 2015
Ankara

Introduction

The possibility of properly political action is an ancient question that has been continuously rearticulated through changing conditions. This question of the political is still as urgent as ever in these neoliberal times. Often dubbed 'post-political', current conditions have sparked incisive if sometimes despairing analyses of how and why truly political collective action seems so difficult in the current historical juncture of ever-spreading marketisation and militarisation (Badiou 2012; Bauman 2012; Diken 2009, 2012; Harvey 2005; Žižek 2010, 2011, 2012). Much is said of the debilitating and even violent effects of individualisation from both Marxist and poststructuralist perspectives (Dikeç 2007; Harvey 2003; Mouffe 2005; Rancière 2010; Žižek 2008a, 2008b). But one of the most tantalising but undeveloped aspects of this body of scholarship has been the affective aspects of post-politics. This book offers a systematic theoretical analysis of not only some of the effects of post-politics on political subjectification, but of how its affective logics are integral to its regimes of power, regimes which help condition the field of power in which political subjectification takes place. It theorises the ideological, political, and affective dimensions of post-politics, and its relationship to neoliberalism. Furthermore, discussions of these regimes have largely been confined to the triad of sovereignty-discipline-government familiar from Foucault (2007, 2008) and the regime of control suggested by Deleuze (1995). This book argues that these regimes alone are insufficient to account for the peculiar violence of neoliberalism. It proposes an additional regime, 'terrorism', with its associated affect of 'spite', in order to explore the special relationship between neoliberal capitalism and terrorism.

Whereas this book conceptualises the post-political nature of neoliberalism, many—but not all—of neoliberalism's characteristics are generic to capitalism, and so this book often makes use of the past to make sense of the present. There are different temporal chapters of neoliberalism. And post-politics is a very recent form of neoliberalism. If neoliberalism seeks to expand market-based economic rationalities into all spheres of life (Davies 2014: 244; see also Brown 2015), then post-politics is the current rationality of replacing politics with economics. By seeking to render the political a technical rationality, a calculated and strategic behaviour, post-politics seeks to suppress not only the political but also the ability to debate and critique. It produces a vision of society in which conflict and antagonism are replaced with economic evaluation and measurement. Post-politics is, in short, hostile to politicisation and radical social change.

The book, therefore, seeks to draw the past of counterrevolutionary events, a memory of the trauma of the failure of revolutions historically, to illuminate the post-political nature of contemporary neoliberal societies. As Walter Benjamin (1969: 261) pointed out in the advent of fascism, revolution 'is a tiger's leap into the past', which enables human subjects to fulfil some historic task by linking the present to the time of the virtual. In the process, moments of the past and moments of the present eventually coalesce meaningfully, disrupting the continuum of history and thus providing the subject of history with a theoretical and practical framework for altering the present. And so this book theorises post-politics, based on some retrospective analyses of some key moments in its history and development. It puts relevant theoretical and cultural productions from the past century and more in conversation with current intellectual and historical developments. It examines the specific mechanisms through which post-politics is constituted and explores how it suppresses the political by depoliticised managerial reason. Post-politics is a conscious project of colonisation of politics by economics. It seeks to replace conflict with technique, antagonism with statistical frameworks. In that sense the book is meant as an unmasking of the 'political' logic of post-politics.

And so this book theorises post-politics and historical social regimes and their affective structures. It contends that the analytics of neoliberalism cannot be thought of without post-politics. In other words, post-politics is central to sustaining the dominant neoliberal ideology. Post-politics envisages a society in which lives inhabit a time all of their own, unrelated and unbothered by disruptive 'revolutionary' events. As such, it does not give us, '*all of us*, the space and time to become something else, the right and opportunity to experiment, to enable lines of flight, to forge solidarities' (Amin *et al.* 2000: 26). Post-politics—the institutionalised reaction, the depoliticised expert administration—is the clear logic beneath this process.

The ideal of a world without conflict, antagonism, and radical political change is the problem of post-politics. It is precisely for this reason that confronting post-politics must be a political question, for politics proper is always an intervention into a particular situation, against specific agents and rationalities. If conflict, antagonism, and social change are invisible in contemporary neoliberal condition, the challenge of politics today is to make them appear. The task of politics is, in other words, to shift conflict and antagonism to their proper place. But in what form?

At this point in my discussion, it is perfectly helpful to focus on agonism as a common good that can accommodate conflict, passions, and creative destruction.

Agonism

Agonism is a political theory which, following the ancient Greeks, asserts contest and struggle as the proper bases for politics. In doing so, it challenges some of the fundamental commitments of liberal theory as embodied in procedural/aggregative model (e.g. Schumpeter) and consensualist/deliberative democracy (e.g. John Rawls and Jürgen Habermas). In both models, the primary aim is to achieve a 'rational' consensus by means of free discussion (Habermas 1996; Rawls 1996). Theorists of agonism, however, are sceptical of the possibility of a consensus-based liberal politics. Hence, they specifically focus on what Chantal Mouffe (1996: 247) calls the 'ineradicable character' of 'power and antagonism'.

It is worth noting that there are different versions of agonism, such as the work of Ernesto Laclau, Chantal Mouffe, and William Connolly, but I want to exclusively refer to Connolly's work when I use the term 'agonism'.[1] Heavily inspired by Nietzsche, Connolly's work on identity/difference guides us to construct a politics of adversaries rather than enemies, which would entail an ongoing process of conflict, antagonism, and affect. To articulate Connolly's work in the context of post-politics, I aim to build up a critical approach, returning him to agonism via Nietzsche's *agon,* thus showing the weak sides of his agonistic politics. Conversely, I assert, radical politics based on Nietzsche's *agon* should accommodate conflict and a will to struggle.

William Connolly is a significant exponent of agonistic pluralism. In *Identity/Difference* (2002), he follows a Nietzschean tradition, suggesting that agonistic democracy is capable of mediating the two poles of identity/difference. By both demonstrating the centrality of identity and difference with regard to life while being aware of the dangers of the identities getting dogmatised, Connolly also folds 'care for the protean diversity of human life into the strife and interdependence of identity/difference' (2002: x). Connolly's thesis can be divided into three main propositions. He suggests as a first step that life requires identity. Second, he argues that identities create and maintain differences. Identities are formed by way of constitutive others; they refer themselves to a 'constitutive outside'[2] against which they define themselves. That is to say, identities are structurally incomplete; they are always marked by a constitutive outside which both constructs and deconstructs them. The third proposition is what Connolly calls 'the second problem of evil', which 'emerges out of solutions to the first one' (2002: ix). The second problem of evil, according to Connolly, 'flows from diverse political tactics through which doubts about self-identity are posed and resolved by the constitution of an other against which that identity may define itself' (2002: x). 'To explore this territory,' Connolly writes, 'is to struggle against the evil done by attempts to secure the surety of self-identity' (2002: x).

The two evils of identity/difference, Connolly argues, must be protected. Identity can be the source of 'the second problem of evil', but it is also a defining dimension of life. In this sense contemporary politics does not seek to eliminate identity from the domain of life, for 'to do so would be to work against a public ethos of deep pluralism' (2002: xxii). It is in this respect that Connolly proposes agonistic respect as a constitutive element of politics and society, which consolidates identity through the constitution of difference. Agonistic democracy is based on agonistic respect which 'is a civic virtue that allows people to honor different final sources, to cultivate reciprocal respect across difference, and to negotiate larger assemblages to set general policies'. Agonistic respect is a fundamental political virtue in a society 'in which partisans find themselves in intensive relations of political interdependence' (2002: xxvi). As such, it seeks to combine tolerance with the possibility of 'selective conflict' in its practice. But how can agonistic respect flourish in a society? Agonistic respect 'flourishes most when it becomes a reciprocal virtue cultivated by interdependent partisans' (2002: xxviii). However, agonistic respect for the other is not enough to establish an 'expansive ethos of pluralism'. It also needs to involve the civic virtue of 'critical responsiveness' (Connolly 2005: 127). According to Connolly, whereas agonistic respect 'speaks to relations between already crystallized constituencies', critical responsiveness 'speaks to the relation a crystallized constituency pursues to a disqualified minority struggling to migrate from an obscure or negated place below the register of legitimate identity to a place on that register' (2002: xxviii). To embrace critical responsiveness as a civic virtue 'exposes the extent to which a positive ethos of political engagement exceeds the reach of any fixed code, austere set of procedures, or settled interpretation of moral universals' (2002: xxx). Predicated upon the notion of agonistic respect and critical responsiveness, agonistic democracy thus opens up the space for agonistic relations of adversarial respect (2002: x, 86).

Connolly's work is a significant attempt to link agonism with identity and difference. His understanding of agonism, however, is not devoid of difficulties. In order to clarify this point, we need to take a closer look at Nietzsche's *agon*. As is well known, God dies in Nietzsche's world. But Nietzsche is indeed far more interested in asking what happens when 'God is dead.' Nietzsche points out that if God is dead, then so is Man, or 'at least the conception of humanity favoured by the guardians of social order' (Eagleton 2012: 8). Thus, killing God is not sufficient to get rid of him entirely. A nihilist world is prone to new gods, myths, and idols. Hence, his main concern is to create the Overman whose life is full of passion for greatness in a world without Gods. The Overman is one who revolutionises the idea of himself without pretending that God is still alive. For this to happen, however, the Overman should engage in the art of the struggle because struggle is the essence of life. In his early essay 'Homer's Contest', it becomes obvious that Homer's contest occurs, for Nietzsche, in an 'uninterrupted spectacle of a world of struggle and cruelty' (1954: 34). Thus, Nietzsche values the Greeks for their embrace of cruelty, violence, and destruction, the very affects that made the Greeks' accomplishments achievable. Nietzsche's *agon,* too, is a channel for our destructive affective capacities. The Overman, for instance, is the agonal spirit incarnate (see Thiele 1990: 12). He bears a 'spiritualized enmity' that does not 'stretch out languidly and long for peace desire peace' (Nietzsche 2005: 173). In his world, strife is not the great-vote winner, but it is actually the best policy because from strife, from struggle 'man emerges . . . stronger for good and evil' (Nietzsche 1986: 163). Life is a struggle, a conflict between two necessary aesthetic elements: Dionysus and Apollo. As Apollo creates boundaries, Dionysus transcends them; Apollo is life-preserving, Dionysus life-creating.

The Overman never finishes his labours. And the *agon* provides him the opportunity to enjoy cruelty and transcend boundaries. Which is why the formulations such as the 'full release of . . . hatred as a serious necessity', 'the tiger charged out', or 'the cruelty of the victory' (Nietzsche 1954: 34–39) refer to will to power, the supreme immanent principle of Nietzsche's philosophy: '[a will to power]—when you speak of good and evil too, and of valuations. You still want to create the world before which you can kneel: that is your ultimate hope and intoxication' (Nietzsche 1961: 136). Seen in this perspective, life is will to power, which expresses and seeks to expand itself. Life as will to power forces us to destroy old values and set new ones. Values are, however, not *there* in nature, waiting to be discovered, but instead are created, or willed. And it is through struggle that values can be authentically created. To engage in struggle requires us to view values from the perspective of a will to power as an immanent principle. Significantly, however, will to power should not be understood as success, for success can undermine the benefits derived from the contest. How is victory, therefore, measured? Victory is meaningful only when it 'heightens the feeling of power, the will to power, power itself in man' (Nietzsche 1990: 127). Nietzsche asks: 'What is happiness?' He answers: 'The feeling that power increases—that a resistance is overcome' (Nietzsche 1990: 127). In this sense the struggle is permanent.

At this point, I seek to show that Nietzsche's *agon* has an aesthetic dimension with respect to life. Nietzsche tells us that art is 'the true metaphysical activity of his life' (Nietzsche 1967b: 20). Thus, art and struggle are intimately connected. For Nietzsche, intoxication is indispensable for the agonistic struggle, and this applies to action as well. When it comes to politics, Nietzsche's *agon* should be thought of as an exit point which the will to power may take, be it the sublimation of passions or creativity.

As a common outlet for the will to power, a uniquely political *agon* does not desire *power* but *desires* itself. That is, the political *agon* can only be satisfied insofar as the subject desires something other than power. Thus, though Connolly has made important contributions to the theorisation of democratic politics, there is a fundamental difference between his agonistic politics and the Nietzschean agonist. The key problem arises when he attempts to transfer the ontological *agon* to a normative status. For instance, he agrees with Nietzsche that, ontologically speaking, absolute truth is an impossible one. In his hands, however, this becomes a distinctly liberal-democratic and egalitarian normative claim. In brief, Connolly places the emphasis of Nietzsche's *agon* in entirely the wrong place, writing that

> an ethos of agonistic respect grows out of mutual appreciation for the ubiquity of faith to life and the inability of contending parties, to date, to demonstrate the truth of one faith over other live candidates. It grows out of reciprocal appreciation for the element of contestability in these domains. The relation is agonistic in two senses: you *absorb the agony* of having elements of your own faith called into question by others, and you *fold agonistic contestation* of others into the respect that you convey toward them.
>
> (2005: 123–4)

This passage is a good example of how Connolly attempts to institutionalise Nietzsche's *agon,* which demands respect for others' beliefs. My contention is that any attempt to institutionalise and formalise *agon* is doomed to fail. This is, in fact, what Connolly's agonism is about: the *agon* without the struggle. The Nietzschean *agon* is an ability to interpret, that is, to construct a perspective in which life, along with differences, is felt, experienced, lived. The *agon* is, therefore, not submission to an already established institution; it is sustaining the struggle, the contest, while preparing the stage for potential contingencies. Crucially, and contrary to Connolly, the *agon* does not promote a *liberal respect* for institutions or existing differences; it itself is pure *difference*. The *agon* emerges out of a desire to think beyond the existing practices. As such, it demands its warriors create their values against another's with the aim of deciding whose values are life-affirming and whose life-negating values must be ruthlessly destroyed. In this sense, Connolly's agonistic pluralism predicated on liberal respect is insufficient to produce the agony of the perfect struggle, or Dionysian fervour and intoxication. As a consequence, his agonism, and the emphasis on the opening of more political space, becomes a pseudo-agonism which produces no genuine political events and no genuine political space.

Converting difference into otherness, Connolly's agonism, in short, seems to skip the value of struggle and cruelty. Nietzsche, however, repeatedly celebrates confrontation, struggle, and war. For Nietzsche, life simply is will to power, and will to power is a struggle for mastery over life. Paradoxically, however, Connolly does not accept 'the reading of Nietzsche as the consummate philosopher of world mastery' (2002: 185). As can clearly be seen from the following passage, he writes:

> While such a reading is possible, it is not the single or necessary reading to be drawn from a thinker as protean as Nietzsche. It tends to be given by those who endorse strong transcendental or teleological perspectives. They presume that any ethic of care and self-limitation must flow from a teleotranscendental perspective, and that since Nietzsche noisily repudiates such a perspective, the coiner of the phrase 'will to power' must endorse a ruthless philosophy in which a few exercise mastery over other humans and nature.
>
> (2002: 185)

I agree with Connolly that Nietzsche's agonism is not about world domination. And the same goes for will to power. Will to power as a struggle for 'mastery over life' does not entail domination over people. Instead, it asserts confrontation, struggle, and cruelty as fundamental features of life. But, in Connolly's agonistic democracy, they are seen as positive, generative sources of potentiality. Despite that he is heavily influenced by Nietzsche, the insufficiencies of Connolly's ethics thus necessarily becomes indexed to a politics of liberal tolerance in which antagonisms are reduced to agonism and agonistic respect to a general political dialogue. In contrast to Connolly, in his notion of life as will to power, Nietzsche writes: 'The free man is a warrior.—How is freedom measured? By the resistance which must be overcome' (Nietzsche 2005: 213).

What Nietzsche wants is a will to power which is free-spirited, joyful, and life-affirming. In Nietzsche's formulation, if there is to be any normativity in will to power it will have to be active will rather than passive will: the joy felt in courageous wisdom. Hence, and contrary to Connolly, what we need is a radical politics that is at the intersection of affect (a will to struggle) and reason which is constitutive of agonism in a radically political framework. Behind the rational context of any politics there is also an affective force, an intensive desire.

If post-politics is the impossibility of a real change regarding the 'given' situations, then the challenge of radical politics today is to disrupt that givenness. Post-politics is counterrevolutionary because its main task is to displace dissent, rupture, and resistance against the system. Its logic, of course, is political. It is a determinate formation, a principled reaction with tendencies towards the increasing neoliberalisation and militarisation of society. Post-politics is, in short, a complex combination of different types of social regimes and affective structures.

This also explains why a radical politics of event should delve into the complex linkages between historical social regimes and their affective structures that constitute post-politics. Because post-politics is a principled reaction against revolutionary alternatives, and because radical politics is not simply a politics of resistance, any discussion of how to rethink alternate social and political imaginaries cannot proceed without a proper understanding of the established social regimes and the affective logics of post-politics that it seeks to emancipate itself from. Hence the challenge of radical politics: to diagnose the depoliticised conditions of neoliberalism and better understand the relationships between historical social regimes that constitute it, and the affective logic each regime entails and how they interrelate. So what rationalities of power underlie the post-political? How can one theorise the affective logics of the established social regimes?

Social Regime

In this book, I argue that post-politics is unthinkable without social regimes. I use *social regime* to refer to a prevailing social system, pattern, or the set of rules, both formal and informal, that disciplines, controls, manages, regulates the operation of a specific ideology, rationality, 'governmentality', and its interactions with society overall. Above all, a social regime reconceives the political as a field of management and administration through which different techniques and forces attempt to make the existing order function effectively. A social regime assumes society is 'anarchic' and that there is no authority above the existing order capable of regulating, managing, assaying its interactions and the corresponding characteristics such as affects. Because the aim is to create a society without radical conflict, opposition, and antagonism, a social regime assumes that conflict should be shifted, regulated, and, if possible, eliminated through strategies, techniques, and affects. It presses towards consensus-driven managerial solutions to antagonisms and, of course, class conflict and struggle. Thus, it disseminates a depoliticising epistemology, ontology, and norms and rules.

Even though a social regime may at first seem identical to the dispositif, it is in fact a more complex concept. To get closer to an understanding of social regime, we need to highlight the differences between the concept of dispositif and unpick its political logic in relation to 'governmentality'. In Deleuze's reading of the dispositif, we observe remarkable similarities with his own reading of assemblage. In 'What Is a Dispositif?', Deleuze argues that a dispositif can be analysed in terms of

> lines' which enable new forms of objects and subjects to appear. Dispositifs are then composed of 'lines of visibility, utterance, lines of force, lines of subjectivation, lines of cracking, breaking and ruptures

that all intertwine and mix together and where some augment the others or elicit others through variations and even mutations of the assemblage.

(Deleuze 2006: 347)

Deleuze, therefore, links dispositif to a complex network of power relations in Foucault's writing, which enables human beings to 'see and speak' with regard to truth.

In this sense the key to a dispositif is the valorisation of truth; indeed, a dispositif is a heterogeneous ensemble of power relations through which truth creates an ontological surety. As with Deleuze and the concept of assemblage, a dispositif for Foucault is not to be confused with a technical device. Rather, it is a heterogeneous system where the truth of any real is produced. Foucault thus used the term *dispositif* to refer to multiple power relations, norms, values, and discourses that maintain the functioning of power (see Foucault 1980: 194–5).

This book discusses social regime as a more specific type of dispositif. Rather than making a general claim that a social regime is identical to the dispositif, or apparatus and assemblage, I suggest that a social regime is a type of dispositif that, in brief, organises society in a particular way in a specific time and place, according to a particular rationality of power and affective logic. A social regime, by aiming to create a society without conflict and antagonism, is self-transcending. From this perspective, it is produced through counterrevolutionary principles and the corresponding affects that shape human conduct and social and political relations, with the aim of preventing and preempting disruptive events.

A social regime, then, is a specific form of dispositif that is enacted always in response to an urgent threat: the event. By events, I mean revolts, uprisings, riots, insurrections, revolutions—in short any relatively unorganised individual or collective upheavals that threaten to overthrow the existing social order as a whole. Because a social regime is essential to the operation of the existing order, it provides the conduct that organises the social and prevents disruptive events through counterrevolutionary principles and affective logics. Thus, the power of social regimes has to do with the preemptive and regulating strengths they inject into governmentality (see Debrix & Barder 2009: 407). Social regimes are indeed machines *for* governmentality. If the event is the problem, and if social regimes are the answer, the existing governmentality must ensure that the conduct responsible for disruptive events is done away with (before they take actual shape). It is indeed through techniques, rationalities, affects, and by way of organisational and counterrevolutionary social regimes that post-politics takes charge of a life, orchestrates the conduct of conducts, and represses all forms of disruptive resistance, ensuring that the event is an impossible one. The event is, therefore, managed at the governmental level (through social regimes).

Indeed, a social regime is established on the presupposition that life is characterised by pervasive uncertainty. Thus, actions, threats, and affects that are considered potentially dangerous do not only interrupt the present but also have future consequences, and it is therefore in the interests of the social order to govern, manage, neutralise, and eliminate unknown future events. What we are encountering here is an uncertainty in the sense of the market, that is an economic uncertainty in which populations are trained and 'nudged' in the assumption that 'they personally need to become more resilient in the face of potential events, unexpected shocks, financial turbulence, and entrepreneurial innovation' (Davies 2014: 16–7; see also Evans & Reid 2014).

Within this context, the social regime allows us to understand how the post-political nature of neoliberalism works, how it achieves authority, and the role of the economics in maintaining the existing order so that conflict and antagonism do not degenerate to disorder. It is in this sense that the social regime should be approached in terms of an imposed governmentality. In short, social regimes are deliberately established by dominant and hegemonic governmentalities with the aim of getting populations to conform to the existing norms, rules, and requirements through normalisation and regulation of human behaviours and their affects, as well as a combination of war and violence. A social regime is the pursuit of war and violence by corresponding characteristics and associated affects so that the existing order remains intact.

Alongside this, social regimes and their associated affects are complex and plural (Foucault 2007, 2008), distinguished by their capacity to counter the event. Social regimes are thus as plural and complex as post-political neoliberalism. After all, neoliberalism is concerned to keep its own social regimes of governance under continuous control and critical review (Dillon & Reid 2001: 47; see also Dean 1999; Dillon & Reid 2009; Rose 1999). The social regime operates then as a complex and necessarily heterogeneous network of rationalities, tendencies, and affects. Structuring the affects and the corresponding characteristics that shape the operation of the existing order, of life, the social regime avoids, at all costs, the unexpected eventualities that would be the dissolution of the neoliberal order.

It is in this context that the properly ideological function of the post-political nature of neoliberalism is directly evident. Mobilising concrete social regimes—the cultivation of affects such as ressentiment, fear, cynicism, and spite—are central tropes which the integrity of the system is maintained, while, at the same time, a counterrevolutionary logic that accompanies the established social regimes is one which aims to create a society without conflict, struggle, and radical systemic change.

As I elaborate further in the following chapters, proponents of the concept of post-politics have taken as their point of departure two rationalities of power (sovereignty-discipline) discussed by Foucault (1977) in

Discipline and Punish and the regime of control by Deleuze (1995) in his 'Postscript on the Societies of Control'. However, the links between these rationalities of power have only been hastily suggested (see Diken & Laustsen 2005; see also Collier 2009; Diken 2009; Wilson & Swyngedouw 2014). In this book, I reread sovereignty, discipline, control—along with my own proposed regime of terrorism—as social regimes in order to illuminate the corresponding characteristics and the affective logics that are either only implicit or else partially developed in Foucault's and Deleuze's accounts yet are essential to their operation. I focus on the concept of post-politics further by rigorously theorising the links between the four basic types of social regimes of sovereignty, discipline, control, and terrorism.

Furthermore, I link these social regimes within the topology to four distinct affects, which have been proposed as characterising post-politics: ressentiment, fear, cynicism, and spite. Because affective modulation becomes an essential function of contemporary neoliberal society, affects such as ressentiment, fear, cynicism, and spite are necessary to impose a neoliberal way of life on populations. Thus the population is addressed affectively so that it can be rendered governable and manageable for the stable unity of global capitalism and the neoliberal order. In the process, therefore, the affective logics become a generative principle of post-politics. Every social regime of governance generates its own particular affect.

Importantly, the aim is to analyse each affect independently so that their effects can be studied within the established regimes. Thus, ressentiment, fear, cynicism, and spite are explored as different affects without one determining the others. Alongside this, social regimes open up new fields of entry, so that it becomes possible to engage in life with more political energy, to directly manipulate life purely at the level of its affective relations. Thus, when one refers to post-politics, one is effectively pointing towards an entire political economy of affect. In short, social regimes are inseparable from affective relations. Nietzsche writes: 'moral evaluation is an exegesis, a way of interpreting. [. . .] Who interprets?— Our affects' (1967a: 148).

Topologies of Power

In this book, I propose that every social regime is connected with the other social regimes in a specific way without any succession. Rather than viewing sovereignty, discipline, control, and terrorism, for instance, in terms of a dialectical confrontation, social regimes can be seen as inextricably connected and interdependent. One should, therefore, note that this is not a straightforward linear development. Rather than there being an implied redundancy or a logic of temporal developmental succession, there comes into being a dynamic interaction that is called post-politics.

The established social regimes and their associated affects are not pre-given, lying there waiting to be revealed. The effect of such a perspectival analysis is not, then, intended to be solely an 'intellectual' one. Rather, what is at stake is the production of a certain kind of experience, rationality. And we cannot passively wait for the Messiah to come with the ability to recognise the existence of such relations. The real problem we must confront, therefore, is a political one: how to sustain a critical rationality with political intent? How to find the events? The task is to find the events, 'where they are, at their time, and in their element' (Deleuze 1983: 110).

Hegemonic social regimes aim at countering disruptive politics that threaten the dominant system in order to bring about radical structural change in the way they function. This strategy is composed of a diversity of practices and interventions operating through multiple topologies of power. Hence, I employ a 'topological' analysis of 'the patterns of correlation', as Steve Collier has put it, 'in which heterogeneous elements—techniques, material forms, institutional structures and technologies of power—are configured, as well as the redeployments through which these patterns are transformed' (2009: 78). Unlike topography that is based on 'fixity, placement, or grounding', topology appreciates space and life as matter of 'relationality, connectivity, distribution, assemblage, transformation, or supplementation' (Debrix 2015: 444). Topology points to the potential that concerns with how society is organised. It points to how the established social regimes and affects are configured in assemblies of post-politics, without implying that they follow a straightforward linear development. Each of these regimes has its own 'machines', its own spatial and temporal forms of organisation. This specificity of post-politics, in other words, lies in the complex interweaving of social regimes and affects. To maintain its hegemony, post-politics needs to permanently mobilise multiple social regimes and affects in order to shape people's identities and the political/cultural terrain. Thus, it is no good simply criticising the post-political nature of neoliberalism without also understanding the established social regimes, affects and subtlety of the ideas that underpin it. We need new critical tools to analyse it.

Approach of the Book

The key methodological question for theoretical interpretation, then, is how to conceptualise the relationships between regimes of power and their affective logics. Politics and International Relations are the disciplines dedicated to understanding and explaining of why truly political action is foreclosed in contemporary times, and yet they have failed to offer adequate answers to this question. As disciplines, they remain dominated by ideas drawn from traditions of liberal internationalism and political realism, in which political imagination is preoccupied with command and order rather than with disruption and emancipation. Politics and International Relations have become disciplines in which human freedom is largely dependent upon the limit of political order itself. As such, they are incapable of diagnosing the relationships between historical social regimes that constitute the post-political aspect of neoliberalism and the affective logic each regime entails and how they interrelate. This book offers to make sense of these failures by galvanising the resources of an alternative tradition of social and political thought much misunderstood by the disciplines of Politics and International Relations; that of Deleuzean, Foucauldian, Benjaminian and Nietzschean thought. Politics and International Relations seem to exhibit an ever-increasing demand both for work on the problem of the foreclosure of the political and in the development of ideas drawn from Benjamin, Nietzsche, Foucault, and Deleuze. However, they have yet to fully delve into the complex linkages between post-politics and historical social regimes and their affective structures in the ordering of contemporary societies developed by such thinkers. This book does precisely that.

Deleuze/Foucault

First, as argued above, I take as a point of departure a topological analysis that employs Deleuzean/Foucauldian concepts, for they provide us with analytical tools to grasp the truth of the post-political nature of neoliberalism, an immanent target in which different social regimes of power, affects, and knowledge take shape and function. Utilising Deleuzean/Foucauldian concepts, I explore how sovereignty, discipline, control—along with my own proposed regime of terrorism—are combined in 'complex edifices', 'systems of correlation', or 'topologies of power', thus diminishing post-political neoliberalism's political and moral fallout. For Deleuze, for instance, the topological analysis always acts on the present. What is our present situation? What new possibilities of life do we see appearing today? What are new forms of political subjectivation? Above all, one might say, the topological dimension of Deleuze's analysis requires an 'untimely' intervention into history and the present. Untimely in the Nietzschean sense: the aim is to act 'on our time and, let us hope, for the benefit of a time to come' (Nietzsche 1991: 60). In other words, to act against the present that would give life to new becomings.

Deleuze always insists on creating new concepts, which enables us to see the world in a new way, in a process of becoming. A creation of new concepts means that we see the world and time within the perspective of becoming or virtuality rather than within a linear, determinist time. Only on this basis are we able to invent new ways of conceiving time and temporality and create new perspectives on life and being, leading to revolutionary events. This is what history means for Deleuze: everything is historical and contingent, a process of revolutionary becoming.

In doing so, Deleuze thus stresses the importance of the virtual. Philosophy, for Deleuze, is an attempt to grasp the virtual, for it is the virtual that generates the actual. The virtual is real itself in the sense of making future potentialities and possibilities real in the present. In other words, life, according to Deleuze, 'is composed of virtualities, events, singularities. What I am calling virtual is not something that lacks reality. Rather, the virtual becomes engaged in a process of actualisation as it follows the plane which gives it its proper reality' (2006: 388). This is why the event should be understood as the virtual form of what is to come: 'the part that eludes its own actualisation in everything that happens' (Deleuze & Guattari 1994: 156).

For Foucault, in a similar vein, history is made up of two principles which are matter (that is only potential) and form (that makes the object a reality). His genealogy recognises 'the events of history, its jolts, its surprises, its unsteady victories and unpalatable defeats' (Foucault 1984: 80). His genealogical practice is able to 'seek out discontinuities where others found continuous development . . . find recurrences and play where others found progress and seriousness' (Dreyfus & Rabinow 1982: 106). Introducing 'discontinuities into our very being' (Foucault 1984: 88), Foucault's genealogy in this respect serves as a 'grid of intelligibility' that reveals immanencies in historical social regimes and events. What's more, it critically disrupts the given order and challenges its basic premises. It opens up the range of possibilities for thinking and acting, and thus is associated with solidarity and emancipation. In this sense, Foucault's genealogical method is to identify and *intervene*. Genealogy is always immanent to resistance and decidedly political.

Social regimes are historically contingent rather than teleological. Contingent here does not refer to randomness. Social regimes are contingent because there is no inherent meaning guiding their evolution. Instead, their emergence and development is dependent upon contests and struggles marked by different power relations (see Bonditti *et al.* 2014: 163). For Foucault, history is marked by breaks and ruptures rather than continuity or transcendental laws. The motor of history is rooted in immanent forms of struggle, power and adaptation that result in contingent developments (Bonditti *et al.* 2014: 163). Like Deleuze, Foucault is thus careful to note that immanent regimes do not follow a straightforward linear development. Rather, he proposes a reading of history that is against historicism, for historical immanent orders are seen as 'multiplicities', that is, dynamic effects of 'incessant transactions' (Foucault 2008: 77).

To sum up, Deleuze and Foucault offer a reading of history that is against the entire model of linearity, for the established social regimes and the corresponding characteristics are seen as, to borrow Julian Reid's term (2010b: 394), 'moving targets', not rigid ideological rationalities. What unites them is that they both conceive power to be immanent to the social field, not external to it. If we read Deleuze's and Foucault's concepts as an account of immanent regimes that operate through 'incessant multiplicities', then the question of power, the 'political' logic of post-politics becomes available for contestation. As such, Deleuzean/Foucauldian concepts provide us to construct new forms of subjectivities and social relations that are immune to neoliberalism as counterrevolution.

Nietzsche

My conception of political agonism and affect follows Nietzsche and his notion of will to power, the supreme immanent principle in life, which he juxtaposes to God's transcendent judgment. Based on cruelty and struggle, Nietzsche's *agon* takes life as will to power as a guiding principle. In Nietzsche, life as will to power expresses and continuously expands itself, which leads him to identify will to power with freedom. Thus, for Nietzsche, freedom can only emerge insofar as it is understood as a necessity, a necessity which provides and encourages human actors to fulfil life's main purpose: to engage in a ruthless struggle which is to become fully the will to power and thus become free. Significantly, however, will to power does not refer to actual physical force or political dominance. Rather, it is a process of overcoming a struggle. For Nietzsche, life as will to power requires that an organism strives to heighten mere-life; it is the fundamental value, a value on the basis of the enhancement of life conditions, its self-overcoming. Struggle and resistance are required for such a process of overcoming, which is based on *this* life, not denying it.

If the primary value is life as will to power, then the fundamental point concerning will to power is to establish alternative counter-ideals/values to life. Life here, however, is to be understood as a struggle between creation and preservation. All life is therefore the will to 'striving against something that resists' (Nietzsche 1967a: 374). Nietzsche enables us to see life as an immanent principle, a conflict, which has neither an external cause nor a final end. Life as will to power is not to be exhausted in existence; it is a permanent struggle.

Benjamin

Lastly, Deleuzean and Foucauldian topological analysis and Nietzsche's conception of agonism based on will to power allow us to link their concepts with Walter Benjamin's critical approach to historical memory, whose task is to emphasise an intimate relationship between past and present events, by which agonistic history opens up the path to universal redemption. In this sense, the idea of agonistic histories is essential to Benjamin's Marxist analysis of society. Of course Walter Benjamin's dialectical perspective to historical memory and revolutionary events predates Deleuze and Foucault. However, we are still haunted by the spectre of Benjamin, for he provides a negative dialectical perspective that is opposed to any determinist, evolutionist historicism. Seen in this light, the past, for Benjamin, is not simply past, but carries in it signs and traces of another temporality, a promise of a future redemption. Benjamin did not write specifically about neoliberalism or the post-political. His main targets were totalitarianism and fascism. However, from a Benjaminian perspective, in order to understand the past properly, one should not only analyse actual conditions in which post-politics is constituted, one has also to take into account alternate political possibilities that are available in the 'now-time' (Benjamin 1969).

Benjamin's notion of 'now-time' refers to a theologico-political temporality that is entirely different from mechanical, linear time. Simply put, his messianic Marxism (dialectical perspective) enables us to conceive of a different temporality suspending vulgar historicism based upon linearity, succession, and homogeneity. Following the dialectical approach of Benjamin, the task here is to unearth the hidden potentialities (the utopian emancipatory potentials) 'which were betrayed in the actuality of revolution' (see Žižek 2006: 78) and in its final outcome, which is now embodied in post-politics. Today, 'hope is surrounded by dangers' (Bloch 1988: 17). Post-politics is one of them. And 'awakening' from this danger, from this counterrevolutionary moment, is the primary purpose of materialist historiography, and 'dialectical images' are (in Benjamin's case, industrial capitalism) the moments of historical awakening from this hell, the very hell of post-political neoliberalism.

However, this is not the whole story. Benjamin's notion of temporality and dialectical perspective also open up the past to the present, the actual to the virtual, in which the subject of history is capable of escaping the entire model of linearity, the captivity of neoliberal capitalism. As Benjaminian ancestors, we are enslaved by neoliberal capitalism, robbed of our power to act in the present. We can only interrupt the endless parade of current misery by choosing to take on the burden of redemption, recognising the past struggles as our own, rather than sinking into the vicious cycle of guilt and ressentiment of capitalism. 'The enemy', Benjamin insists, 'has not ceased to be victorious' (Benjamin 1969: 247). We should never forget the debt we owe to those who came before us. We can achieve what they did not because 'even the dead will not be safe' unless the enemy loses. And if our dead are not safe, then neither we are. Hence the importance of Benjaminian 'moment of danger', which is not an injunction to remember the past struggles but a call to action: to strive to make good in the now for emancipation, to complete the struggle by honouring 'correctly'.

If we follow Benjamin, we are left with two conflicting philosophies of history: the one represented by post-political neoliberalism refers to a worldview as power and hegemony, and the other by revolutionary events. What seems for neoliberalism to be consensus, for the history of events is conflict and antagonism. On the one hand, bare repetition, which is counterrevolutionary; on the other, productive repetition, which is revolutionary. On the one hand, the 'enlightened' human being, who is determined by the conditions; on the other, the subject of history who is able to determine the conditions that determines her. On the one hand, the history of progress, which insists on continuity; on the other, the history of events, which insists on discontinuity and thus wants to change the course of history.

So this book seeks to 'think with' Deleuze, Foucault, Nietzsche, and Benjamin on what the post-political aspect of neoliberalism is and how we can resist it. The point here is not to correct Foucault with Nietzsche, Deleuze with Benjamin, but to bring them together to generate a rich account of post-political neoliberalism and radical politics. Through my empirical discussions I put social and political theory in conversation with them, all of whom I contextualise as crucial to understanding the dominant hegemony and radical social change. The book, in short, brings together these diverse figures not in a 'dialogue' but in a 'debate'; a debate which allows for both collective solidarity and confrontation among the theorists mentioned above in its own framework (see Diken 2012). I am particularly interested in the way in which these figures and their radical theories take as their point of departure some significant common aspirations (freedom, struggle) and unite against common enemies (e.g. hegemonic ideologies, neoliberalism, capitalism).

Chapter Outline

The substantive chapters of the book start with Chapter One. Taking as its point of departure Marx's analysis of not only history as farce, but politics as farce in *The Eighteenth Brumaire of Louis Bonaparte*, the chapter argues that Marx's diagnoses of the French counterrevolution allow us to understand the very foundations of post-politics. However, the chapter does not suggest that the lessons of *The Eighteenth Brumaire*, or Bonapartism are identical to the current developments in contemporary society. Rather, the point of comparison is confined to the lessons of the relationship between neoliberal capitalism and creeping militarism. Post-politics is as much about expanding the processes of capital as it is about war and violence.

It then focuses its critique on Jodi Dean, arguing that she fails to treat post-politics as a complex and historical regime of power relations, instead asserting it as crude and stable 'fact'. The chapter, therefore, explores how the established social regimes and related affects continue to play a major role in relation to the political.

Chapter Two examines the concept of sovereignty. Taking Deleuze's notion of sovereignty as its point of departure, it reactivates the concept of sovereign power by establishing its relevance to contemporary society. The main argument is that sovereign political power is a radically contingent power in which 'cruel acts' manifest themselves. Sovereignty is a social regime, a set of governmental practices and rationalities that is more than merely a piece of land or territory.

Furthermore, this chapter develops ressentiment as the main affect that pertains to sovereignty. Yet, in social and political theory this link remains surprisingly underresearched. The main contention is that the social regime of sovereignty cannot be thought of without ressentiment as it creates pacified and oppressed subjects who cannot act.

The chapter also deals with cinema, focusing on Pier Paolo Pasolini's final film *Salò*. *Salò* poses significant questions regarding the sadistic torture as a form of sovereign political power. Contrary to liberal democratic interpretations that consider torture as a form of insanity, as a juridical problem, the chapter discusses torture as the most privileged actualisation of state terror, for it reveals the nature of sovereignty and its rational consciousness. Torture is a rational necessity that defines postpolitical neoliberalism in general and sovereignty in particular.

Chapter Three proposes to rethink Foucault's *Discipline and Punish* by exploring the profound mutation from sovereign power to contemporary neoliberal governmentality. First, it examines the birth of neoliberalism that is based on the market. It addresses the idea of competition as a defining feature and ideal of neoliberalism. It argues that the Benthamite panoptic prison is crucial to the development of disciplinary and economic aspects of neoliberalism and the capitalist labour market. Second, it explores how the rule of law (*Rechtsstaat*) plays an important role to get rid of various forms of 'disruptive ideas'. Third, the chapter develops *fear* as the main affect of discipline, arguing that it is the essential condition and a positive element of neoliberalism.

Moreover, this chapter focuses particular attention on the theological reasoning of modern biopolitics. It explores modern paradigms of government and economics as to the ways in which they stand in basic continuity with the prophetic-apocalyptic tradition. It argues that the always-present possibility of a 'terrifying event' is what defines modern biopolitics' legitimacy. In a revision of Foucault's account of biopolitics, the chapter argues that modern biopolitics is a measured attempt to combine the neoliberal order and legitimacy of a neoliberal economic theory in order to decrease resistance. Modern biopolitics is both *katechontic* (preventing radical structural change and delaying the coming of end times) and as figured around the *eschaton* (the end time).

To flesh out these arguments, in Chapter Three the relationship between discipline and neoliberalism is approached through *kettling*, a controversial police tactic that turns a legitimate protest into a 'violent disorder'. Kettling is a political technology, deployed and mobilised in the exercise of power. The chapter traces the emergence of kettling in relation to the challenges to post-political neoliberalism posed by new social movements. Kettling is a complex spatial strategy of crowd discipline within established territories. It is an answer to new social movements, which use digital technologies.

Chapter Four examines the continuing relevance of Deleuze's framework about the 'society of control', relating it to neoliberal capitalism. The social regime of control manages and regulates life in its productive new capacities. The chapter, in this context, examines the role of the biopolitical production of infinity, that is to say a factical finitude of life as an immanent quality, which is another name for the desire to subject the potentialities of life itself to the pernicious logics of capitalist accumulation.

The chapter then develops *cynicism* as a crucial concept for the examination of the affective politics of neoliberal capitalism, arguing that the cynical individual is able to participate within the existing order without internally accepting its truth-value. Cynicism legitimises and ultimately (re)produces individuals based on market defined self-interest(s).

Furthermore, this chapter discusses debt as a dispositif, as a technique of governance, which predetermines political outcomes. Debt is a future acting, restricting and curtailing human imagination. It details how neoliberal capitalism establishes a regime of indebtedness, exploiting and alienating human beings. Debt is as much about biopolitical control as it is an extension of capital.

Chapter Five theorises a new affect, *spite*, which is defined as a willingness to cause harm for harm's sake. With spite, everything is pushed to its boundaries, to its outermost limit. The chapter suggests that spite has become one of the major affective dimensions of post-politics. The question is, however, what corresponding social regime would produce the distinctive affective modality of spite. The chapter contends that spite corresponds to a fourth, paradoxical social 'regime'—terrorism.

To exemplify and supplement the main arguments, the chapter examines Islamic terrorism. Islamic terrorism uses spite as a strategy, as the spectacle of death against 'the pacified life' on offer in post-political neoliberalism. It documents how Islamic terrorism has become a depoliticised gesture, that is, nihilistic quality of the violence that leads to a state of disengagement from politics as purposive, collective action. The chapter then explores convergences and divergences, differences and similarities between post-political neoliberalism and Islamic terrorism, arguing that they are two aspects of the same cycle of bare repetition, that is, repetition without real political change.

Chapter Six confronts the consequences of the previous discussions and asks what kind of radical critique is needed to resist post-politics. Firstly, it explores what critique means in neoliberal times. To exemplify the arguments, the chapter deals with cinema. It focuses on Harold Ramis's film *Groundhog Day*, in which a cynical TV weatherman is stuck in a time loop that makes him relive the same day over and over again. Utilising the movie, it explores how critique can arise from bare repetition.

In particular, it examines the relationship between critique and political spirituality, arguing that political spirituality is strictly inseparable from the concept of parrhesia—truth telling—and subjectivity. It then explores how spirituality connects parrhesia with the care of the self, the virtual with the actual, without falling back on either cynicism (post-politics) or spiteful destruction (Islamic terrorism).

The Afterword explores the actuality of political spirituality in the context of Gezi revolt. It discusses Gezi as an example of political spirituality, an attempt at linking truth telling and subjectivity. As such, Gezi enables us to see the world and time within the perspective of virtuality rather than a linear, determinist time. It explores the alternative political possibilities of Gezi as a revolutionary process.

Notes

1. Agonism is, after all, a classical concept used by more than one advocate. It is also referred to as 'strong democracy' (Barber 1984); 'virtu politics' (Honig 1994), and 'deliberative neo-pluralism' (Mansbridge *et al.* 2010).
2. In *Hegemony and Socialist Strategy* Laclau and Mouffe (1985) also argue that the political field and identities are constructed through the production of a determining outside. In other words, the very domain of politics and identities establish themselves through the naturalisation of the 'pre-'or 'non-'political. In Derridean terminology, this is called the production of a 'constitutive outside'.

1 Post-Politics
A Theoretical Intervention

In 1848, Louis Bonaparte, nephew of Napoléon Bonaparte, was elected president of the new Second Republic of France. Defending the work of the revolution of 1848, promoting prosperity for all, he promised glory and greatness for a nation which supposedly characterised his uncle's reign. Because the constitution limited the president to a single four-year term, and because he failed to secure the three-fourths majority required for constitutional revision, he staged a coup d'état on December 2, 1851. The coup provides the occasion of Marx's insightful book *The Eighteenth Brumaire of Louis Bonaparte* (1852).

What follows is an analysis of the post-political as a 'political' formation, juxtaposed against Marx's account of the 1851 coup d'état by Louis Bonaparte. The first part of the chapter introduces the argument of Marx's *Eighteenth Brumaire* as a model for understanding the foundations of contemporary politics. Part two examines the depoliticised conditions of contemporary neoliberal society through the concept of post-politics. This is precisely a moment of Benjaminianism in the sense that the analysis inserts the past into the 'now-ness' of a present danger, which is post-politics. Aiming to redeem the past generations of the oppressed, a Benjaminian approach allows us to grasp the truth of post-politics, a truth which is found in present-day-life (Benjamin 1999a: 297). After Benjamin, then, what do we see? It is important to stress that Benjamin's concept of history does not see in history happy promises. Looking at contemporary society through the lens of Benjamin, what we see is a moment of danger, or post-politics as a counterrevolutionary logic that grows incessantly, with its social regimes and their associated affects. In front of such danger, Benjamin's concept of history would like to help; an interruptive history which illuminates and actualises new possibilities. From a Benjaminian perspective, the possibility of revolution and dialectical history is what matters.

In this precise sense, one should not forget the face of the past (the spectre). It is true that we see a past that is full of traumatic experiences and counterrevolutionary events. Whereas 'the history of the victors' sees the past as something that we should all leave behind, a Benjaminian approach allows us to see history that includes danger and catastrophe, but wants to liberate it from chains. Benjamin sees the past capable of interrupting and thus stopping counterrevolutionary logics that produce non-events in which misery, injustice, and reaction are continuously (re)produced. It is the past which reveals a new dimension of history. That is the difference.

Hence, the importance of Benjamin's concept of history in which the past (nineteenth-century France) has a new meaning that can rise in light of the present (post-politics). Let me add that I do not mean to equate the political lessons from nineteenth-century France with the current developments in contemporary society. Rather, I use Marx's diagnoses of the French counterrevolution in order to understand the tenuous relationship between the economisation and the evident militarisation of society. In doing so, I aim to show the emergent link between an analysis which does not forget the past, and the object of its attention, which emerges as a flash in the present, becomes present: 'knowledge comes only in lightning flashes' (Benjamin 1999b: 456).

Model: The Eighteenth Brumaire of Louis Bonaparte

> Hegel observes somewhere that all the great events and characters of world history occur twice, so to speak. He forgot to add: the first time as high tragedy, the second time as low farce.
> (Marx 1852/2002: 19)

When Marx wrote of *The Eighteenth Brumaire of Louis Bonaparte* (1852/2002), the main question to which Marx was responding was how the revolution of 1848 had led to Louis Bonaparte's coup d'état and the subversion of democracy. To explain these events, Marx divides Louis Bonaparte's (farcical) rise and rule into three separate phases, in which different alliances of classes and groupings rule. In the first phase—called the February Period—King Louis Philippe, whose rule Marx identifies with the finance aristocracy, is forced to abdicate by a broad coalition, including the republican bourgeoisie. This alliance is modified by the removal of the 'proletariat' from the centre of the revolutionary stage. The second phase is brought on by the fall of the republican bourgeoisie, which gives rise to the Party of Order as the ruling alliance. The Party of Order is a bourgeois formation, representing two antagonistic wings of the two bourgeois factions—the landlords (Legitimists) and the industrialists (Orléanists). For Marx, their rule is made possible only in the framework of republicanism. This is why not royalism but the parliamentary republic becomes the common denominator of the two bourgeois factions. for it is the best possible political shell for the common class interest, the interests of the capital. Eventually, however, republican institutions are discarded by the Party of Order, that is, by 'capital', in the name of 'order'. This is the key to understanding the different role of the bourgeoisie in 1848 as compared to 1789: in 1789 the bourgeoisie played a 'progressive' role by allying with the people against the monarchy, the aristocracy, and the established church, whereas in 1848 they had become much more conservative by doing everything in its power to prevent the spread of potential socialist revolutions.

The third phase ends in a coup d'état, which brings Louis Bonaparte to power. The alliance behind Bonaparte comprised of the various factions—from finance capital, the Legitimist landed aristocracy, to the industrial bourgeoisie, the lumpenproletariat, the state officials, and the army. As a result, the victory of 'order' succeeds in conquering democracy's 'disturbance of order' and Louis Bonaparte declares himself emperor of France. In the process, Bonaparte profits from the myth of his uncle as the symbol of the revolutionary ideals of liberty, equality and stability. In exploiting this legend, Bonaparte projects himself as a man who would rule above class interests, the divisions of French politics, for the reconciliation of all classes.

Significantly, as Marx argues, there is something special about France where the head of the executive—with a bureaucracy of more than half a million civil servants, a complement of a half million officials alongside an army of another half million—controls a state apparatus which 'restricts, regulates, oversees and supervises civil life from its most all-encompassing expressions to its most insignificant stirrings . . . where through the most extraordinary centralisation this parasite acquires an all-knowing pervasiveness' (Marx 1852/2002: 53). This is a process in which the '*material interests* of the French bourgeoisie are intertwined in the most intimate way' with the maintenance of the machinery of state (Marx 1852/2002: 54). With the support of the bourgeoisie, Louis Bonaparte needs the widespread and ingenious machinery of the state, 'the fearsome parasitic body', in order to repress other classes. For this reason, the bourgeoisie is 'compelled by its class position both to negate the conditions of existence for any parliamentary power, including its own, and to make the power of the executive, its adversary, irresistible' (Marx 1852/2002). It thus finds the everyday business of democracy useless and stigmatises any popular agitation as 'socialistic'. By now decrying as 'socialistic' what it had previously extolled as 'liberal', the bourgeoisie thus confesses that 'its own interests require it to dispense with the dangers of self-government'; that in order to 'retain its power in society intact its political power would have to be broken'(Marx 1852/2002: 57).

In the name of saving society 'from being destroyed', from 'anarchy', the bourgeoisie betrays its 'progressive' past to try to safeguard capitalist class interests by invoking, in Bonaparte, a leader who contradicts them. Hence they cry out: 'only theft can still save property; only perjury, religion; bastardy, the family; only disorder, order!' (Marx 1852/2002: 107). Put differently, the bourgeoisie—so much afraid of the revolutionary working class and socialist ideals—is willing to sacrifice democracy in order to maintain a state of 'order'. However, whereas the main protagonist of *The Eighteenth Brumaire* is the French bourgeoisie, Marx points out that Louis Bonaparte is able to garner the support from the smallholding peasants as well as the petty bourgeoisie and the lumpenproletariat. Bonaparte's strength lay in his ability to be able to depict himself as 'all things to all men'.

It is precisely when he becomes aware of himself as a man 'superior' to his bourgeois rivals, as an 'authority' over them, that Louis Bonaparte attains a position which enables him to become the master of the society, an 'original author', in his own right (Marx 1852/2002: 64). And, as Marx argues in another passage, it is this 'abject dependence' which enables Louis Bonaparte to represent each class against all the others in turn (Marx 1852/2002: 101). Because they are unable to enforce their class interest, a master, Bonaparte, must represent them. But herein lay the central dilemma of Bonaparte's rule: he wants to be seen as the 'patriarchal benefactor of all classes', but, in this, he is spectacularly unsuccessful because he could not 'give to one class without taking from another' (Marx 1852/2002: 108). Thus, in the final analysis, Bonaparte is a 'floating signifier', whose true loyalty lies with himself, his clique, the clandestine police force and standby army who keep him in power. And the rest is a total failure:

> The constitution, the national assembly, the dynastic parties, the blue [right-wing] and the red [left-wing] republicans, the heroes of [the Algerian wars in] Africa, the thunder from the grandstand, the sheet-lightning of the daily press, all the literature, political names and intellectual reputations, the civil law and the penal code, *liberté, egalité, fraternité*, and the ninth of May 1852 [when Bonaparte's presidency was supposed to expire, but didn't]—all that has magically vanished under the spell of a man whom even his enemies would deny was a sorcerer.
>
> (Marx 1852/2002: 23)

Bonaparte's coup is undoubtedly illegal and brutal. As a result, the revolution of 1848 becomes an empty gesture, embodying a dialectic of 'purification' and 'destruction'. The authoritarian regime the coup establishes is an exceptional period of 'dictatorship' where the rule of law is suspended. The state power, therefore, unconditionally authorises itself to exercise an absolute power in order to suppress other classes. Anticipating states of emergency in modern times, thus restoring the security state by manifesting it at its most spectacular, the 'obscene' message of the 'unlimited governmental power' imposed by Louis Bonaparte is thus: 'laws do not really bind me, I can do to you whatever I want, I can treat you as guilty if I decide to do so, I can destroy you if I want to' (Žižek

2006: 337). Consequently, the process of promising peace and national honour culminates in a brutal and decidedly unbourgeois regime of banditry that seizes the reins of power. It is the army, 'personified by its own dynasty', which must 'represent the *State* in antagonism to the *society*' (Marx 1986). In fact, the bourgeoisie renounces power in favour of a gangster regime (Carver 2002: 152), for Bonapartism is about enforcing and preserving capitalist exploitation.

The aim of Bonapartism is to recognise popular sovereignty whilst placing it under a specific authoritarian regime in the best interests of the bourgeoisie. At the heart of the regime's policy is technocratic and administrative romanticism, which is seen as crucial in building a competitive economy. Thus, the entire bureaucratic-military machine is deployed to safeguard the managerial-technocratic 'bourgeois order', to support the government's candidates, and to counter opposition. Salvation seems to be offered by the security state. The oft-proclaimed desire for liberty is compounded always by social fear. 'Liberty' depends both on the curbing of the personal power of the Emperor and on the preservation of order (Carver 2002: 156–7).

The French as a whole nation thus sees not the emergence of a democratic society but the return of a demoralising defeat at the hands of a popular 'reaction under the leadership of Louis Bonaparte' (Thoburn 2003: 54). Under the repetition of Napoleon in Louis Bonaparte, the revolution leaves no room for rightful actors on the scene, bourgeois and proletarian, 'making way for a troupe of substitute comedians whose burlesque performance reaches its climax in the triumph of the clown Louis Napoleon' (Rancière 2004: 93). What we have here is a repetition with difference that is 'enriched by the notion of a decline from heroism to foolishness': '. . . the London constable [Louis Bonaparte], with a dozen of the best debt-ridden lieutenants, after the little corporal [Napoleon Bonaparte], with his roundtable of military marshals! The eighteenth Brumaire of the fool after the eighteenth Brumaire of the genius!' (Marx 1852/2002: 19; see also Carver 2002: 120). The result is a deeply retrogressive situation, wherein, 'it seems that the state has merely reverted to its oldest form, to the shameless, bare-faced rule of sword and cross' (Marx 1852/2002: 22). The 'threat' of the socialist revolution leads the bourgeoisie to the conclusion: 'better an end to terror than terror without end!' (Marx 1852/2002: 89). Its logic, of course, is political. This is a history which produces a period of 'crying contradictions'. In the end, nothing changes and everybody occupies exactly the same position as in the beginning. Hence, Marx writes on the Second Republic:

> Passion without truth, truth without passion; history without events; development driven solely by the calendar and wearisome through constant repetition of the same tension and release; antagonisms

which seem periodically to reach a peak only to go dull and diminish without resolution.

(Marx 1852/2002: 34)

As a result, the class struggle is foreclosed, the antagonism and conflict are merely weakened and transformed into harmony, all corners of society are framed and measured by economic terms, and the entire political structure is delimited to the actual reality by preventing potential 'revolutionary' events from occurring. Louis Bonaparte's ideal is a society without conflict, antagonism, and radical social change.

Because the lessons of the French counterrevolution are past, they can never be experienced again in unmediated form. But *The Eighteenth Brumaire of Louis Bonaparte* can be experienced now and in the future. It is here that one should return to Benjamin's concept of history, for it allows us to generate an interrelationship between past and present events. Here the implicit issue is the construction of a *critical* analysis that interweaves Marx's arguments of *The Eighteenth Brumaire* with post-politics, how 'history is referred to its 'making'—political praxis' (Tiedemann 1983: 84, 91). By juxtaposing Marx's analysis of the 1851 coup d'état and post-politics, I argue that there is a direct relationship between past and present events, a certain relationship which enables us to see the future as a new radical possibility, which goes beyond just the temporality of the present. For Benjamin, then, an interruptive philosophy of history makes sense only insofar as the past *critically* examines the present conditions. This analysis is of course 'dialectical': 'for while the relation of the present to the past is a purely temporal, continuous one, the relation of what-has-been to the now is dialectical: is not progression but image, suddenly emergent' (Benjamin 1999b: 462). Following Benjamin, the dialectical image is the moment of awakening from hell, the very hell of post-politics as a counterrevolutionary system. It identifies with the oppressed of the past and present as a crucial strategy in overcoming the time-continuum of post-politics.

Benjamin's main concern is to seek the future in the past that journeys in the present. In this respect, *The Eighteenth Brumaire of Louis Bonaparte*'s temporal status in a continuous present is 'still journeying' (Marx 1852/2002: 98). Rereading Marx's cutting descriptions of Bonaparte and of French politics with an eye focused on contemporary society, the late post-political politics comes to mind again and again. But, to reiterate, by juxtaposing these two historical realities I do not mean to suggest that the political lessons from nineteenth-century France should be equated with the current developments in contemporary society. The point of comparison is confined to the lessons of the relationship between neoliberalisation and the increasing militarisation of contemporary society.

Past makes its present appearance as an interruption of the present. And 'articulating past historically means appropriating a memory as it flashes up in a moment of danger'. This danger for Benjamin is what 'threatens both the content of the tradition and those who inherit it' (Benjamin 2003: 391). By 'those who inherit it' Benjamin means the tradition of the oppressed, those who are aware—through a dialectical perspective—of this very danger and the meaning of liberation. Hence the importance of *The Eighteenth Brumaire* which enables us to see history as both a moment of danger and hope in which 'time takes a stand and has become to a standstill' (Benjamin 2003: 396). Through an analysis of *The Eighteenth Brumaire* as the clash between the past as a moment of danger and hope arises, then, a new mode of critical thought, where the present remembers the past and liberates the oppressed. In short, *The Eighteenth Brumaire* allows us to introduce an 'untimely' intervention into the counterrevolutionary aspects of the present conditions, which is post-politics.

The Eighteenth Brumaire has relevance today on its 164th anniversary for many reasons. First, if Napoleon Bonaparte is a floating signifier who can be classified as a tragic hero, then the emptiness of the imitative acts of Louis Bonaparte can be qualified as 'low farce' (Martin 2002). In this way, Marx tries to 'demonstrate how the *class struggle* in France created circumstances and relations that made it possible for a grotesque mediocrity to play a hero's part' (Marx 1852/2002: 77). Crucially, however, Marx declares that the tragedy of Napoleon Bonaparte is that of society, not of the man. Likewise, the farce of Louis Bonaparte is tragic, not for the man but for the society, for it is the society that is both the victim of Bonaparte's rumblings and a cause contributing to them (Riquelme 1980: 69). As Marx rightly observes, though Louis Bonaparte was 'the most simple-minded man in France', he had 'acquired the most multiplex significance. Just because he was nothing, he could signify everything to save himself' (1850: 81).

Cutting to the chase, Marx's argument is that the reign of Napoléon le petit is not 'real' history but merely a parody of non-events, a farce (Riquelme 1980; see also Diken 2012; Žižek 2006). There are two kinds of repetition, which helps us understand history as a 'paradox'. On the one hand, there is 'productive' repetition that creates something new. On the other, there is bare repetition that parodies 'the old' (Marx 1852/2002: 12). Thus, repetition can dramatise the 'spirit' by awakening the dead, as part of a new struggle, or make the ghost of revolution 'walk about again' (Marx 1852/2002: 12). Productive repetition resurrects past events, whereas bare repetition takes an empty form of history, the consequence of which is farce (Diken 2012: 84).

In this sense, revolution occurs twice: first as tragedy, as a productive repetition, which can create something new; then as 'farce', as counter-revolution (Marx 1852/2002; Žižek 2009). Counterrevolution is bare repetition that is built on harmony and consensus, whereas revolution is productive repetition which seeks to disrupt harmony and consensus

(Diken 2012: 84–86). Simply put, counterrevolution as bare repetition produces non-events within the given, whereas revolution disrupts that givenness. When the spirit of revolution is forgotten, what remains after is bare repetition, a society characterised by the absence of revolutionary events.

Neoliberalism was conceived at the creation of a new world order. It legitimatised sovereign states who were supposed to defend 'liberal' values both at home and abroad: freedom of speech, all being equal access to prosperity, the ability to challenge governments, the elimination of torture and other cruel sovereign acts. Neoliberalism, in short, asserted values that would improve the lives of human beings and generate prosperity for people living through it. Soon after the collapse of the Berlin Wall, it became institutionalised, declaring 'the end of history' (Fukuyama 1992; see also Jameson 2003). It started to exercise its hegemony, especially in economic and military matters, a power which is constituted by a complex and open ended social regimes. The first Gulf War and 'the war against terror' post 9/11 consolidated the hegemony of neoliberal power, in the hands of dominant sovereign states. Today, however, the hegemony of that power seems to have broken down. The neoliberal world order, in short, is now under siege and being pushed back. Its hegemony is now weaker than ever. As the threat of political and moral decline continues, however, it becomes increasingly authoritarian and thus violent (Bigo & Tsoukala 2008; Diken 2009; Dillon & Reid 2009; Duffield 2011; Evans 2013; Evans & Reid 2014; Hardt & Negri 2004; Springer 2015).

After the broken promises (more democracy, less war and state, equality for all), what sets is an authoritarian neoliberal society in which radical conflict and 'true events' are foreclosed. What we are encountering today is nothing else than an authoritarian liberal populism that 'identifies singular actors as the immediate causes' of non-events (see Lavin 2005: 443). The ideology of authoritarian liberal populism allows and even compels heroes to emerge in the popular consciousness, which produces a moment of historical possibility on which the subjects are able to capitalise (Lavin 2005: 443). It compels us to identify individual heroes to appear as the authors of non-events, the consequence of which is farce. It should, therefore, come as no surprise to those of us that McCarthyism, Thatcherism, Reaganism, Bushism, Mulroneyism, Harperism, Putinism, Erdoganism, and Obamaism have become the rule, not the exception. Although these 'isms' have different objects, the common denominator that exists between them all is the fact that they have presented themselves as the 'kinder gentler' face of neoliberal capitalism. What a scene! What a farce!

Second, the Bonapartist coup of 1851, while 'not an exact parallel' to what happened post 9/11, also shows the drive for total domination by the neoliberal security state. Precisely in this sense the text exposes the shallow structure behind the fragile facade of liberal (bourgeois) democracy and its political allies that supposedly protect democratic liberties. In this age of ID cards, biometric passports, poster bans, military-style borders, fences and checkpoints around 'security zones', armed predator drones, Guantánamo, Border Agencies, Home Office, Patriot, and Terrorism Acts (Agamben 1998, 2005; Elden 2009; Graham 2004, 2010; Graham & Marvin 2001; Gregory 2006; Lyon 2001, 2003), Marx's critique of bourgeois democracy still rings true. Despite its rhetoric, the bourgeois understanding of liberal values can all too easily sink into authoritarianism at the first opportunity. Thus, citizenship rights may be suspended in the name of 'democracy', innocent civilians can be killed by unjust, illegal, and immoral drone strikes to save 'freedom', and torture can 'reasonably' be legalised to preserve human dignity. Instead of legal rights and legal systems based on universal citizenship, post-political neoliberalism is based on 'states of exception', pervasive surveillance, tracking and DNA database technologies, which give governments virtually unchecked powers to preemptively profile the entire population, thus determining how the situation might be understood (Agamben 2001, 2005; Aradau et al. 2008; Bell & Evans 2010; Dillon 2007; Dillon & Reid 2009; Evans 2013; Evans & Hardt 2010; Rose 2007). The neoliberal security state, in other words, is an exceptional state, and so are its characteristics. With the normalisation of the 'state of exception', suspension of basic rights, ideological cultivation of a culture of fear and cynicism, and fundamental separation of bad and good circulation, or the included and the excluded, the aim is to prevent the event, an event which threatens to overthrow the system as a whole (Agamben 2005; Badiou 2008; Diken 2012; Evans 2010, 2013; Swyngedouw 2009a; Taşkale 2011; Žižek 2008b, 2012). The dimensions of the neoliberal security complex now beggar the imagination.

The post-political nature of neoliberalism, in order to defuse the fear of potential revolutions, demands a constant auditing of biopolitical control over life to determine which lives are desired and productive and which lives are dangerous and need regulation (Aradau et al. 2008; Aradau & van Munster 2008; Dillon & Reid 2009; Reid 2012). With post-political neoliberalism, in other words, life becomes the enemy of life itself because it is where the event takes place. Worried about the possibility of the event, post-politics is a politics in which neoliberal capitalism seems to have become a second nature, and where security and militarisation have become productive and generative aspects of social life (Dillon 1996). In other words, a neoliberal consensus has been built around the indispensability for capitalism and the politics of security that posits order as an absolute value. For that reason, Marx's text reveals the thin line between democracy and authoritarian populism, demonstrating how they mirror each other too closely (Carver 2002; Cowling & Martin 2002; Jessop 2002). Those who are supposed to safeguard our essential democratic values threaten to destabilise democracies or perhaps even usher in a new era of global authoritarian rule, so as to retain its social power. Today, that is a danger that lurks more than ever under the surface of post-politics, which operates within multiple rationalities and affects, and above all, within the overall socio-economic context of neoliberal capitalism.

Third, under Bonaparte's rule, politics was reduced to an instrumentalist or technocratic rule. Similarly, in post-politics everyday life has been subjected to increased technocratic control, ensuring that social movements cannot be seen to take root and thrive, and that those who challenge the system politically and ethically can never, under any circumstances, be perceived to win (Graeber 2011). Politics is, therefore, reduced to a technical-pragmatic exercise in implementing and managing developments that are regarded as inevitable, performed by an elite coalition of diverse experts, consultants, economists, strategists, risk managers, business elites, and gurus (Bavo 2007: 7; see also Davies 2014; Stavrakakis 2007). This is a process in which politics operates according to a single economic logic, a violent process in which economic competition and free market appeared to become unquestionable, naturalised backgrounds. Reducing qualities to quantities, post-politics empties out the authentic cores that constitute politics, namely conflict and antagonism. Post-politics is, therefore, the current colonisation of politics by market-based techniques of evaluation.

Marx's analysis of *The Eighteenth Brumaire* is sharp and vivid. While 'not drawing an exact parallel' to Bonapartism, present-day readers will find some resonances in contemporary politics. My own is to think of the capitalisation and militarisation of society and then to grasp the truth of post-politics. As a peculiar form of neoliberalism, post-politics configures all aspects of life in economic terms. For this reason, it expresses itself as an inability to think conflict and struggle in politics. As a principled counterrevolutionary formation, like Bonaparte's rule, it aims at defusing the idea of event. If happiness, as Benjamin illustrates (2003: 390), is liberation from pseudo-events, that is, 'farce', which occurs as counterrevolution, the task is to remember the chains of the past in order to liberate the present. Only on this basis can it be possible to break the misery and counterrevolutionary aspects of the present and create something different from what already *is*. The past that I am interested in is the farcical character of *The Eighteenth Brumaire* that, as principled, reactionary logic, now reappears in a different guise, as one of the dominant modes of thinking in contemporary society: post-politics. According to Benjamin, the historical consciousness of what-has-been starts with a 'political awakening', which offers an interpretation of past and present events. Hence I suggest that *The Eighteenth Brumaire* is a text that comes to the present from the past and awakes the oppressed in the very core of the present, a remembrance. What precisely does post-politics stand for in the current historical conjuncture between the present and the past? This will be the central question addressed in the second part of the chapter.

Post-Politics: Some Definitions

A common complaint about the late capitalist society is that it has been profoundly depoliticised in this way, and a number of thinkers have begun to describe this process as 'post-political' (Bavo 2007; Crouch 2004; Diken 2009; Mouffe 2005; Swyngedouw 2009a, 2009b; Wilson & Swyngedouw 2014; Žižek 1999). At this point, the respective positions of Chantal Mouffe, Slavoj Žižek, and Jacques Rancière I find especially telling because they help us better understand how post-politics is characterised by a propensity towards harmony, towards a consensual arrangement in which antagonism, radical structural change, the event, seem to be ignored. As key thinkers of post-politics, they are concerned with the evacuation of the political and explore the emancipatory potentialities that are set against post-politics.

Let us start with Chantal Mouffe. Mouffe argues that post-politics imposes consensus and excludes the 'passions' from politics. In a post-political vision, she suggests, the dimension of antagonism based on affect vanishes. For this reason, the post-political vision leaves no room for affective or passionate form of politics. Post-politics, according to Mouffe, cannot accommodate deep difference; it does not produce difference (in the sense of antagonism, dialectic) but rather a deliberation, which denies passion in favour of consensus. In this sense, Mouffe proposes 'agonistic pluralism' as a fundamental ingredient of public culture and politics that involves 'a vibrant clash of democratic political positions' (Mouffe 1996: 16, 2005: 14, 20–1).

All of this brings us to the distinction between 'politics' and the 'political'. Whereas, according to Mouffe, politics refers to 'the set of practices and institutions through which an order is created, organising human coexistence in the context of conflictuality provided by the political', the political refers to the potential emergence of new forms of antagonism, understood as a distinctive political experience in which particular identities can be constituted and refuted (Mouffe 2005: 9).

Whereas the political refers to the distinctive experience of antagonism, politics necessarily involves an agonistic struggle for hegemony. Post-politics, in this sense, refers to a situation in which antagonisms are *repressed*. And, insofar as politics is politicisation, politics without antagonism is a depoliticised politics. The aim of an adequate democratic theory is, in contrast, to defuse antagonism and affirm democracy, that is, to provide the possibility for antagonism to be transformed into 'agonism', so that conflict takes a form 'that does not destroy the political association' (Mouffe 2005: 19–20). Whereas antagonism designates a we/they relation 'in which the two sides are enemies who do not share any common ground', agonism designates a we/they relation 'where the conflicting parties, although acknowledging that there is no rational solution to their conflict, nevertheless recognise the legitimacy of their opponents' (Mouffe 2005: 20).

Another key thinker of post-politics is Slavoj Žižek. He argues that the post-political is a principled 'political' formation that 'forecloses' the political, preventing the 'politicization' of particular conflicts and identities. According to Žižek, post-politics is the attempt 'to depoliticise the conflict by bringing it to its extreme, via the direct militarization of politics' (1999: 29). In contrast to Mouffe's approach, Žižek conceptualises post-politics as operating through the *foreclosure* of class struggle, ensuring that events do not occur. For Žižek, however, class struggle can never be truly eliminated. Conflict and struggle are the system, the system is conflict and struggle. Post-politics, Žižek argues, is marked by a false hope that struggle and alternate political possibilities might be resolved, allowing the system to go on as far as it can. However, Žižek reminds us forcefully that there is always an alternative that is never assimilated. This unassimilated rest, in Žižek, is revolutionary struggle. Though post-politics tries to occlude the very possibility of alternate social imaginaries to the existing order, conflict and struggle nevertheless remain significant elements of revolutionary politics.

Also worth mentioning in this context is Rancière's interpretation of post-democracy. Rancière uses the concept of post-democracy to refer to what Mouffe and Žižek call post-politics. He defines post-democracy as 'a political idyll of achieving the common good by an enlightened government of elites buoyed by the confidence of the masses' (1999: 93). Post-democracy is a consensual arrangement that operates not through repression but through *disavowal*. For Rancière, post-democracy operates within a *given* socio-spatial distribution of things and people. This givenness, this existing order of things, is nothing other than the police order, or what Rancière (2001) calls 'partition of the sensible'.

Rancière argues that 'conflict' is tightly controlled by the police order with the object of replacing a democratic configuration of politics with a post-democratic consensus that eliminates real dispute, the very possibility of demonstrating 'acts of subjectivation' and 'contestation' that might interrupt the existing order. In this sense, 'consensus is the reduction of politics to the police' (Rancière 2001). The post-democratic police order insists on circulation: 'Move along! There is nothing to see here!' (Rancière 2001). Assembling around a consensus, the 'police' is a process of counting, of managing who and what counts, and the manner in which they count. The police, then, may be understood as a distributional power in service of the ends of neoliberal order. In such an order, antagonisms are only permitted if they do not interrupt and challenge that distribution which permits them. The police refers to the 'distribution of the sensible', that is to say, the legitimisation of inequality as common sense. It is established against the equality and operates through disavowal under the banner of consensus.

For Rancière, the real question, therefore, is: if the police is based on a particular regime of representation, what would constitute a genuine democracy, a proper political democratic sequence? Politics proper can only be expressed in adversarial terms and a coming together which can only occur in conflict (Rancière 2007: 49). It breaks out of the prevailing distribution of the sensible. It asserts yelping dissent and rupture as the proper bases for politics. A proper political act, for Rancière, perturbs the existing legal order, the police, and gives word to the Wrong, to those who are not included, whose statements are not comprehensible in the ruling political/police space. Hence, a proper political act claims, in the name of equality, a place in the order of things, demanding 'the part for those who have no-part' (Rancière 2001). Politics proper, according to Rancière, only occurs when the existing order is questioned and interrupted.

To summarise, Mouffe theorises post-politics as a hegemonic order that represses antagonism, Žižek as a specific form of depoliticisation that forecloses class struggle, and Rancière as the distribution of the sensible, the police order that disavows equality. Broadly speaking, however, they all refer to a situation in which politics is reduced to the economic, to a depoliticised expert administration, and the space of legitimate political debate is compromised by the coordination of interests, whereby all problems are left to experts, social workers, and technocrats, that is, to an elite coalition of diverse experts.

In this literature on post-politics, therefore, there is a great deal of recurrence or repetition in the precise meaning of the term. One significant exception is Japhy Wilson's and Erik Swyngedouw's newly edited book *The Post-Political and Its Discontents: Spaces of Depoliticisation, Spectres of Radical Politics*, where they provide a series of theoretical approaches to excavating the dynamics through which post-politics comes into being. But in their work, too, the links between historical social regimes and the corresponding affects have only been hastily suggested. The clarification of the affective dimension and the historical social regimes are crucial to the meaning of post-politics. So this literature on post-politics has limitations and only indirectly relates to social and political theory and IR. Though the literature of post-politics is fascinating and valid, it fails to grasp the complex interplay between sovereignty, discipline, control and terrorism at a theoretical level and conceptualise their affective logics. This book rigorously theorises the complex linkages between post-politics and its affective structures and historical social regimes. It employs a topological analysis that aims to explore how the established social regimes are configured in assemblies of post-politics, without implying that they follow a straightforward linear development.

As noted before, productive repetition redeems past events, whereas bare repetition simply parodies the past, the consequence of which is 'farce'. Productive repetition (tragedy) is revolutionary, for it is a resurrection of past events, bare repetition (farce) is counterrevolutionary, for it is a repetition without difference or consequence that produces non-events. The farcical character of post-politics derives from the fact that it builds upon harmony and consensus; what it produces is nothing other than pseudo-events within the confines of the given. Its aim is to repress all forms of disruptive resistance, ensuring that revolutionary subversion is an impossible one. In this sense the post-political politics is an old trick repackaged, but with some flimsy social democratic window dressing (Mouffe 2000: 93): in mid–nineteenth-century France it was socialism for the Party of Order; in McCarthy's day it was anti-communism coupled with the national security state; and today it is post-politics which is not a positive politics, actively pursuing a new social project, but 'a reactive politics, whose motivating force is defence against a perceived threat' (Žižek 2008b: 41).

In short, it is its counterrevolutionary aspects that make post-politics farcical. Hence, it endlessly promises to bring democracy and prosperity, and advocates 'consensus' within the bounds of an existing order. The only subject position this farce allows is that of individual types/heroes who have the ability to capitalise historical moments in which they live without disrupting the givenness, the very possibility of legal normativity. Post-politics is the current project of suppressing the politicisation of subjectivities.

The fact that we live in a post-political society, that politics has been suffocated and foreclosed, has also received severe criticism. One might think of Jodi Dean's work (2009) on Rancière, where she argues the shortcomings of his conceptualisation of post-democratic politics. Dean's article, entitled 'Politics without Politics', is a significant attempt to demonstrate the weaknesses and the inadequacies of the sign of 'democracy' as it is currently constituted for left political aspiration. Dean's article examines the end of ideology thesis, which Rancière associates with the triumph of democracy. Referring to Rancière's idea of post-democracy 'as the art of suppressing the political', Dean (2009: 22) claims that this argument is incapable of handling the current conjuncture. While it is worth noting that he speaks of the cause of depoliticisation, Rancière, according to Dean, can't explain the specificity of neoliberalism (Dean 2009: 22). Thus, the arguments for post-politics and de-democratisation 'are at best unconvincing and at worst misleading' (Dean 2009: 23). Because left political theory should undo the damage neoliberal ideas and polices have created, Dean suggests that 'the claim that we are in a post-political time is childishly petulant'. For this reason, post-politics might not be a helpful term to grasp contemporary reality. As a term, post-politics, Dean argues, obfuscates the political moves and struggles that produce the current conjuncture, and 'prevents us from understanding them as such' (Dean 2009: 23).

Nevertheless, Dean argues that post-politics might be a useful description for two reasons. First, it refers to a specific problem in left political theory: 'the fantasy of a politics without politics' (Dean 2009: 24).

Thought in this way, post-politics becomes a term that refers neither to governance, nor to consensus, but rather to an identity politics that the left tends to embrace. For Dean, the left embraces identity politics based on inclusion and recognition results in naturalisation rather than the politicisation of identity. Second, post-politics is also a useful descriptor 'as an accentuation of the depoliticization of democracy' (Dean 2009). Dean seems keen to argue that in contemporary society, to demand democracy is to demand what already exists, that is, the givenness of the partition of the sensible. To this extent, as Dean seems to hint, democracy sustains, rather than challenges, the hegemonic relations in a given political constellation. Basically, this means that democracy is not the solution; it becomes a common denominator on which both left and right agree. Democracy, in short, takes the form of a fantasy that leads to a politics without politics.

At this point, Dean gives the example of the American right in order to structure and strengthen her critique of post-politics. She argues that the right has been engaged in the political, reframing the constitution, reversing the steps that had been taken towards greater race equality, redistributing the wealth to the wealthy, undermining habeas corpus and enforcement of the Geneva Conventions, expanding unwarranted state surveillance, lobbying aggressively to make evangelical Christian beliefs a part of schools' curricula so that creationism and climate change denial will be taught in the classrooms and so on. Given that these are all political achievements, the claim that we live in a post-political society, according to Dean, does not have political grounds. As such, post-politics is inapplicable to the United States post 9/11 as it fails to acknowledge 'the collapse of regulation in the financial sector, the rise of private security forces, and contemporary practices of surveillance wherein state agencies rely on private databases' (Dean 2009: 24).

While I find Dean's argument elegant and persuasive, it results, however, in an analysis that fails to grasp the governmental rationalities and the affective logics of post-politics. Let us start with the right's engagement in the political. To be sure, the American right once managed to transform politics; they set the pace for 'political change'. How did we get here? Contra Dean, I argue that the right's engagement in the political is a result of post-political politics, an emergency politics in which fear/security becomes a way of life (Badiou 2008). We live in emergency times, a new era in which the exercise of state power refers to a depoliticised expert administration. In such a situation, the only way to introduce passion into politics, the only way to energise people and increase their self-awareness is through fear (Žižek 2008b). The right seeks to mobilise fear and ressentiment on the part of relatively privileged groups in relation to the 'threatening others'. Reducing politics to affects, it boils down all political issues to the fear of external threats: immigration, crime and terrorism, economic downturn, foreign trade, as well as socialism and

Islamism (Obama is a Muslim and a socialist). 'Increasingly reckless, anarchic and strident', the American right, as columnist Gary Younge observes, 'is living in a parallel world where fear and rage drive out the facts' (2010: 31). The right, in short, articulated its lack of political conviction by trying to mobilise the 'fear of the fear' and ended up naturalising rather than questioning the capitalist order and free-market policies.

The right-wing politics, like post-politics, relies on the denial of a radical, utopian dimension to politics and depicts the given reality as the only reality. With regard to George Bush, as Dean herself suggests, 'right-wing politics attempts to restore a ruptured society to its original unity' (2006: 126). Having a general suspicion of social change, the American right plays a given game that relies on the manipulation of fears in a populist fashion, which sustains rather than challenges the already-held beliefs that structure neoliberal capitalism. Radical social change, it believes, should be cautious and pragmatic. The American right seeks to sustain the existing values (neoliberal capitalism, the market, conservatism), with no ambition of overcoming their positivity; it seeks to preserve particular relations of power. Committed to capitalist power relations, it defends privilege from those who threaten it (e.g. the power of employers and managers over workers). The American right, in other words, pivots on an essential commitment—defence of privilege and inequality. Thus, it is really 'successful' in 'politicising' the notion of the public good and replacing it with a free-market ideology precisely through naturalising and establishing a consensus around neoliberal capitalism.

In this way enforced consensus becomes an invariant of politics, and most significant issues inherent to the system cease to create scissions, taking the politics of fear and the market order merely as an unquestionable social and economic goods. In the final analysis, therefore, nothing really political happens; the outcome of the mobilisation of the American right does not change anything, and, in contrast to productive repetition, no perspective takes place. Precisely in this sense, and contrary to Dean, the 'political success' of the American right should not be seen as 'politics proper'. Politics proper aims at disrupting the situation as a whole. What we see in the American right, however, is bare repetition, that is, farce, which produces non-events within the confines of the neoliberal order and the market. In the end, therefore, the right does not provide an alltogether different perspective on social change, and everybody returns to the same position as in the beginning.

As for the private security forces and the contemporary practices of surveillance: one of the central characteristics of post-politics is that it is primarily security oriented. Contrary to Dean's claim that post-politics fails to grasp the rise of military-industrial complex, that it is unable to acknowledge the rise of the contemporary practises of surveillance, post-politics focuses on depoliticised expert management and designates security as the overriding responsibility of the modern state. By making security one of the central features to modern governance (Agamben 2001), post-politics redefines populations as vulnerable and 'resilient' that must be protected (Evans & Reid 2014). If security is one organising principle of post-politics, resilience is another. If security comes to be a fundamental dispositif for managing the society, resilience manages the imagination. In the process, therefore, the affective logic becomes a generative principle of formation for rule. The post-political is a determinate political formation with distinctive social regimes and affects towards ever-increasing militarisation and the economisation of society. The key question then is how to conceptualise the relationships between regimes of power and their affective logics. As I propose in this book, the discursive framing of post-politics and established social regimes has enormous implications for society and politics. Yet, in Dean's analysis, this remains underresearched. Installing 'communicative capitalism' as the power of agency, and 'drive' the only affect, does not seem relevant precisely because they fail to acknowledge the complex linkages between post-political neoliberalism, and historical social regimes and their affective structures.

For instance, in order to explain liberalism's 'constitutive inability', Dean refers to Lacan's discussion of drive as a 'constant thrust', which 'forbids any assimilation of the drive to a biological function, which always has a rhythm' (Lacan, quoted in Dean 2010: 4). Lacan's conception of drive, Dean argues, 'expresses the reflexive structure of complex networks' (2010: 30). And beyond the law 'are the reflexive circuits of drive' (2010: 30). In this context communicative capitalism, according to Dean, 'thrives not because of unceasing or insatiable desires but in and as the repetitive intensity of drive' (2010: 31). By making communicative capitalism operative, drive therefore disengages subjects from a political act of resistance and transformation. For this reason, as Dean argues, 'under conditions of the decline of symbolic efficiency, drive is not an act'. Politically speaking, the challenge is, according to Dean, to produce 'the conditions of possibility for breaking out of or redirecting the loop of drive' (2010: 31).

For Dean, therefore, 'the structure of biopolitics, biopolitics' underlying dynamic and shape, is drive' (2010: 4). Drive can still help us clarify 'how it is that biopolitics is a politics of reversal, repetition, and return', an activity wherein action and reaction merge together (2010: 4). Emphasising three features of the Lacanian notion of drive, that is to say, drive as failure 'which does not reach the goal to enjoy', drive as a 'compulsion to repeat' and drive as 'creative destruction' (2010: 4–5), Dean seems to be saying that drive has a force of loss and capture, which strengthens the specificities of both liberalism and neoliberalism. Drive allows us to understand how people are 'captured in the population', a biopolitical capture that neoliberalism uses and extends its hegemony.

This understanding of drive as a force, as an affect that sustains neo-liberalism is also prone to problems. Drive may be an important affect that enables us to see biopolitics as by-product of fundamental change in terms of 'governmentality', but it is insufficient to understand how human beings are captured in the population, a biopolitical capture that neoliberalism amplifies and extends. Neoliberalism, as Foucault states, is 'the general framework of biopolitics' (2008: 22). Only on this basis will be able to understand the true meaning of neoliberalism and biopolitics. Neoliberalism relies not only on a circuit of fear and danger but an entire political economy of affect. Because it produces and organises different social regimes, its functioning also requires multiple differentiated affects in which subjects are managed and governed through a biopolitical capture. The established social regimes are a kind of sustaining the hegemonic power of the system, a mechanism which consists of affects and emotions. Neoliberalism relies on *this* interplay between different social regimes and the affective circuit they generate, intervening in its management. In other words, it is as much about mobilising concrete social regimes as it is about regulating multiple affects.

Precisely in this sense, it cannot be reduced either to drive, or the stimulation of fear and threat. Neoliberalism is not stable; it is continually transforming itself. In short, it is a dynamic ideology, a heterogeneous and multi-faceted project. And it is necessary that our analysis targets this nexus of relations between different regimes of power, a multiple political economy of affect, life and security/militarisation/war that is its heart. The affective logics are tendencies or incitements inherent to regimes of power, but they cannot determine in any final way the concrete experiences of those logics, such as perceived emotions. Just as each social regime is connected with the other social regimes in a specific way, each affect is connected with other affects without any developmental succession. Closing down possibilities rather than opening them, Dean, however, seems to offer drive as the only stable category of the political economy of affect. The biopolitical attempt to manage life in its productive new capacities, to maintain completely a population and life, requires a force that exceeds the capacity of drive as a sustaining force. Interventions are, after all, conducted in order to affect life so that the individual will behave in the desired way. The post-political nature of neoliberalism's dynamic oscillation between the established social regimes, its compulsive circulation from one affect to the other, indicates that we reground the affective logics differently, that an analysis of extra dimension of affect is necessary for any social and spatial analysis of neoliberalism. What truly matters is an analysis that explains the dynamics of power and the established social regimes, which directly manipulate and intervene in life purely at the level of its 'affective relations'.

Dean also argues that the claim that we are in a post-political time is 'like the left is saying, if we don't get to play what we want, we're not going to play' (2009: 23). But do the regimes and affects characterising post-politics completely foreclose the possibility of politics? No, of course not! Conflict and antagonism are prior to politics and are never entirely eradicated. The reign of post-politics does not mean the end of politics; it does suggest, however, that the traditional models of politics are no longer valid, and that new models are called for. What gives rise to post-politics is also what gives rise to possibilities for radical political change. But Dean leaves this point fundamentally untouched, and she fails even to treat post-politics as a complex and historical regime of power relations, instead asserting it as crude and stable 'fact'. Post-politics is a moving target. And 'moving targets are, nevertheless, targets of a kind. Harder to hit, but more rewarding for it' (Reid 2010b: 394). In this sense, multiple governmental rationalities and their associated affects are means to, and methods of, post-politics. What is then needed is a dynamic topological perspective that aims to explore the complex interplay between sovereignty, discipline, control and terrorism at a theoretical level, and conceptualise the relationships between complex and historical regimes of power relations and their affective logics. Topology refers to virtualities as well as conditions of possibility that are actualised in concrete situations; the topological approach is a theoretical strategy through which I propose to characterise, link together, and analyse different social regimes. Today, post-politics, the established social regimes and related affects such as ressentiment, fear, cynicism, and spite continue to play a major role in relation to the social. We need a dynamic topological approach to analyse them.

Post-politics oscillates in between present and future, to make sure that 'disruptive events' do not take place. Post-politics in this respect actually precludes the gesture of politicisation proper. More importantly, and contrary to Dean, the post-political consensual order takes as foundational the inevitability of neoliberal capitalism and the idea that radical dissent and antagonism can only exist within the bounds of neoliberal consensus (as long as they do not attempt to radically challenge the very foundations of neoliberal capitalism). In the process, politics is boxed into a technocratic managerialism, which leads to the effective silencing of egalitarian movements and genuine social change.

The Euro Crisis

When Syriza won Greece's parliamentary elections in January 2015, it was an absolute shock to the European Union. Syriza is an acronym, meaning 'Coalition of the Radical Left'. More importantly, the party won the election using a campaign platform that was remarkably clear on one major issue: end the brutal austerity measures imposed by 'the Troika', the European Commission, the International Monetary Fund, and the European Central Bank. Syriza's promises and policy views were a direct threat to the consensual mode of politics in the Eurozone. The neoliberal Troika was terrified.

After the electoral victory, the Troika's economic and politico-ideological war against Greece escalated. They did everything they could to deprive Syriza of power. In fact, they wanted 'regime change and total humiliation', as Krugman put it (2015). Tired of the endless negotiations and unable to write off the debt, the Syriza government announced a referendum on the EU proposal of new austerity measures for July 5, 2015, which resulted in a clear 'OXI (NO)' vote victory against the Troika. The day after, however, Syriza leader Alexis Tsipras performed an unexpected U-turn and announced that his government was ready to resume the negotiations with the Troika. Days later, Greece agreed to a bailout deal with the Troika, a deal which is the same as the one the Greek people heroically rejected in the referendum. The Greek Parliament also approved the bailout deal, which wanted Greece to privatise its assets and 'depoliticise' its public administration. Though Syriza won the referendum by a clear majority, they acted as if they lost it. Twenty-five MPs resigned and formed a new party called Popular Unity. The hope that the Syriza government would change the neoliberal establishment was dashed.

It is true that Syriza abandoned most of its promises and accepted to implement the same neoliberal austerity measures they were supposed to end. However, the crisis also exposed lies and the hypocrisy of the consensual-neoliberal European Union. At its most radical, it shows how neutral expert administration, an undemocratic rationality, effectively governs the entire political process. Žižek writes:

> Strategic decisions based on power are more and more masked as administrative regulations based on neutral expert knowledge, and they are more and more negotiated in secrecy and enforced without democratic consultation. The struggle that goes on is the struggle for the European economic and political Leitkultur (the guiding culture). The EU powers stand for the technocratic status quo that has kept Europe in inertia for decades.
>
> (2015a)

The EU treatment of Greece is post-political politics at its purest. What we are witnessing is the managerial-technocratic bourgeois order whose only role is to impose 'necessary regulatory measures' to keep neoliberal capitalism intact. So we are forced to believe that 'we are all in this together' and austerity measures are necessary to tackle the debt. In other words, the debt can and must be paid by cutting jobs, reducing wages and living standards, smashing the trade unions, and destroying public services. This is the 'successful solution' to debt crisis that experts, economics, politicians and media have come up with. What we have here is a creation of a veritable sense of shared guilt, which aims to justify austerity policies imposed by the Troika. Austerity is, however, a class-driven strategy, a form of capitalist governance, aiming to revive financialisation. Austerity is therefore intimately connected to the logic of finance. It aims to 'feed a process of accumulation and expropriation that is centred on financialisation' (Fumagalli & Lucarelli 2015: 6). It destroys the lives of ordinary people, 'by diverting disposable income into the financial sector, thereby guaranteeing that economic shrinkage, not growth, takes place in the real economy of goods and services. A war of finance against not only the working class but uniquely, industry as well' (Coats 2015). Austerity is a carefully calculated political strategy for the common class interest, the interests of the capital. It is an ideological shell, a perfect cover for neoliberal capitalism in which 'the enrichment of the few comes the impoverishment of the many' (Coats 2015).

The Greek case also shows that the depoliticised and technocratic managerial order is not the exception but the rule in contemporary society. As we also witnessed in Greece and in Italy in 2011, elected, if flawed, prime ministers were forced to resign in favour of unelected economic experts, of technocrats, for they could not push through all of the necessary draconian austerity measures. In the Italian case, for instance, Berlusconi was toppled neither for corruption nor for rising unemployment, xenophobia, or for having sex with underage girls, but because the markets thought he had to go, whereas in the Greek case former Prime Minister George Papandreou threatened to give the people a say on austerity plan, through a referendum. This means that in a crisis, so-called democratic principles and institutions may be entirely scrapped in favour of technocracy, of 'safe pair of hands', backed by the full force of the capitalist state, for the sole purpose of implementing neoliberal policies. It also illustrates how sovereign decision (permanent state of exception) is intermingled with market-based economic rationalities. More troubling, though, is that the suspension of parliamentary democracy in favour of 'unity governments', of the rule by the ideologically neutral technicians, 'is viewed not as a problem but as an affirmation that these nations mean business' (Guardian Editorial 2011: 26). This is a modern debased version of the political that relies on expert knowledge and administration, thereby reducing politics to 'a professional spirit of an engineer fixing an aeroplane' (Guardian Editorial 2011: 26). In post-politics, the political no longer represents itself in terms of purely political aims, dissent, and rupture. Rather, dissent is rendered complicit within the logic of the existing order, for instance, being accommodated by consumer capitalism. Thus, large-scale social and political problems are given depoliticised solutions in which human beings are reduced to 'a pure disembodied gaze' observing their own 'absence':

> As Lacan pointed out, this is the fundamental subjective position of fantasy: to be reduced to a gaze observing the world in the condition of the subject's non-existence—like the fantasy of witnessing the act

of one's own conception, parental copulation, or the act of witnessing one's own burial, like Tom Sawyer and Huck Finn.

(Žižek 2010: 80)

The aim of Bonapartism was to place sovereignty under specific security regimes in the name of order, of bourgeoisie. At the heart of regime's policy was technocratic management, which was supposed to be a catalyst for the development of a competitive economy. As such, the political debate was reduced to a farcical exchange without taking on an antagonistic form. Similarly, the aim of post-politics is to protect the neoliberal order whilst placing it under specific social regimes. The farcical character of post-politics derives from the fact that it is based on a technocratic management, which is viewed as the only viable alternative for the development of a market capitalism based on competition. The Bonapartist politics was largely restricted to the wealthy members of the regime, and not necessarily across 'class' lines, for a share of political and economic power. Thus, politics was locked into a 'technocratic management', represented by older and newer elites. In post-politics, in a similar way, politics proper is prohibited and restricted to experts, scientists, gurus and technocrats who shape the social environment. In this, there is no proper content of politics; the political space is closed down by criminalising or ridiculing dissent. Post-politics is farcical in the sense that it is deployed to safeguard the managerial-technocratic 'bourgeois order', for it is the best ideological shell behind which neoliberal capitalism continues on its brutal, militarised, unjust, and destructive way.

Militarisation of Society

While post-politics sacralises the liberal market, it also mobilises all sorts of military/security complexes, a process in which the state of exception has become the rule (Agamben 1998, 2005). The militarisation belies the seemingly pacific façade of 'consensual' post-politics; indeed, contemporary society now seems to be formed in the image of militarisation. What we are witnessing is the emergence of 'the new military urbanism' as the organising principle of contemporary society (Graham 2010). In a sense, therefore, the exception has become the norm: military urbanism has permeated 'the sphere of the everyday, the private realm of the house' (Misselwitz & Weizman 2003: 272).

Indeed, militarisation of society is central to depoliticised consensual post-politics that has characterised the past few years. Especially since 9/11, this process has been accelerated. This is not to say that the militarisation of society did commence on September, 12, 2001. Processes of urban militarisation and securitisation are nothing new; they predate 'the war on terror'. Thus, one could argue that the 'war on terror has been used as a prism being used to conflate and further legitimize dynamics that *already* were militarizing urban space' (Warren 2002: 614). In effect, there is a particular relationship between the histories of the city and political violence. For instance, war, for Virilio (2002), is at the origins of the foundation of cities. War, according to Virilio, is not only to be understood as 'warfare' but as a means for thinking about the way in which society itself is constituted. War, in this sense, is an 'absolute immanence' that political sovereign power 'ceaselessly fails to capture in performing the kinds of biopolitical manoeuvres upon which forms of civil pacificity are built' (Reid 2005: 5). As an absolute immanence, 'pure war' enables the state to establish homogeneous cities under the auspices of purity and safety. Indeed, methods of discipline and control—coupled with processes of urban militarisation—served to normalise war and preparations for war as central elements of the material, political-economic and cultural constitution of cities and urban life (see Graham 2012: 137).

To understand the importance of militarisation and war as the organising principles of societies, it might be useful to read Clausewitz from a Foucauldian perspective. Such a Foucauldian perspective suggests that in *On War* (1993), Clausewitz did not simply define the conjunctive relation of war to society and politics as the art of strategy. He provided a theory of strategy upon which complex power relations operate within contemporary societies (Foucault 2003; see also Reid 2003). The primary significance of Clausewitz's strategic thought, according to Foucault, was its basic principle upon which a new form of political power had emerged, that which Foucault described as 'governmentality' (Foucault 2007, 2008; see also Reid 2003: 2). Clausewitz's theory is valuable as it outlines the modern role of warfare in what Foucault (1998) called the strategy of power. As Foucault provides an analytics of power that permeates the morphological networks of contemporary society, so Clausewitz helps us better understand the networking of 'the liberal way of war' (Dillon & Reid 2009). In this sense, militarisation and war take on positive characteristics of neoliberalism that takes on the task of the management of life in the name of the entire population and life.

Post-politics, then, is as much about *economisation* as it is about the *militarisation* of society. It is as much about expanding the processes of capital as it is about war and violence. These two registers are intimately connected. Today the post-political nature of neoliberalism increasingly centres on securitising and militarising the architectures and circulations of the city (Dillon & Reid 2009; Graham 2012). The struggle for contemporary society now coincides more and more with the struggle for the liberal way of war, for the ability to provide security is especially useful in maintaining a liberal way of life. However, as Agamben (2001) shows, security consists not in the prevention of crises and catastrophes but rather in their continual production, regulation, and management. Therefore, by making security central to modern governance, there is the danger of producing a situation of clandestine complicity between terrorism and state terrorism, locked in a deathly embrace of mutual incitement. When security becomes the organising principle of politics, and society and law is replaced by the state of exception, a state 'can always be provoked by terrorism to become itself terroristic' (Agamben 2001).

The state of exception is always reactionary. Its declaration is a form of violence. We know very well from Schmitt (1985) that the political involves a permanent struggle between order and 'chaos'. This is why the state of exception is declared to save the condition of normality (order), that is to say, to avoid a true exception (Žižek 2002: 108). The state of exception is always counterrevolutionary because its main task is to displace dissent and resistance against the existing order. It holds together as a response to an 'urgent threat': how to protect order against the fear of disorder. Post-politics is nothing else than the materialisation of the state of exception as a reactionary political principle.

We seem doomed to repeat history. In its desire to protect a liberal way of life through militarisation, war, and violence, post-politics takes the empty form of farce, bare repetition. Post-politics is counterrevolutionary because it is a compulsion to repeat. For Marx, tragedy refers to disharmony and interruption, whereas farce is built upon harmony and consensus. In this sense farce is a constellation of non-events which produce no difference within the bounds of a given hegemonic discourse. The farce of Louis Bonaparte was tragic, not for the man but for the society. Likewise, the farce of post-politics is tragic, not for the man but for the society. It is its counterrevolutionary tendencies that make post-politics farcical. Just as Louis Bonaparte subverted democracy and disavowed class antagonisms in order to bring 'freedom' in a mode of futurity, in the interest of the capitalist class, post-politics recognises freedom and democracy only in a conservative way, specifically as market freedom. Both are authoritarian populist regimes that allow individual heroes to emerge in the popular consciousness (Bonaparte–Bush Senior and Bush Junior). Both depict their societies as the end of history (the 'end' being Bonapartism in one case and neoliberal capitalism in the other). Both mobilise the repressive state apparatus in order to subvert democracy and disavow class antagonisms. In both, political debate is reduced to the managerial-technocratic 'bourgeois order' without taking the form of antagonism. And in both the politics of security/fear appears as the ultimate mobilising figure; two militarised societies, two preemptive strategies, two counterrevolutionary regimes, one Bonapartist, one post-political, which depict the given reality as the only reality, pushing the idea of radical social change to the background.

Just as Bonapartism signified the 'depoliticisation' of the political, post-politics signifies a naturalisation that rejects the political nature of given questions. However, neither engineering nor militarisation, politics always involves antagonisms which require us to make a choice between conflicting alternatives. It represents reclaiming the terms of debate in wider society. Post-politics, by contrast, has eliminated a genuine political space of radical conflict and disagreement. It should be clear how in such a climate there is hardly room for a genuine political gesture: that is, the positioning of those groups who have no space in the current or future police order. At this point, a naïve, but nevertheless crucial, question is quite appropriate: is consensual post-political order a peaceful order? Absolutely not. Because post-politics is based on a consensual order by excluding those who understand themselves as increasingly alienated and abandoned by neoliberal forms of power and rationality, this provokes greater violent insurgent activism. Because the system is unable to handle political and mass civic participation, it operates culturally and ideologically through the demonisation of dissent, or the moral castigation of all radicalism as 'bad', as 'terrorism'. Are we not witnessing the same ideological operation in the ongoing revolts against the system all around the world? If you build a system on the assumption that there will be no radical dissent, critique, and fundamental conflict, what happens when antagonism and dissent do appear, and begin to articulate themselves as political alternatives? In this sense, the violence we have seen against protesters (Occupy Movement, the Arab revolts, the Indignados, the Québec student strike, Gezi, etc.) exposes the brittleness of the post-political nature of neoliberalism and its refusal to accommodate radical socio-political conflict and antagonism in politics. What such hypocrisy shows is that the 'intimate' partnership between democracy and neoliberal capitalism has come to an end.

All of which leads to a problem: when the political, and the real democratic subject, is foreclosed, the blind violence tends to be seen as the only 'political' (re)action for the affective staging of active discontent. Thus, even though post-politics represses the political, such a repression is bound to lead to a 'return of the suppressed', to violent expressions of discontent and hatred but also to the return of new forms of anti-immigrant and anti-Marxist racism, as in the case of the Norwegian terrorist Anders Behring Breivik, who killed 77 people in Norway in July 2011. Which points to a problem: we live in a society in which 'the only available alternative to enforced democratic consensus is a blind acting out' (Žižek 2011).

Consequently, late capitalist consensual governance and debates signal a depoliticised politics 'where administrative governance defines the zero-level of politics' (Swyngedouw 2009b: 225–6). It is at this point that one should return to the historical lessons of *The Eighteenth Brumaire*. The most astonishingly original analysis of Marx in the text is not the idea that human subjects make history, albeit in well-determined conditions. The novelty is rather quite different: 'traditions from all the dead generations weigh like a nightmare on the brain of the living' (Marx 1852/2002: 19). That is to say, we agents in the present 'are compelled by the imagery and symbols of the past when they come to fulfil some historic task' (Cowling & Martin 2002: 4–5). The nightmare world of tradition that Marx refers to is nothing else than 'farce'. The 'new' that comes to be actualised in the present always gives a comforting 'familiarity' in which the spectres of the past are continuously summoned up. Marx's theory, in other words, is that history is a parody of events which have to be thrown away in the dustbin. Similarly, in contemporary society, we have post-politics which is not the product of 'real' history but merely of a 'farce', a dusting off of long-dead historical form. Post-politics is a 'political' formation, a principled counterrevolutionary logic that aims to defuse, disperse, and suppress radical social change.

History, then, is revealed to be a tissue of farcical non-events, which are not identical in nature but inextricably merged with their effects. Failure to be conscious about the past events results in a pseudo-history that is static rather than dynamic. The greatest danger for our understanding of history thus resides in the entire model of linearity and the violence that accompanies it. No doubt this is a form of temporal hegemony to which we are subjected and by which we unwittingly become a silent accomplice to the dominant. As it appears in Marx and Benjamin, the ruthless critique of linear progression provides an opportunity for correction to homogeneity of history and vulgar progressivism. Seen in this way, one cannot address the present independently of the past; the present is always in relation to the past. Benjamin speaks of 'our defeats', Marx speaks of 'inheritance', and they are talking about the same history, if not exactly the same thing. For both Marx and Benjamin, this insight is vital, for it allows us to think of the relation between time and politics in non-linear terms.

Thus, juxtaposing *The Eighteenth Brumaire* and post-politics, I aim to reinforce the act of remembrance and farce as dynamic principles of history and politics; dynamic principles in which the past (Bonaparte's rule, the French counterrevolution) and the present (post-politics) converge and unearth the real dialectics of history (Benjamin 2003: 396). I propose a 'critical' reflection in which a moment in the past (*The Eighteenth Brumaire*) and a moment in the present (post-politics) coalesce, subverting the non-linearity of history and thus providing with a theoretical and practical model for interrupting the present. And this is where Marx's text discloses its close 'political' relationship to Benjamin's philosophical revitalisation of material history.

The reign of Bonaparte was based on a 'depoliticised politics' where socialist ideals, revolutionary events, were equated with terrorism. As such, the official plebiscite campaign was accompanied by affects (e.g. fear) created by carefully established security regimes. Its logic, of course, was political because it was a reactionary counterrevolutionary logic that aimed at suppressing revolution. In short, the Bonapartist regime was a principled 'political' formation with different social regimes and affects towards militarisation and technocratic romanticism in the interest of the capitalist class. Similarly, the post-political is not simply an absence of politics. It is a determinate formation with tendencies, rationalities and affects, towards ever increasing securitisation and managerial consensual governing in the interests of the market. But what rationalities of power and affects underlie the post-political? This will be examined in the next chapter.

2 Sovereignty

The previous chapter gave a general overview of the debates concerning the functioning of post-politics in contemporary society. Taking as its point of departure Marx's analysis of not only history as farce but politics as farce in *The Eighteenth Brumaire*, it showed that post-politics is the current project of foreclosing the political. However, the crucial question raised by the last chapter was: what rationalities of power underlie the post-political; how do we understand the relationships between sovereignty, discipline and control, and their corresponding affects? Research has yet to fully delve into the complex linkages between post-politics and historical social regimes and their affective structures. In addition, radical politics must diagnose and confront these modalities of post-politics and the affective logic each regime entails and how they interrelate.

This chapter examines the concept of sovereignty, arguing that sovereign political power is one of the vital regimes to the development of post-politics. Here, I take as my point of departure Deleuze's notion of sovereignty. This is for two reasons. First, because sovereignty always involves the effort to reduce multiplicity to unity, difference to sameness; the concept of sovereign power requires itself an updated understanding on which to resist that capture operation globally. Nevertheless, sovereignty is a vengeful regime that generates ressentiment (Nietzsche 1996). The immediate exercise of vengefulness is the privilege of sovereign political power whilst victims (slaves) are burdened with ressentiment. Following Deleuze, the problem is not simply that of how to criticise sovereignty as a concept, as a social fact, for 'those who criticize without creating, those who are content to defend the vanished concept without being able to give it the forces it needs to return to life . . . are inspired by *ressentiment*' (Deleuze & Guattari 1994: 28–9). Rather, the problem is how to reinvent/reactivate concepts by giving them a space to breathe so that new forms of life come into being (Deleuze & Guattari 1987). Thus, the central purpose of this chapter is to reconceptualise sovereignty by mapping its relation to contemporary society.

Control over a territory has long been one of the fundamental organising principles of sovereignty as exemplified by the signing of the Treaty of Westphalia in 1648. According to the Westphalian vision of sovereignty, political power should not be separated from territorially defined state sovereigns. However, the conjunction between sovereignty and the exclusive control over a territory has changed in contemporary societies. Though sovereignty is often associated with territory, developments such as 'globalisation' (Appadurai 1996) and 'the war on terror' (Amoore 2006; Bigo 2006; Elden 2009) suggest that the emphasis on territories as spaces as a normative precondition for sovereignty is highly questionable (Agnew 2005; Agnew & Corbridge 1995; Brenner 2004; Cox 1991). As Saskia Sassen argues, global financial markets centred on 'cross-border flows and global telecommunications has affected two distinctive features of the modern state: sovereignty and exclusive territoriality' (1996: xii). Thus, the Westphalian sovereign state model in political geography and international relations theory, which have generally linked sovereignty with the notion of territory, which views territory as an area of land claimed by a country, is insufficient to analyse the realities of contemporary society.

This chapter argues that sovereignty can be examined in a similar fashion to territory—through contingency. Thus, we can think sovereignty as a *contingent* regime without dependence on traditional notions of territory (Elden 2013). By territory, I do not only mean national borders, lines on a map, or the physical manifestation of place. Rather, I argue that territory is to be understood as the product of a set of governmental practices than a pre-given object or physical space. The notion of territory is not absolute. It is not only defined by a 'physical space'; rather, it defines physical spaces 'through patterns of various relations'. After all, 'every type of social relation can be imagined and constructed as territorial' (Brighenti 2010: 57). In other words, territory is both a social, political, and affective process. It is always in relation to governmental practices by which things can be ordered and managed. Thus, the mainstream view that interprets territory as merely 'land' or a static 'terrain' must be challenged (Elden 2013). This, however, in no way means that we should conceive of sovereignty without territory or borders (Brenner & Elden 2009). In fact, every social regime requires a territorial endeavour. Once a social regime is set up, territory-making becomes the norm.

Territory is a dynamic concept, a heterogeneous multiple. It is a 'process, made and remade, shaped and shaping, active and reactive' (Elden 2013: 17). In other words, it is a vibrant concept, 'a juridico-political' power that is concerned with resources and the means for their management and 'circulation' (Foucault 2007: 176). For this reason, territory should be seen as a 'political technology': the 'government of populations'. For Foucault, therefore, governmentality is about population, along with security mechanisms, the discourses, rationalities of power, and the disciplinary technologies. Thus, the population 'is not the simple sum of individuals inhabiting a territory' (Foucault 2007: 70) but dependent on a series of variables that includes the 'climate', 'the material surroundings', 'the intensity of commerce and activity', and 'the circulation of wealth' (Foucault 2007). In this sense, territory is a governmental response to the problem of population. From this perspective, sovereignty is not only inseparable from territory but also from various set of practices, such as 'civil society, population and the nation' by which it becomes as 'a way of governing, a way of doing things, and a way too of relating to government' (Foucault 2007: 277; see also Elden 2007: 574). We should therefore stop using the notion of territory as the key element to define contemporary sovereign power. Sovereignty is a social regime, a set of governmental practices and rationalities that is more than a bounded entity, terrain, and territory.

Thus, following Deleuze, we need a reconceptualisation of sovereignty, for it allows us to avoid falling into the 'territorial trap' (Agnew 1994), a logic which is static and has become unable to grasp changes and transitions that occur in contemporary society. One way out of this trap, then, is to analyse sovereignty as a *contingent* concept that is able to grasp the dynamics of contemporary society. Today, with the war on terror and foreign interventions, 'boundaries may remain fixed, and considerable efforts may be undertaken to preserve existing territorial settlements' (Elden 2010: 759). Yet sovereign political power within them is held to be quite contingent in the sense that it does not only seek to simply acquire the whole territory but also to create 'zones of indistinction' (Agamben 1998). According to Agamben, the sovereign, through the use of force and violence, imposes a political order, creating an inside and outside. The outside, or zone of indistinction, is a place where the dividing line between the legality and illegality, citizen and outlaw, law and violence, war and peace, life and death tends to disappear. It is a place where administrative lawlessness becomes normalised as part of the workings of corrupt sovereign and financial power. Contemporary sovereign power seeks to create new market dynamics and thus increase the impacts of global capital flows. This, however, cannot be done without preemptive violence and war upon which sovereignty was founded (Lefebvre 1976, 1991; Mbembe 2001). Sovereignty, therefore, needs to be seen in relation to war and violence, an intersection which cannot be separated without contingency.

Crucially, therefore, sovereignty is a social regime which attempts to appropriate, or capture, war and violence and utilise them for its own purposes (Deleuze & Guattari 1983). The overall suggestion here is thus that sovereignty is best understood not through 'territoriality' (Elden 2010) but through an examination of the relation between contingency and war and violence. In short, sovereignty must be approached as a concept itself rather than simply through territoriality, which hinders our ability to understand the social, historical, affective, and geographical specificity of sovereignty, both as a social regime and a political form.

Understanding sovereignty as a contingent social regime, as the political control of power relations, allows us to account for a range of modern society. Hence, the importance of Deleuze.

In *A Thousand Plateaus*, Deleuze and Guattari provide an alternative to thinking of the concept of territory as a geographically bounded space (1987: 88). They argue that a territory (geographical, political, and conceptual) is associated with a continuously changing configuration of multiple social regimes. Each territory is the compositions of different flows, encounters, and affects. Thus, territory is never fixed, neither by national borders nor by physical manifestations of place. Rather, it is marked by dynamic movements and social processes. As dynamic configurations, various interrelated assemblages form a historically specific territory, where 'deterritorialisation', and in reaction to that, 'territorialisation', take place. State sovereignty cannot deterritorialise from some relations without (re) territorialising on some others. On this basis, then, the focus of sovereignty is not exclusion per se but the creation of ordered social and political relations and more secure life cycles, which refer, above all, to relations of dominance. State sovereignty is a social regime of capture, an instance of (re)territorialisation, which always hegemonises and stabilises new configurations of deterritorialisation. Whenever a state sovereignty, an organisation, an institution stop resistance, reterritorialisation takes place.

At this point, it is important to show the difference between Foucault's and Deleuze's analyses of sovereignty. Foucault argues that political sovereignty emerges as a 'realisation' of war and power (1977, 2003). Furthermore, Foucault's concept of sovereignty is pluralised, fragmented, relational, and closely related to various set of governmental practices spread throughout society. In this way, he aims to historicise the concept of sovereignty through discursive modalities over time by showing the transition from the (classically modern) idea of the state to the governmentalised apparatuses and the set of practices. Deleuze's analysis of state sovereignty, on the other hand, is related to both war and resistance. Indeed, Deleuze offers an account of sovereignty in which war is a property to be appropriated and institutionalised by the state. For Deleuze, therefore, it is important to grasp the 'appropriative' character of state power, for it provides us new analytical weapons to resist the cruel contingency of political sovereignty. Referring to the work of anthropologist Pierre Clastres, he argues that some primitive societies used war as a means of preventing concentrations of power which may give rise to forms of state (1987: 357–9). As a response to this challenge, nomadic peoples nevertheless seek new ways to preserve the uniqueness of their way of life so that the relation between them and the earth—the agent of all social production—continues to exist. Hence they attempt to create strategic mechanisms to ward off the state apparatus.

Indeed, one of the central concerns of Western civilisation is precisely the issue of the control of movement. The state is a territorialising machine and 'the permanent settlement of population is, along with taxes, perhaps the oldest state activity' (Scott 2009: 98). The state has always sought to marginalise and supress the nomadic peoples; this is why the nomads have been at war against the state and its plan to 'appropriate' them, civilise them and turn them into permanent settlers (Scott 2009: 98). And this also explains why space is so important at preventing 'unwanted' movement and controlling populations: 'it is through the prevention of motion that space enters history' (Netz 2004: xi). If the history of Western civilisation is the history of ordered and more secure life cycles, the foundation of the state is made possible not through the destruction of nomadism but of its 'appropriation' (Deleuze & Guattari 1983: 194, 225, 327). In this regard, the Western model of sovereignty derives its strength not so much from its denial of nomadic multiplicity but from the integration and regulation of nomadism for the development of a unity (see Reid 2010a: 413). The state, or sovereignty, endlessly attempts to appropriate, or capture, nomadism and utilise it for its own purposes. Thus, sovereignty employs a different 'regime of violence', a 'lawful violence', which consists of judicial and penal institutions of capture and punishment and the repressive state apparatus of the armed forces and police.

Thus, rather than start from the analysis of the role of radical politics in Deleuze's thought, it is necessary to focus directly on sovereignty's 'cruel contingency' and contemporary processes of 'capture' that create ressentiment. In Deleuzean political theory, an admission of certainty is seen as problematic. Deleuze's political theory urges us to recognise sovereign power in terms of changing socio-historical circumstances. Once this has been achieved, we can move on to the next step of creating for ourselves the capacity to confront the 'cruel' contingency of sovereign political power, as well as to counteractualise certain kinds of transformative agency for radical politics. If radical politics is a response to the problem of sovereignty, it can become an 'event' only when it succeeds in creating new forms of life that can overcome ressentiment and counteractualise identities and affects. In this sense, any understanding of post-politics and radical politics is incomplete without an understanding of sovereignty and ressentiment. However, we must first examine more rigorously how sovereignty came into being. And it is this that I shall turn to next.

From Primitive Society to the State

> [They] come like fate, without cause, reason, consideration, or pretext; they appear as lightning appears too terrible, too sudden, too convincing, too 'different' even to be hated. Their work is an instinctive creation and imposition of forms; they are the most involuntary, unconscious artists there are—wherever they appear something new soon arises, a ruling

> structure that lives, in which parts and functions are delimited and coordinated, in which nothing whatever finds a place that has not first been assigned a 'meaning' in relation to the whole. They do not know what guilt, responsibility, or consideration are, these born organizers; they exemplify that terrible artists' egoism that has the look of bronze and knows itself justified to all eternity in its 'work', like a mother in her child. It is not in them that the 'bad conscience' developed, that goes without saying-but it would not have developed without them, this ugly growth, it would be lacking if a tremendous quantity of freedom had not been expelled from the world, or at least from the visible world, and made as it were latent under their hammer blows and artists' violence.
>
> (Nietzsche 1989: 86–7)

This is how Nietzsche speaks of a new socius, of a new social regime, with its blond men and its own conquerors, who have the ability to wage war and inflict their own institutional cruelty upon its victims, especially upon the formless, the crowds, for the crowds aren't true social formations inasmuch as they are ephemeral gatherings of people, living and dying with the moment. Neither subjects, nor objects, they are the *anti-organisation* par excellence. The new socius, however, is more enduring than the crowds, and it is precisely the ability to perform endurance than spontaneous irruptions that makes the state, state and distinguishes it from the primitive socius. The new regime, the state, replaces the old primitive socius with its own distinct character: 'a terror without precedent, in comparison with which the ancient system of cruelty, the forms of primitive regimentation and punishment, are nothing' (Deleuze & Guattari 1983: 182).

For Deleuze and Guattari, the first social regime to capture and code the flows of desire is the primitive social machine. Invented by the 'primitive peoples', it is the 'machine of primitive inscription, the 'megamachine' that covers a social field' (Deleuze & Guattari 1983: 141). The primitive society is built on the collective investment of the organs, not directed at whole persons or their privatised organs, which are referred to as the earth, as the original condition of all production. The earth thus appears to be the agent of all *social production*. It is this deterritorialisation that forms the basis of Deleuze and Guattari's concept of the full body, or the body without organs.[1]

For Deleuze and Guattari, there are two kinds of relationships between people in groups: affiliations and alliances. The primitive society mobilises both types towards its own purposes. Filiation is by nature intensive, inclusive, and polyvocal, whereas alliance is extensive, exclusive, and segregative (Buchanan 2008: 24–5). Thus, filiation and alliance 'are like the two forms of a primitive capital: fixed capital or filiative stock, and circulating capital or mobile blocks of debt' (Deleuze & Guattari 1983: 146), that is, a debt which is measured in blood and inscribed on the body. Even though processes of circulation produce differences in rank and prestige, they are without 'net investment', without forming a system of exchange or a hierarchy with groups self-elevated above others. In this sense, the primitive society is without a state and an exchange economy.

The primitive social machine does not exchange but inscribes, marks the bodies with rituals of cruelty, which consists in 'tattooing, excising, incising, carving, scarifying, mutilating, encircling, and initiating' (Deleuze & Guattari 1983: 144). The primitive habitus is a place where violence is normative, if not common, and marks on the body as a result of violence or disease have a significant role in communication (Mellor & Shilling 1997: 48). The body has this role in communicating because knowledge is acquired through *figural* and carnal knowing. That is, in this medieval route to knowledge, the body is the central organising principle. Thus, open, mobile, and finite debt emerges from the process of savage inscription on the body. However, no *ressentiment* or *revenge* arises from the finite blocks of debt. To put it bluntly, *ressentiment* does not exist in primitive societies because pain, as a festive occasion, as a fundamental ingredient of active life, is very public phenomenon. It is shared and part of the belief system that supports active participation in community life. In short, pain itself has meaning.

The longing for contact through pain is believed to be not only necessary but also the proper order of social relations between the community and God. Thus, punishment takes the form of compensation, or the repayment of a debt. In wars, for instance, the injured party demands satisfaction, which involves punishing the offender, the debtor's body. Yet the logic of this kind of 'exchange', according to Nietzsche, is not, cannot be a direct compensation for the damage done. Instead, 'a kind of pleasure—the pleasure of being allowed to vent his power freely upon one who is powerless, the voluptuous pleasure . . . the enjoyment of violation' (Nietzsche 1989: 65). Punishment, then, is considered as a festive occasion, a transgression in which cruelty is gratified, and where the carnivalesque activity takes place. Hence, Nietzsche writes: 'without cruelty there is no festival: thus the longest and most ancient part of human history teaches and in punishment there is so much that is festive!—' (Nietzsche 1989: 67).

As a segmented society, the primitive socius exists as a nomadic space of connections. However, as we have seen, in their preservation of a style of life tied to the earth, nomadic peoples and movements 'attempt to ward off the social-political processes of unification on which political sovereignty relies' (Reid 2010a: 411). But how does the state sovereignty occur? At this point, Deleuze and Guattari follow Nietzsche's claim that the state is brought from the outside by 'some pack of blond beasts of prey, a conqueror and master race' (Nietzsche 1989: 86). In this sense, they treat the state as a 'virtual concept'. Rejecting the orthodox Marxist anthropology's and other Western models' interpretation of primitive society which states that societies evolve almost linearly, ultimately enabling the state apparatus to come into existence, Deleuze and Guattari argue that the state does not occur in a linear way (from nomadic to agricultural) but is born as an idea, which replaces the old primitive social regime and its essential elements: 'the State was not formed in progressive stages; it appears fully armed, a master stroke executed all at once; the primordial *Urstaat*, the eternal model of everything the State wants to be and desires' (Deleuze & Guattari 1983: 217).

The actual state does not come into being as a result of the internal dynamics of the primitive territorial machine but is imposed from without. As Deleuze and Guattari insist, 'the death of the primitive system always comes from without; history is the history of contingencies and encounters' (Deleuze & Guattari 1983: 195). Thus, they propose a history written from a contingent and critical point of view, which provides a point of intersection between past and present. This is a remarkable achievement, for it leaves no room for historicism that posits a determinate mode of thought. In other words, social regimes are not considered as successive stages in the sense that one can occur as a result from the effects of another. Rather, Deleuze and Guattari argue that all social regimes (territorial, despotism, and capitalism) coexist within the perspective of becoming or virtuality: 'all history does is to translate a coexistence of becomings into a succession' (Deleuze & Guattari 1987: 430).

In short, the state is a virtual existence that proceeds from the abstract to the concrete (Deleuze & Guattari 1983: 221), conditioning both what comes before and what follows: the primitive system and capitalism. From this perspective, the state comes into being not by suppressing but subordinating the determinate relations of the primitive system to its own system of alliance and filiation, which is based on the despotic will, that is, God's chosen peoples (Deleuze & Guattari 1983: 89). The State, in other words, comes into being by capturing nomadic space of connections and coding the flows of desire. For Deleuze and Guattari, the task is therefore to inquire about meaning behind the coding of every aspect of life, ranging from the daily practices and the biological life to the metaphysical. Anthropologists have of course been engaged in this task for a century or more, but mostly with a view to trying to decipher the social purpose behind the codes and what they mean to the people whose lives are determined by them. Deleuze and Guattari take a different route. They are not concerned with what native people think; rather, they are interested in the operations of the unconscious. In other words, what is important is to discern the *machinic* processes, that is, the modes of organisation that link the differentiation and distribution of material flows, desires, affects, and so on, to the human body as a living system (Deleuze & Guattari 1987: 435; see also Patton 2000: 88). To be sure, the conception of the machinic, or the territorial machine, overturns the vulgar assumptions that have conditioned anthropology for a long time. Contrary to the orthodox Marxist anthropology and other Western interpretations which claim that, in the primitive society all relations between subjects are ultimately exchangist, Deleuze and Guattari argue that society is inscriptive, not exchangist.[2] In this sense, the process of capturing and coding the flows of desires is not enough by itself to establish a social regime; it is merely the means. Because the nature of the individual relations is changed, it requires a social regime to come into being.

As a result, the nature of the whole system is changed, a new hierarchical structure is installed, and these changes make both the despot and the new machine, the State, the new paranoiac: 'for the first time something has been withdrawn from life and from the earth that will make it possible to judge life and to survey the earth from the above: a first principle of paranoiac knowledge' (Deleuze & Guattari 1987: 194). The despot becomes the new body that replaces the earth as the body without organs of the social, possessing all the organs of all the subjects. From now on everything seems to emanate from the despot. As a consequence, life becomes politicised and absolutely subject to sovereign power, a power in which 'it is permitted to kill without committing homicide and without celebrating sacrifice' (Agamben 1998: 83).

Because a new bureaucracy replaces intertribal alliance and all stock becomes the object of accumulation, debt is rendered infinite and becomes a debt of existence on subjects themselves, including their very lives, in the form of tribute to the despot (Deleuze & Guattari 1987: 197). That is to say, there is a transition in sovereignty from marking bodies with rituals of cruelty to imposing infinite debt. All meaning thus arises from the sovereign because all debt is owed to him. Thus, it is debt that rather than the sovereign will that holds the despotic regime together. In using terror, the despot also acquires the monopoly on violence that is inscribed on the bodies of the subjects. In the shadows of sovereign violence is born a new city, a city of blood, 'where power spoke *through* blood: the honor of war, the fear of famine, the triumph of death, the sovereign with his sword executioners, and tortures; blood was *a reality with a symbolic function*' (Foucault 1998: 147). The system of cruelty as principle and practice now becomes an integral part of the state apparatus that renders debt infinite to the despot, to God, and to society.

> Examine what Christianity calls 'redemption': It is no longer a matter of discharge from debt, but of a deepening of debt. It is no longer a matter of suffering through which debt is paid, but a suffering through which one is shackled to it, through which one becomes a debtor forever. Suffering now only pays the interests on debt; suffering is internalized, responsibility-debt has become responsibility-guilt.
>
> (Deleuze 1983: 141)

Sovereignty demands only obedience and holds only the power of death over its members. In this way law and sovereignty are completely merged without 'designation', which makes it possible to make arbitrary decisions, thus creating an empty space around the despot. The despot acquires 'the right to punish', which then becomes a very aspect of sovereignty to make war on his enemies. The purpose of punishment is not, then, to restore justice but to reconstitute sovereign power. This is why, quoting Muyart de Vouglans, Foucault asserts that

> the right to punish . . . belongs to that absolute power of life and death which Roman law calls *merum imperium*, a right by virtue of which the prince sees that his law is respected by ordering the punishment of crime.
>
> (1977: 48)

Ressentiment

How, then, does sovereignty relate to the 'social' and its affective structure? I shall argue that *ressentiment* is crucial to understand such an evaluation of state sovereignty. Yet, in social theory, this link remains surprisingly underresearched. A social regime does not exist without affects it brings into play, for every regime of governance invokes its own particular affect. In a revision of Deleuze's and Foucault's understanding of sovereignty, I argue that sovereign political power cannot be thought of without ressentiment because it is not ressentiment that generates vengefulness but sovereign vengeance that generates ressentiment. Any analysis that claims to explain sovereignty without paying full heed to the momentum of this thoroughly important affect will be fundamentally incomplete. The remainder of this chapter aims to address this absence by demonstrating attention to the affective logic of sovereignty.

Within the enjoyment and the renunciation of pain, of punishment, which is turned into a sovereign law, the subjects are ruled by the threat of death, by terror. Punishment is no longer experienced as a festive occasion but as the vengeance of the despot: 'in the execution of the most ordinary penalty, in the most punctilious respect of legal forms, reign the active forces of revenge' (Foucault 1977: 48). As the limitless vengeance of the despots' is increased and exercised on the pacified subjects, it generates *ressentiment*, the main affect that pertains to despotism. As mentioned before, the finite blocks of debt in the primitive society does not cause ressentiment, but within the matrix of terror, of despotism, ressentiment is born as a kind of passivity or impotence: desire becomes reactive. Under the tragic regime of infinite debt, as Deleuze and Guattari powerfully demonstrate, 'the eternal ressentiment of the subjects answers to the eternal vengeance of the despots' (1983: 214–5). The state terror, with its right to punish, with its elevation of death to a permanent threat, and with its subordination of desire to the providence of God sovereignty, thus forms a massive pacification and creates subjects who are essentially reactive. Hence, the importance of Nietzsche and his ideas of master-slave morality, which could help us better understand the genealogy of ressentiment.

For Nietzsche, ressentiment is a state of 'deeply repressed . . . vengefulness' (1989: 34). Three elements are crucial in this regard. First, the 'man of ressentiment' desires to live a certain kind of life which he sees invaluable: thus, the priest, a member of the nobility, values a life that includes political supremacy (see Reginster 1997: 286). Second, the man of ressentiment becomes aware of his complete inability to fulfil this aspiration: he is inspired by his 'weakness' or 'impotence'. Third, he retains his arrogant attitude or his 'lust to rule' (Nietzsche 1989: 33). Because his 'will to power' remains 'intact', he retains his certain values or pretensions, and refuses to accept his inability to realise them (Reginster 1997: 287). Crucially, therefore, his soul oscillates between a desire to live the life he values and his belief that he is unable to satisfy it. He dreams of a future revenge, that he 'will be better off someday' (Nietzsche 1989: 47). In this sense, the man of ressentiment is one who does not act (Deleuze 1983: 111).

If sovereignty is characterised by an eternal vengeance, ressentiment refers to a repressed vengefulness. Sovereignty is marked by action, the man of ressentiment by reaction; he is rendered an inert subject and subordinate to an absolute sovereign power (vengeance). This coincidence of action (vengefulness) and reaction (ressentiment) means that sovereign power is per definition the arbitrary and external power, that it does not abide rules. Thus, in exceptional circumstances such as 'disorder', the law can be suspended (Agamben 2005: 42). In this sense, sovereignty is conditioned by the exception—that is, the ability of the sovereign to stand inside and outside the law at the same time.

In this sense, the state of exception is not any power whatever of sovereignty but its central aspect, which is why it is not only bound up in the self-founding power of the logos or raw power-as-property but also in subjectivation and affection: the sovereign is s/he which is also subjectified as vengeful, whereas victims who are subjectified through ressentiment are marked by reaction. In short, sovereignty is not only a rational social regime but also an affective one.

How does the state of exception function in contemporary society? And how does one make sense of ressentiment in the context of state sovereignty? In what follows, I argue that cruel manifestations of the modern state, which are intimately connected to the state of exception, have become normalised in contemporary society. In a sense, therefore, contemporary sovereign power has transformed the logic of exception into a form of sociality. The state of exception is no longer a historical anomaly but the normalcy itself. However, this normalcy is not only about states of exception. Post 9/11, we are also witnessing the increasing justification and legitimisation of torture as a form sovereign vengeance, and this is a theme to which I shall turn next.

Salò

Pasolini's controversial final film *Salò* (1975), based on Marquis de Sade's *The 120 Days of Sodom* (1785), poses significant questions regarding the intersection between sadistic torture and sovereignty. The film is divided in four segments, heavily inspired by Dante's *Inferno*: Ante-Inferno, Circle of Manias, Circle of Shit, and Circle of Blood. *Salò* focuses on four corrupt sovereigns after the fall of Italy's fascist ruler Benito Mussolini in 1944. Four fascist libertines—the Duke, the Bishop, the Magistrate, the President—kidnap the most beautiful young people in town and take them to a villa, to an enclosed space called The Republic of Salò, a Nazi puppet state that became the last stronghold of Benito Mussolini (Pugliese 2013: 60). From now on, the Republic of Salò becomes a fascist enclave from which there is no escape. Thus starts extreme abuse, torture, and the murders of young men and women for the sake of perverted lust and extreme pleasure. The fascist captors welcome the beautiful young Italians to hell with the following words:

> You herded, feeble creatures, destined for our pleasure. Don't expect to find here the freedom granted in the outside world. You are beyond reach of any 'legality'. No one knows you are here. As far as the world goes, you are already dead.
> (Pasolini 1975)

The young victims' bodies become sites of repressive pain and sexual pleasure, bearing the scars of sovereign vengeance. Thus, *Salò* shows us that the appeal of pleasure is inseparable from the appeal of sovereign violence, which is at once served and kept at bay by a minor festival of the arts. Reminiscent of the rituals of primitive system of cruelty, Pasolini almost succeeds in making the sadistic torture part of an entertaining spectacle. This festivity is, however, unlimited and protected by an unrestricted law of sovereign power. Thus, sadistic violence can go 'as far as the world goes', carrying to a point 'where it is no longer anything but a unique and naked sovereignty: an unlimited right of all-powerful monstrosity' (Foucault 1998: 149). What we encounter in *Salò* is what I call the limitless 'enjoyment of cruelty', which makes torture the vengeance of four corrupt despots. Sovereign cruelty punishes the victims' bodies without any guilt, while sexual pleasure becomes a weapon of total domination. Whereas physical beauty becomes a symptom of vulnerability, sovereign power becomes a total form of fascism, a repressive desublimation of nihilism.

Torture is widely considered as a form of madness, as an unethical practice that is confined to corrupt administrations or totalitarian systems. In this view, torture is conceived as an 'illiberal act'; it is 'irrational' (see Dershowitz 2002; Luban 2005). It is also viewed as a juridical problem, as one of the basic principles of human rights (see Kelly 2009, 2011; Langbein 2006; Todorov 2009). I suggest that both approaches misunderstand and simplify the role of torture; they fail to grasp the true purpose of torture within sovereign political power. Torture, I assert, is one among many manifestations of sovereign as domination. Thus, on the eve of the publication of his memoir, *Decision Points*, which is believed to 'contain anecdotes seemingly ripped off from other books and articles', George W. Bush was still describing waterboarding as 'highly effective', saying it provided 'large amounts of information' (quoted in McGreal 2010: 7). Torture, therefore, needs to be considered in relation to other cruel manifestations of state sovereignty: for example, the destruction of ecological systems; the risk-security complex; the state of exception; and the complete animalisation of human beings carried out by neoliberal biopolitics. And yet, torture is not one among these various forms of sovereign power. It is the most privileged actualisation of state terror, for it reveals the nature of sovereignty (and its rational consciousness).

I contend that torture is the extreme systemic expression of the logos of sovereign domination. Torture is a technique of sovereign domination; it is not an extreme expression of lawless vengeance, for vengeance is political. It is for this reason that it is widely practiced in secret. Torture is a smaller system which is representative of a rational sovereign law; it is a tool of governance, with the aim of eliciting information from and humiliating the 'enemy'. As a tool of war and sovereign domination, torture is, therefore, intimately bound to 'the liberal way of war' (Dillon & Reid 2009). Liberalism consists of various interrelated social regimes, which, although said to be committed to 'peace-making', is nevertheless also dependent upon violence, a permanent state of emergency, and constant preparedness for perpetual war (Dillon & Reid 2009: 7). Seen in this light, war, violence, and society are mutually constitutive and the liberal way of war is 'a war-making machine whose continuous processes of war preparation prior to the conduct of any hostilities profoundly, and pervasively, shape the liberal way of life' (Dillon & Reid 2009: 9). The main object of the liberal way of war is *life itself* because it is what threatens life itself. For this reason, 'everything is permitted' to the liberal way of war.

Seen in this light, to try to understand the liberal war and violence without law is a serious mistake. Rather than representing a limit upon state violence, laws have in many ways underpinned an expansion of neoliberal governance (Neocleous 2014). What's more, law and war are intimately connected in varied and revealing ways. Cicero once said, '*inter arma enim silent leges*': in times of war, the law falls silent). This no longer captures the reality of contemporary society, however. As Craig Jones has put it, 'far from "failing silent", law constantly intervenes in and gives shape to war' (2015: 2). For instance, war on terror is but one instantiation of the project of liberal order-building that unites war, violence, and law (Neocleous 2014), and space comes to play a central role in activating and actualising this intersection.

Consider, for instance, Guantánamo Bay and the Abu Ghraib prison, where torture is systemic. The sort of sovereign political power being deployed is not only a sovereign 'who decides on the state of exception' but also a social regime which transcends land, terrain, or national borders. Far from being a legal 'black hole', Guantánamo Bay, for instance, is not only a carefully constructed legal territory but also the product of a set of governmental practices by which things can be ordered and controlled. In this sense, Guantánamo emerges as a new form of cruel and contingent sovereignty that deterritorialises and (re)territorialises, expands its capacities to act as beyond its own borders and territories (Reid-Henry 2007; see also Margulies 2004).

In this sense, contemporary sovereign power is not territorially limited; it spreads through contingent acts and practices, bringing about a type of reterritorialisation as deterritorialisation (Hardt & Negri 2000). This, however, does not mean the end of territories as such. On the contrary, deterritorialisation always goes hand in hand with (re)territorialisation, creating new markets, identities, and regimes of power, as well as new territorial configurations (Brenner 2004; Sparke 2005). Sovereignty is as much about 'selective openings' (deterritorialisations) as it is about 'closures' (reterritorialisations). Whereas someone, something, or somewhere is included, someone else, something else, or somewhere else is also excluded (see Brighenti 2010: 65). In the process, however, violence, permanent states of exception, and war become a powerful force in making and unmaking of territory. Hence, contingent sovereignty is intimately bound up with the liberal way of war. We should, therefore, begin to examine the relation between deterritorialisation and (re)territorialisation, on the one hand, and war, violence, and other cruel manifestations of sovereign as domination, including torture, on the other (Butler 2004; Comaroff 2007; Gregory 2006).

It is in this context that Guantánamo should be viewed as the sort of space which makes possible the territorialisation of the war on terror alongside a deterritorialisation of domestic jurisdiction (Reid-Henry 2007: 639). Simply put, it reinforces 'a deliberate spatial separation' of sovereign law and violence within spaces of exception. And it is by enforcing this spatial separation that the cruel contingency of sovereign political power is deployed alongside the law. Thus, Guantánamo reminds us that the real politics of contemporary sovereignty lies not in putting boundaries and territories up, but in blurring them (Reid-Henry 2007: 644). The cruel contingency of state sovereignty would suggest asking not only 'where are the territories of sovereignty' or 'where are spaces of exception' but also 'how does sovereignty's cruel contingency operate in contemporary society'? As Agamben writes: 'the precise scope and location of sovereignty and its jurisdiction is never final, but always fleeting' (1998: 55). The functioning and the operation of new forms of sovereign power cannot be understood only in terms of its territories, but in terms of its cruel and contingent effects (its scope).

How, then, are we to understand the relationship between torture and the detention of enemy combatants in light of sovereign political power as cruel radical contingency? As discussed before, torture is a tool of cruel sovereign political power, of the liberal of way of war. Hence, it has its own set of theological, philosophical, and political values. The physical destruction of the 'enemy'—from crucifixion employed by the Scythians in antiquity, to the sleep deprivation and mutilated arms of the accused with a blunt knife put into practice during the time of the English Civil War, from public executions during the Middle Ages, to prolonged use of stress positions, starvation, beatings, electrical charges, and extreme cold throughout the Cold War, and 'squeezing of the testicles, hanging by the arms or legs, blindfolding, stripping the suspect naked, spraying with high-pressure water' (HRW 1997) practised by specialised teams in Turkish prisons—in short, what we see before us today is not the expression of incomprehensible horror. It is the exact opposite: the calculated expression and a rational necessity that define sovereign power. It is the same expression that led Pasolini to explore the nexus between torture, the state of exception, and the biopolitics of late-capitalist hegemony. Today's most likely successors of Pasolini's corrupt sovereigns are to be found in the torture chambers of Abu Ghraib and Guantánamo.

In the Republic of Salò, young captors are given the taste of sovereign vengeance at its most radical shape: that of the limitless enjoyment of sovereign cruelty and torture. Beyond reach of any 'legality', 'herded creatures' are reduced to bare life, life devoid of any value. In Abu Ghraib and Guantánamo, similarly, 'enemy combatants' have been given the taste of sovereign cruelty and the 'liberal way of life' at its most effective: that of the limitless enjoyment of sovereign vengeance, violence, and systemic torture. Reduced to bare life, they are effectively stripped of all rights. Systemic torture starts at the top and trickles all the way down, creating victims who are not able to act. Ressentiment is a peculiar reaction in which the subject's immediate responses (anger, spite, revenge) against the oppressor are muted and thus take a detour through sublimation, inward suffering. Hence, the favourite destination is not the courtroom but the camp where torture is practised secretly. Creative forms of torture find expression in waterboarding, sodomy, and fucking. This is the paradigm of sovereign political power, of reign, that makes post-political neoliberalism and capitalist power operative. That is to say, torture is fundamental to the operation of neoliberal capitalism as a whole. It is one of the fundamental engagements of the war against everything. The bare life of victims has come to define contemporary society in the war against terrorism.

Second, the metaphor of the Republic of Salò as a fascist enclave in an inaccessible place signifies a state of exception, or the space of exception where legal order is suspended. The violence of sovereignty in both the Republic of Salò and Abu Ghraib and Guantánamo (as spaces of exception) demonstrate that space is one of the central media of struggle, and is therefore to be seen a fundamental political issue. For Lefebvre, for instance, 'there is a politics of space because space is political' (1976: 33; see also Elden 2007: 822). Each concrete space, territory, and spatiality is a site of conflict and struggle (Soja 1989). Considering the interrelation of the space as the place of conflict and space as an object of power and struggle provides us with an important dimension for grasping the truth about the war on terror. Today, modern sovereignty is no longer founded on a distinct territory. Because acts of governance are distributed among the established social regimes and relations of power, it is now everywhere. Sovereign political power 'is in no case complete; it is also, openly or surreptitiously, everywhere contested and eroded, facing ever new pretenders and competitors' (Bauman 2010: 138). Legitimising torture and creating global spaces of exception, the violence of sovereignty undoes territory so that the rule of law becomes ineffective. In the eyes of the sovereign power, the preservation of the territory necessarily entails the disruption of another territory (war on terror). Put differently, the insistence on territorial preservation goes hand in hand with the insistence on wholly contingent sovereign power: 'the stress on territorial preservation is enforced most strongly at the very time territorial sovereignty is disrupted' (Elden 2007: 827).

Whereas sovereign power wants to completely enforce its own territory, it wants to assert the cruel contingency of sovereignty over territory elsewhere. Contingent sovereignty does not seek to simply acquire the whole territory but only to create 'grey zones' or 'zones of indistinction' (CIA prisons in Eastern European countries) and facilitate capital flows and access underground sources (Elden 2007; Harvey 2003). In this, modern sovereignty is looking to preserve its own position while at the same time expanding capital flows in order to support the neoliberal economic order. This also explains the relation between mobility and immobility. Whereas some are literally 'arrested' and legally abandoned through spaces of sovereign exceptionalism, others enjoy limitless mobility. While some die as 'disposable "nobodies", disappearing in the night, others die as sacrificial "everybodies" in well-publicised cataclysms' (Dienst 2011: 70).

Torture Is Political

It is worth noting that Pasolini succeeds in presenting torture as a constitutive act of political and military organisation of the state. By denunciating acts of collective torture, *Salò* therefore reveals one of the secret aspects of sovereign order that attempts to legally legitimise torture as a way of social control. The 'anthropological genocide' of *Salò*, a term used by Pasolini himself (quoted in Chiesa 2007: 209), takes place in a villa, decorated with a magnificent art collection of futurism, cubism, art deco, etc. The masterpieces of the artistic vanguards make you feel bad because they are the key to what he is thinking. Pasolini hates modernism and makes the masterpieces of the artistic vanguards, or modern art, look fascist (see Jones 2005). Thus, we get the message loud and clear: modernism does not erase violence and torture; rather, it incorporates them into the biopolitics of capitalism. Life itself is continuously being destroyed by the biopolitics of modern capitalism and sovereign power to which no moral ideal is attached. In this sense, *Salò* presents torture as one of the supreme expressions of modernism and sovereign domination.

Furthermore, the politicisation of torture in *Salò* metaphorically anticipates the state of exception on the basis of which the legal and moral order of a sovereign exceptionalism might be constituted. In other words, just as the state of exception and institutional regimes of cruelty are the basic characteristics of the Republic of Salò, the justification of torture and the practice of permanent detention have become the rule in contemporary society. Recall the victims of Guantánamo and Abu Ghraib in orange boiler-suits, who were urinated on, sodomised with chemical light and broomstick, in short, the victims who were tortured to death. What is more, Guantánamo and Abu Ghraib are spaces where absolute sovereign power operates through absolute suspension: suspension of humanity and the Geneva Conventions regulating the treatment of prisoners of war. These practices were supposed to be stopped in neoliberal societies, but torture is a permanent aspect of sovereignty which keeps returning in spaces of exception. In this sense the political (and sadistic) torture of *Salò* signifies a rationalisation of what has hitherto been an exception.

The political torture presented by *Salò* has another aspect. Torturers are normal (not mad and bad) sovereigns because the bodies of the victims are inscribed by signs and regimes of sovereign violence that is seen as 'legally legitimate'. In this way, the sadistic torture coincides with reactive subjects who are rendered obedient and subordinate their desires to sovereign political power. Victorious only in perversion, the torturers derive pleasure from inscribing signs and regimes of sovereign violence on the bodies. In effect, signs and traces of sovereign vengeance become an integral part of oppressive norms that give rise to the creation of a legal sovereign state. Pasolini thus shows how torture is the interior dimension of the state apparatus, according to which political philosophy, from Hobbes to Schmitt, has defined the absolutist idea of state sovereignty.

Nevertheless, *Salò* does not only denounce torture, it also anticipates the crimes of state sovereignty. Torture as political: this is the contemporary dimension of torture as an instrument of sovereign domination and repression. As mentioned before, Pasolini presents these dimensions of torture by means of four segments: Ante-Inferno, Circle of Manias, Circle of Shit, and Circle of Blood. Circle of Blood is particularly illuminating in this regard. At issue here is a kind of torture that is political, which is replete with sadistic violence, gore, blood, and death: precisely the sort of torture that military dictatorships in Latin America and Turkey put into practice and is being practised in the torture chambers of the 'liberal way of war'. Circle of Blood symbolises torture as a paradigm for the intended destruction of the integrity of the humanness.

In the final sequence of scenes, an orgy of political torture is practised in a courtyard. While the young victims are subjected to most brutal and almost unendurable torture and eventual execution, the fascist sovereigns derive greater sexual pleasure and enjoyment from watching them suffer. Aroused by the display of suffering, the libertines begin to suffer with the victims they've once degraded, tortured, and exterminated. Who's torturing whom? What goes there? What does it all mean? The fascist sovereigns and the victims enter into a zone of indistinction, making it impossible to distinguish between obedience to the law and its transgression. Thus, the entire system would start to break down. But one of the libertines and a fully aroused soldier watch this deadly and inverted scene from an enclosed balcony and through a set of binoculars. The screams, the cries, the pains, and the sufferings of the victims cannot be heard. Orff's *Carmina Burana* is played in the background. We begin to witness eroticism, beauty, and the suffering in silence. The camera then shifts from the suffering bodies to the fascist libertine, who is being masturbated by the soldier. The scene focuses on the voyeuristic and masturbatory victimiser, who sits with his back to the camera. All of a sudden, the victimiser turns out to be an anonymous viewer. He becomes us, the audience. Voyeurs of the voyeurism of others, we are—by this conclusion—both distanced from and become part of the film's politicisation of sadistic violence. The sadistic pleasure of *Salò* is projected onto the audience: we are shocked and disgusted at sadistic violence, and are shocked and disgusted all the harder when we realise that we all ourselves become a silent accomplice to violence committed by the global sovereign order in our everyday lives.

Notes

1. A body without organs (BWO) is a process that is directed towards 'pure becoming'. In this sense it is opposed to the organising principles that structure, appropriate, and thus hegemonise the collective investment of the organs,

experiences, and states of becoming. A BWO is a non-organismically organised body, a limit of a given process of destratification, where matter-energy flows come into play immanently without reference to a transcendence. A BWO refers to absolute disorganisation of organs, which is nothing else than a process of pure becoming: it is 'what remains after you take everything away' (Deleuze & Guattari 1987: 151).
2. 'We see no reason in fact for accepting the postulate that underlies exchangist notions of society; society is not first of all a milieu for exchange where the essential would be to circulate or to cause to circulate, but rather a socius of inscription where the essential thing is to mark or to be marked. There is circulation only if inscription requires or permits it' (Deleuze & Guattari 1983: 156).

3 Discipline and the Birth of Neoliberal Governmentality

In the preceding chapter, I theorised an updated understanding of sovereignty that is no longer founded on a distinct territory. I argued that, because technologies of government are distributed among the established social regimes and relations of power, sovereignty is now everywhere. Furthermore, I suggested that sovereignty cannot be thought of without ressentiment, as it creates an intricate relationship between the sovereign and the victim. Sovereignty, in other words, is a dynamic radical contingency because it is in that contingency that the forceful and brutal sovereign presence manifests itself.

However, state sovereignty constitutes only one of the four principles embodied in post-politics. Post-politics is also organised according to discipline, which constitutes a differentiation between an inside and outside. Discipline is one of the most central elements of Foucault's analytics of power. This chapter proposes to rethink Foucault in order to make sense of discipline that he began to understand but at the same time has evolved very rapidly over time. Foucault proposes a fragmented and relational concept of power that allows us to examine a non-sovereign-centred potential for disciplining subjects. The chapter explores this slow but profound transition from sovereign power to neoliberal governmentality, which is based on high levels of disciplinary normalisation upon life. Foucault, in *Discipline and Punish*, argues that discipline works through situated contingencies where individualised bodies are ranked and assayed according to 'a political anatomy of detail' (Foucault 1977: 139). Furthermore, his argument suggests that the biopolitics of fear is central to the operation of disciplinary neoliberalism. Biopolitics, I assert, should be viewed as an eschatological, katechontic response whose mission is to pacify life in order to delay the event, and it is towards these Foucauldian considerations and their implications for a discipline and neoliberal biopolitical governmentality that I now turn.

The Rise of the Disciplinary Regime

> And yet the fact remains that a few decades saw the disappearance of the tortured, dismembered, amputated body, symbolically branded on face or shoulder, exposed alive or dead to public view. The body as the major target of penal repression disappeared.
>
> (Foucault 1977: 8)

Above the punitive city hangs the body of the condemned, bearing the ritual marks of sovereign vengeance. The body of the criminal, tortured on the scaffold, signifies the power to punish. Sovereign power is, in short, a certain power upon life where 'the law can be inscribed, a life capable of reading and following the proscriptions and prescriptions of those inscriptions' (Dillon 2002: 78). Thus, for a long time one of the crucial aspects of sovereign power has been the right to decide life and death—the right of a single sovereign to make life 'live'. The ceremony of cruelty is an exercise of sovereign terror at its most spectacular.

But, as Foucault suggests, this has become only one aspect of sovereign power in a range of mechanisms because the power over life is transformed in the modern West. From the late eighteenth century, as Foucault observes, political power is no longer exercised through the stark choice of taking life or letting live. Wars are still bloodier, killing an enemy is still the objective, and torture is still frequent. Yet, a major shift occurs in the way the right to punish is exercised. Now the wars are no longer waged in the name of the sovereign but in the name of the entire population: 'the right to punish has been shifted from the vengeance of the sovereign to the defence of society' (Foucault 1977: 90). What emerges is a new social regime with a new political authority that takes on the task of the management of life 'in the name of life necessity', ranging from illness, sanitary conditions in the towns, to the problems of security. The mechanisms thus 'shift from exclusion to inclusion', from 'sending the victims outside the bounds of the polity, to a mechanism for spatial partition that allows them to be contained within' (Elden 2007: 564). The new regime is that of discipline, which aims to govern life through a multitude of attempts, turning bodies into information and knowledge. Discipline is an immanent historical reality, 'a quite different materiality, a quite different physics of power, a quite different way of investing men's bodies' (Foucault 1977: 116).

From this moment on, politics addresses the vital processes of man as a self-creature, who speaks, lives, and works. Man as a finite being is to discipline, it might be said, what the state of exception is for the sovereign power of the state. In the new disciplinary regime, man is conceived as a being that is finite, but this finitude turns out to be a source of knowledge, meaning, and history. At once a subject and an object, man is the being who produces himself. Here, Foucault's argument closely parallels Marx's definition of man as a species-being. Consider the famous lines in *Economic and Philosophical Manuscripts*, where Marx defines species-being in the following terms: 'man is a species-being not only in that he practically and theoretically makes his own species as well as that of other things his object, but also . . . in that as present and living species he considers himself to be a universal and consequently free being' (1970: 31). What fundamentally separates Marx from Feuerbach is his insistence on the historicity of man, namely that man does not come into being as the object of consciousness, but is produced practically by the concrete factors of social life due to labour. Thus, labour itself distinguishes us as a species-being because 'the practical creation of an objective world, the treatment of inorganic nature' is proof that 'nature appears as his work and his actuality' (1970: 32).

For Foucault, similarly, man—who is supposed to be an a priori, transcendent figure outside history—turns out to be a historical category, a product of power and knowledge. Man as a transcendent category, who is supposed to be ahistorical, thereby becomes the historical itself. Thus, with the disciplines, man (and his body) appears 'as object and target of power' (Foucault 1977: 136). Or, to say this differently, the new body is not a 'mechanical body'; it is now conceived as man-the-machine, 'composed of solids and assigned movements' (Foucault 1977: 155). The new machine body has two registers: 'the anatomico-metaphysical register, of which Descartes wrote the first pages and which the physicians and philosophers continued', and the technico-political register, 'which was constituted by a whole set of regulations and by empirical and calculated methods relating to the army, the school and the hospital, for controlling or correcting the operations of the body' (Foucault 1977: 136). Their point of intersection is the docile body, intersecting the analysable body with the manipulable body. In the process, therefore, man emerges as a 'theoretical' object whose body, whose decipherable depth and actualities could be formed and corrected through mechanisms of normalisation (Foucault 2003: 38). Utilising these mechanisms, the primary target of discipline is to manage the situation and maximise individual efficiency and productivity. Through production of self-regulating individuals, society begins to become, as Foucault (1991a) would explore in his governmentality writings, a space that, to a certain extent, has to be left to itself in order to achieve maximum efficacy.

Inseparable from these issues is the integration of the system of observation into a tightly connected circuit. The disciplinary social regime belongs to the level of the diagram of power and forces, acting on 'the potentiality of danger that lies hidden in an individual and which is manifested in his observed everyday conduct' (Foucault 1977: 126). In other words, the very principle of strategic danger is crucial to the operation of discipline. Without danger, no such discipline; without discipline, no such danger. As a result, danger becomes a formative, productive aspect of disciplinary action. Within the matrix of the potentiality of danger, discipline can be viewed as an abstract machine in which power relations emerge and operate in different physical spaces, such as schools, hospitals, military barracks, prisons, and so on. It is in this context that the panoptic prison emerges as the form of punishment, as an apparatus of knowledge. Let us recall Bentham's vision.

The Panopticon

> Thou art about my path, and about my bed: and spiest out my ways. If I say, peradventure the darkness shall cover me, then shall my night be turned into day. Even there also shall thy hand lead me; and thy right hand shall hold me.
>
> (Bentham, quoted in Miller 1987: 5)

When Jeremy Bentham first used the above verses of the 139th Psalm, what he had in mind was creating a semblance of the 'image of God'. Bentham was a utilitarian who used an 'architecture of choice' (Bentham 1995)—by which he meant that the authorities should give an appearance of choices so that the prisoners have the illusion of autonomy but end up behaving in the desired way. Thus, he believed the panoptic architecture could be applied to any physical space, including schools, workhouses, and prisons. The principle was that the inspector sees everyone 'without being seen' (Bentham 1995: 101), ensuring everyone is making the right choices.

Bentham wanted to achieve a system of utilitarian thought that avoids dangerous 'concert among minds' (Bentham 1995: 48), so that any challenge to the system does not take place. The goal was to maximise general utility and to minimise harm. With the emergence of the idea of the panopticon, the power to punish becomes institutionalised, and death is just the reverse side of life. The punishment is no longer seen as a crucial aspect of sovereign power but as a technique, as a 'procedure for requalifying individuals as subjects, as juridical subjects' (Foucault 1977: 6). Because discipline deals here with an attempt to alter man, nothing is allowed 'just to exist'; thus, all circumstances, including that of chance, must be controlled, weighed, compared, evaluated, calculated, banished, organised (Foucault 1977: 25–6; Miller 1987: 5). In short, everything must be technically argued out. This is, no doubt, a new discourse, a new knowledge of the body that will overlook no single detail. After all, you cannot govern the society (and life) without knowing something about it. Discipline works through minute controls of the body; it is a life problem that must play out, hence, a whole learned economy of the 'strategy' of the body through the institutions such as schools, hospitals, barracks, and workshops.

This, however, does not mean that the disciplinary techniques disrupt sovereign political power and violence. Rather, the new 'strategy' of the body now finds itself recombined with the internalisation of the sovereign gaze. The primary goal of the new strategy is, therefore, not confinement, enclosure, disclosure, but the true and faithful *obedience of the subject*. With the emergence of the panoptic prison, therefore, it becomes possible to develop a disciplinary regime which produces the individual as a governable and economically productive but politically inert commodity. In other words, the panopticon idea also paves the way for the development of a global political economy, under a strong interventionist state. The development of the capitalist economy and the neoliberal state introduces systematic surveillance in order to better discipline and control the labour process and relationships. Put simply, surveillance is an integral feature of the capitalist market (Foucault 1977, 2007, 2008; see also Aradau & van Munster 2007; Bigo & Tsoukala 2008; Dillon & Reid 2009; Gill 1995; Retort 2005; Rose 1999). In the emergence of Taylorism and scientific management, for instance, similar surveillance practices of worker are widely used to supervise workers and managers, as well as to constitute and expand labour processes more systematically. What is crucial in this context is Taylor's articulation of the raison d'être of global capitalist management: managers are supposed to act as 'information specialists, as close observers', and disciplinary analysts and planners of 'productive' labour processes (Webster & Robins 1993: 245). Taylor writes:

> The deliberate gathering in on the part of those on the management's side of all of the great mass of traditional knowledge.... The duty of gathering in of all this great mass of traditional knowledge and then recording it, tabulating it and, in many cases, finally reducing it to laws, rules and even to mathematical formulae, is voluntarily assumed by the scientific managers. And later, when these laws, rules and formulae are applied to the everyday work of all the workmen of the establishment, through the intimate and hearty cooperation of those on the management's side, they invariably result ... in producing a very much larger output per man, as well as an output of a better and higher quality.
>
> (1947: 40)

This connection between Taylor and the panopticon is also recognised by De Gaudemar when he writes that 'the principles set out by Taylor scarcely go beyond those set out by Bentham' (quoted in Webster & Robins 1993: 245). In both Taylorism and the panopticon, we find the same mechanisms of surveillance and disciplinary control. The very principles of the panopticon become intensified through Taylor's capitalist management and thus extended throughout society. In this sense the panopticon is the precursor of global capitalist management. Consequently, the panopticon (surveillance) and the disciplinary regime are incorporated more firmly into the labour process.[1] The disciplinary panoptic sustains the political economy of capitalism, especially the free (competitive) market. It is not just what is done by a strong interventionist state but what is *allowed* by this state in a 'free market' society.

Indeed, the key to the capitalist political economy is the cooperation of free trade and competition, and a strong governmental apparatus. Free trade is productive as long as it is protected by an administrative social regime. In other words, free trade and competition require a centrally organised and a disciplined social regime that facilitates and expands free-market policies, capital, and labour. In order to sustain an individualised society with economic freedom, the Benthamite political economy and disciplinary mechanisms of normalisation[2] go hand in hand in order to modify human behaviours and promote responsible, reliable, and rational 'acts'. So, on the one hand, there is an active and strong interventionist apparatus with discipline, panopticon and surveillance practices, and on the other, a market economy (economic freedom), competition, individual pleasures, and good acts. Thus, the panopticon is crucial to the development of a neoliberal governmentality that aims to intensify surveillance while at the same time produces self-governing 'harmless' individuals according to the established norms.

Yet the panopticon itself is insufficient to solve the conflicts inherent to society. Neoliberalism entails spreading the free market to all aspects of society as the basis for the production of new forms of life: it extends the process of making the free market a general matrix of social and political relations by taking as its focus not exchange but competition. As such, it is precisely this extension of market relations to all spheres of society that compels individuals to internalise the logic of surveillance and control from the panopticon, for there is no escape from failure in the neoliberal logic of market-based competition. After all, one cannot legislate away inherent systemic problems, because in the eyes of neoliberal governmentality the only solution to such conflicts, problems, is competition. Free trade and competition work better than an authoritarian governmentality precisely because they compel human beings to compete and come up with 'better' solutions to conflicts and problems. The Benthamite panoptic prison, therefore, gives the way for the materialisation of competition as an eidos. The 'invisible' panopticon must regulate the society overall by perpetuating a culture of competition that promotes capital and labour in accordance with free market policies. Thus, in the absence of a 'visible' authoritarian governmentality, the political competition solution is anything but clear and convincing. The panopticon is adopted by the market order and becomes invisible, but its effects are tangible, operating through a culture of competition as an 'eidos' (instead of a natural given). The striking similarity between them is that both rely on individual freedom understood as 'economic freedom' from a *given* menu. In the panopticon, the confinement is actualised by the cells and physical barriers. In the case of the market order, the cells are now socially constructed, given by property rights and competition. As a result, competition as an invisible 'watchtower' spreads across all aspects of life and thus becomes an organising force through which human beings engage into a continuous activity of capital and labour. That is, life that is conducted in market relationships as competition. But what is competition? 'Competition is an essence . . . a principle of formalization. Competition has an internal logic; it has its own structure. Its effects are only produced if this logic is respected' (Foucault 2008: 120). Competition therefore must be produced and protected.

According to Foucault, by competition we must always understand the market order and inequality rather than equality of exchange. To favour competition is never to favour equality. If exchange works by equivalence, competition implies inequality (see Dardot & Laval 2013: 83). The task of neoliberalism is to develop the concrete spaces in which competition as an organising principle can take shape and function. 'So it is a matter of market economy without laissez-faire, that is to say an active policy without state control. Neo-liberalism therefore should not be identified with laissez-faire, but rather with permanent activity, vigilance and intervention' (Foucault 2008: 132). Because competition is essential and valuable, then it must be continuously (re)produced and supported. Competition regulates conflicts and problems inherent to society and the neoliberal market whose logic must be 'respected'. Significantly, for Foucault, the new—as distinct from the eighteenth century—disciplinary paradigm announces a new phase of liberalism. Contrary to classic liberal governmentality, which believes that the economy is somehow natural, that things can develop on their own without any intervention, that markets can just happen, the economy is understood by neoliberalism as an effect of a legal order. 'The juridical gives form to the economic, and the economic would not be what it is without the juridical' (Foucault 2008: 163). Thus, and contrary to classical liberalism, neoliberalism realises the need to create the market. Whereas liberalism is founded on exchange and no state intervention, neoliberalism is founded on competition and thus inequality (Foucault 2008: 118–9). It entails 'a market economy without laissez-faire'; it is market with 'permanent vigilance, activity, and intervention' (Foucault 2008: 132). The market, therefore, has to be created and maintained. This is the key point that distinguishes classic liberalism from contemporary economic liberalism.

The Rule of Law (Rechtsstaat)

But how could competition as an eidos be extended from the realm of the market and become the regulative principle of society? At this point, Foucault makes reference to the rule of law (Rechtsstaat) as a concept which may literally be described as 'state under law'.³ The rule of law plays a central role in constituting a disciplinary normalisation that is based upon economic order. With the constitution of the rule of law, the sovereign no longer has the power of life and death. The new sovereign is different in that it is not based on the juridical power of coercion. The function of the state, then, is elevated to a status that guarantees freedom, particularly a domain of economic freedom. Neoliberal 'freedom' is economic, not political. The old values of liberty, equality, and fraternity are displaced by capital accumulation and the economisation of human relations and life. The state, therefore, will exist to guarantee and protect economic freedom.

What is the ultimate purpose of the rule of law? The rule of law is a response to the needs of the market, but market expansion creates more opportunities for conflict and political dissent. Conflict and dissent cannot be resolved by the market but require a rule of law under which the intervention and arbitration are carried out. In establishing the rule of law, the liberals see the possibility of getting rid of various forms of 'disruptive ideas', including socialism. Or, to put it even more succinctly: it is the fear of 'potential disruptive events' that creates the rule of law. Neoliberalism views society as a battlefield. Revolution is always in the air. Neoliberalism is wary of dangerous multitudes, the crowds who shun the unity of the system and create disorder. The aim of the constitution of the Leviathan (Hobbes) and the state of exception (Schmitt) was to transform the multitude into the 'people'. However, the multitude can always reappear within the state. Thus, dangerous multitudes should be transformed into 'ordered multiplicities' so that resistance does not occur, that the event does not take place, for the multitude is 'anti-state', 'anti-people'. Hence, Hobbes writes: 'when they rebel against the state, the citizens are the multitude against the people' (quoted in Virno 2004: 9).⁴ The fear of the multitude, the fear of the event reconfigures neoliberal economic theory in the same sense that Hobbes and Schmitt treated a state of exception that is war operationally as a political kernel of the law, as a condition for the establishment of an absolutist state. This is also the way how the rule of law institutionalises a culture of competition as an eidos.

All that society needs is formal law that paves the way for the enterprise society subject to the dynamic of competition, but also that banishes the state intervention in the economy, and in society overall. For neoliberalism, the rule of law is valued, 'but on the extrinsic and contingent grounds that it is beneficial for enterprise' (Davies 2014: 191). Law makes sense only insofar as it structures and expands competition and capital accumulation. What is then needed is more market and less politics and the state, for a state 'under the supervision of the market' is preferable 'than a market supervised by the state' (Foucault 2008: 116). The market, in other words, governs the state. Crucially, therefore, the rule of law is not only used to do away with the threat of 'disruptive socialist ideals'. Instead, it becomes a general strategy to transform the society into an economic battleground. The battleground means that the liberals also use the rule of law to ward off the other aspect of the savage, 'that other natural man or ideal element dreamed up by economists: a man without a past or a history, who is motivated only by self-interest and who exchanges the product of his labor for another product' (Foucault 2003: 194). In effect, with the constitution of the rule of law the liberals see the possibility of warding off both two senses of the savage, 'who emerges from his forests to enter into a contract and to found society, and the savage Homo economicus whose life is devoted to exchange and barter' (Foucault 2003: 194). Homo-economicus is the ideal figure of the liberal market. For this reason, the rule of law 'constitutes a social body, which is, at the same time, an economic body' (Foucault 2003).

Just as neoliberalism creates markets, it also realises the need to create homo economicus as a form of subjectification. Within neoliberalism, therefore, 'we are everywhere homo economicus and only homo economicus' (Brown 2015: 33). Homo economicus approaches everything as a market of winners or losers. In this figure of homo economicus as a grid of intelligibility, the noble savage who carries an inscriptional subjectivity is now gone. Gone also is the classical economy of crime and punishment. Sovereignty rules men as subjects of right, whereas the rule of law supplements the disciplinary panoptic power with the management of individuals qua homo economicus. Summarising rather crudely, neoliberal economic theory manages individuals qua homo economicus that is based on the dynamic of competition. Homo economicus therefore is the key to understanding neoliberal economic theory. Homo economicus is a person 'who is eminently governable' (Foucault 2003: 270). Nowhere is this personal-social-economic transformation more aptly expressed than in how homo economicus responds to sovereign power:

> This is what the man right, *homo juridicus*, says to the sovereign: I have rights, I have entrusted some of them to you, the others you must not touch. . . . Homo economicus does not say this. He also tells the sovereign: You must not. But why must he not? You must not because you cannot. And you cannot in the sense that 'you are powerless'. And why are you powerless, why can't you? You cannot because you do not know, and you do not because you cannot know.
> (Foucault 2008: 283)

Homo economicus reveals a reality that transcends all the limitations of sovereign power, including the economic domain, because the sovereign is incapable of mastering the new emerging society. The emergence of homo economicus changes how sovereign power must work; it demands a new society, a new social regime, which cannot be founded on ruthless, cruel sovereignty as having a power of life and death. Neoliberalism declares that what's important about the market is competition, so the state should protect and secure market mechanisms that facilitate competition. As a result, permeated by state-phobia, competition becomes the organising and regulatory form of state and society. What emerges in the process of transformation of the noble savage to the savage homo economicus as a 'free' subject with its passions, and a 'freedom' that is deprived of justice and equality. Freedom is valuable insofar as it is met with competition. 'No freedom without competition, no competition without freedom' becomes the mantra of neoliberalism. Indeed, neoliberalism is not satisfied with respecting or guaranteeing any kind of freedom. Neoliberalism is, in short, 'consumer of freedom' (Foucault 2008: 63), and it is valuable only insofar as other freedoms exist: 'freedom of the market, freedom to buy and sell, the free exercise of property rights, freedom of discussion . . . and so on' (Foucault 2008: 63). Neoliberalism governs *for* the markets, and governing for the markets means that 'sovereignty and law become supports for competition, rather than rights' (Brown 2015: 66). As Vatter succinctly puts it:

> In neoliberalism, the law is no longer intended to organize citizens as law-giving subjects into a free people (civitas). Instead, the law favors negative liberty ('free choice' and 'pursuit' of self-interest) which, in turn, compels subjects to conduct themselves with respect to each other by following those legal norms that structure the spontaneous order of the free market (societus). This neoliberal conception of law refuses to see citizens as equal members of a people, in accordance with a constitution. Instead, it sees them as nothing more than specimens of a population who are subject to a normative order: a normative order on which they become entirely dependent (alieni iuris).
> (2014: 178)

Neoliberalism wants absolute dependency on the normative order and markets. You are not allowed to challenge the *nomos* behind this normativity, even if you are continuously told that you are 'free'. In fact, you are free insofar as you express your consumer satisfaction within a given space, which is the market. You are free to express brand preferences; you are not free to mobilise politically. In neoliberalism, freedom is judged, limited, and subject to 'forms of coercion, and obligations relying on threats etcetera' (Foucault 2008: 64). All that matters, in the end, is organising 'the conduct of conducts' that require techniques and, above all, a way of speaking the truth of neoliberalism 'about the nature of times through the truth of the end of times' (Dillon 2011: 784). In other words, neoliberalism always charges itself with delaying the end of a temporal order of things, of life. Neoliberalism is a truth teller. And 'if the truth teller is the truth, then the truth is for everyone, and if what the truth teller says is true, then it follows that the conduct of conduct, from the individual to the collective, should be aligned or align itself with the truth' (Dillon 2011: 784). What is now played is a new 'game of truth': market. The market becomes a 'site of veridiction', a new reality which connects up 'of a regime of truth to governmental practice' (Foucault 2008: 37). The central concern is to colonise social life by market relations so that all spheres of life can be better managed and ordered. Neoliberalism is thus about modelling all social relations that are still viewed as outside the market according to market rationalities—even when the particular relations in question have not actually been commodified. It declares that 'markets know best'. Reconfiguring life to resemble markets is a hallmark of neoliberalism. The market circulates the truth of neoliberalism to sustain its power as well as its legitimacy.

In the new governmental practice, the neoliberal subject as homo economicus is a subject who must be left on its own. In this process, the individual is addressed affectively. The universalisation of competition means that any way of life that does not fit with neoliberal economic forms is rendered valueless. What is sought, therefore, is a 'society subject to the dynamic of production' (Foucault 2008: 147). To facilitate competition, however, discipline should not naturally restrain human beings and their passions. On the contrary, their wants, desires, passions, and instincts should be duly noted, turned into a liberal dialogue. If human beings are motivated by passions, which lack the idea of equality for all, there should be no control of their actions. After all, how could disciplinary regime ever obtain the knowledge that would enable it to produce faithful and law-abiding subjects?

Interestingly, but not surprisingly, neoliberalism has a model of the state that guarantees economic freedom. However, neoliberalism is not about the state leaving the society and economy alone. The state therefore has never disappeared; it has always been a guardian, maintainer of order. Here one should shamelessly repeat the major lessons of Marx, Weber, and Polanyi: 'the modern market does not operate on its own, but has always backed by the state' (Dardot & Laval 2013: 6). Neoliberalism views society as a site of conflict and war, aiming to prevent disruptive events by state apparatuses, by dispositifs of power, such as the panopticon.

Sovereignty centralises power as a way of dealing with fears of dangerous events. With neoliberal discipline, fear is what must be (re)produced by social regimes of power to secure a life to make life live. In other words, 'fear rules'. The process of competition combined with flexible labour markets, economic freedom understood as the free choice constrained within a competitive jacket, and socially constructed barriers (property rights), contribute to the pervasiveness of a threat and the actualisation of fear. The next part of the chapter argues that fear is what enables secure and docile bodies to thrive in the marketplace. Furthermore, the disciplinary regime mobilises the spectre of danger and threat in order to normalise and organise populations. The effects of this (re)productive mobilisation of fear are central to the disciplinary neoliberalism.

Biopoliticised Fear

Because affective modulation of people becomes an essential function of neoliberalism, fear is necessary to impose discipline on population and the multitude. Addressing bodies from the angle of their affectivity, the growth of disciplinary society depends on effective means of enforcing rules by punishing those who break the rules—by creating, in effect, a 'culture of fear' in which control is achieved by a collective fear of punishment, including loss of livelihood, economic status, etc. Thus, citizens begin to experience fear, wrapped in the perpetual anxiety, which glorifies reaction rather than action: 'the fear snowballs, as the reaction runs its course' (Massumi 2005: 37). It is here, in that immanence, that disciplinary neoliberalism coincides with its affective potential: 'fear becomes a generative principle of formation for rule' (Dillon & Reid 2009: 86). Having fear as a habitual posture becomes a way of life.

Fear is the essential condition and a positive element of neoliberal discipline. Life is now lived as a natural 'fear environment' in which there is no relief, no day of rest. The fear of failure/punishment also dissolves trust, one of the binding agents of society togetherness. Thus, with discipline, neoliberal governmentality moulds itself to suspicion, for self-censorship becomes the new normal. At the core of such fear lies 'the sheer weakness, incapacity to resist, vulnerability of the frail' (Bauman 2004: 47). In other words, the disciplinary society addresses fearful bodies 'at the level of their dispositions' towards (re)action, capturing the spontaneity of the individual soul (Massumi 2005: 33). The goal is to convert fearful bodies and fearful subjects into disciplined and ultimately (re)productive subjects of neoliberalism.

Importantly, the fearful subject is not a passive subject but an actively driven subject of neoliberalism, who is continuously produced through its fears and insecurities. Neoliberal markets are most efficient when they are transmitting fear. If sovereignty generates a weak subject of ressentiment whose collective existence is damaged, who does not react, discipline addresses a fearful subject whose freedom is (re)produced in response to insecure and unsafe situations it encounters within the requirements of docile and obedient bodies. What is the political importance of the fearful subject? Two points stand out. First, the subject is always already recognised or recognises itself under fearful conditions. Enslaved by its own fears and anxieties, the subject cannot show a collective political response as fear environment becomes a second nature. Fear braces people together in the terror of not yet being able to answer the question, 'What can we do?' As a result, collective action is restrained as fear becomes an open field for intervention and arbitrary exercises of neoliberal power operating on a continuum with militarisation of society (Massumi 2011). When a response occurs, 'it is on the individual scale of the personal actions of 'everyday heroes' carrying out small deeds of voluntaristic support' (Massumi 2011). Second, the object of discipline is the management of fear and the insecurities that are its foundations. Fear and danger meet the necessities of securitisation, whereas civil and political rights are suspended in the name of the market's future stability. The association between fear and growing state security apparatus—in the interests of the market—becomes almost automatic. What remains is a fearful subject whose ability to understand and make sense of events is suspended, for fear caused by discipline is unresolvable. To paraphrase Engin Isin (2004: 232), what the fearful subject wants is the impossible. It wants absolute security. It wants absolute certainty. It wants absolute safety. It wants to have the perfect body. Yet, because providing absolute security, certainty, and safety is impossible, it cannot tackle its fears; it cannot act. It cannot live a normal life. Since these claims are impossible because they pronounce a space that the fearful subject cannot reach, it cannot overcome its fear. Consequently, fear becomes a permanent feature of discipline, which 'circulates through the capillaries of collective life' by not repressing but producing and intensifying life (see Collier 2009: 81).

Indeed, neoliberalism addresses fearful and 'self-managing citizens' capable of conducting themselves in economic freedom, deprived of the substantive concept of the common good. Thus, 'economic freedom' and fear are intimately connected. Fugacity, instability, and insecurity are elementary ingredients of neoliberal discipline, in which freedom and fear refer to one another. In other words, discipline nurtures fear and makes it subject to an economic calculus. In fact, fear and homo economicus are of a piece: they are indissociable dimensions of the same subjectivity. Homo economicus as rational self-entrepreneur promises manifold options and opportunities to consume, but it also creates a risk-security-aware culture, thus establishing a permanent fear of success, or fear of failure. With disciplinary neoliberalism, the incentives are changed, not by a coercive sovereign authority but motivated by self-interest—fear of failure—for fear (economic failure, fear of failure) is the best way to transform harmful responses into the beneficial, undesirable into desirable; it is an integral part of capital expansion.

To sum up, disciplinary neoliberalism's key concept is less liberty and more fear, for without a persistent sense of fear and danger present in the minds and bodies of subjects, productive and 'inspiring' powers vested in the disciplinary regime may lose its legitimacy. The emphasis on fear and danger is vital to the development of a biopolitics of fear. The managing of fear becomes the scope of biopolitics: biopolitics needs fear to manage it. This is particularly clear when 'danger' is involved. In what

80 *Birth of Neoliberal Governmentality*

follows I argue that biopolitics is precisely the disciplinary (and neoliberal) strategy of pacification and stabilisation of society that takes making live as its objects. For modern biopolitics, only a constantly pacified and administered life is a safe environment. Furthermore, I contend that the coevolving fear of the event is the basis and motive for the constitution of the responsible, reliable, and rational self, for it paves the way for continually growing security apparatus. In between stretches a continuum of 'the event', which becomes a legitimate tool for preemption.

The Political Theology of Biopolitics

> All significant concepts of the modern theory of the state are secularised theological concepts.
> (Schmitt 1985: 36)

As noted earlier, within the matrix of discipline politics addresses the vital processes that sustain human existence: 'the size and quality of the population; reproduction and human sexuality; conjugal, parental, and familial relations; health and disease; birth and death' (Rose 2007: 52–3). This shift in history is what Foucault (2003) calls 'biopolitics'. According to Foucault, biopolitics refers to the political strategisation/technologisation of life for its own productive betterment; the *modus operandi* of power relations that aims to enhance, render productive, promote, compose, maximise, and administer life. Biopolitics is a privileged form of intervention; it is 'the politics of life itself' (Rose 2007).

In volume 1 of *The History of Sexuality*, Foucault proposes (1998) two bipolar diagrams of biopower, or power over life. One pole of biopower works by *individualisation*, that is, on the micro-level of power, which seeks to produce individuality and thus incorporate it into efficient systems. But this pole also makes another pole that works on the macro-level, namely, *biopolitics of the population*, which focuses on 'the species body, the body imbued with the mechanisms of life: birth, morbidity, mortality, longevity' (Rose 2007: 53). Foucault claims that this bipolar technology, emerging in the seventeenth century, seeks 'to invest life through and through', which is 'a question of constituting something like a milieu of life, existence' (Foucault 2007: 30). The development of life therefore necessarily becomes the focus of inquiry.

This, however, tells only part of the story. One should, therefore, raise the more fundamental question: what is the true purpose of biopolitics? My contention is that, because biopolitics is also a regime of truth, that is to side with the forces of neoliberal order, its main purpose is to avoid more apocalyptic and radical change. In other words, the main objective of biopolitics is to defuse any fears of a repeat of the event. Thus, when we examine modern biopolitics, we should pay attention to its theological reason because how to minimise the immanent emergencies and potentially disruptive events is shaped by 'secularized theological concepts'. Biopolitics is one of them. The always present possibility of an event is what defines modern biopolitics' legitimacy. This powerful configuration also makes the fear of the event the currency of neoliberalism.

Katechon

In a revision of Foucault's account of biopolitics, I shall suggest that biopolitics is a measured attempt to combine the existing order and legitimacy of a neoliberal economic theory in order to decrease resistance. In a sense, therefore, modern biopolitics is doing here to the 'sacralised neoliberal order' what Schmitt did to the exception, turning its revolutionary potentiality (Benjamin) into a counterrevolutionary politics of event. Modern biopolitics is therefore *katechontic*. Every epoch has its own Satan and seems to be generating its appropriate katechon. In this sense, the antagonism is between the Satan and the katechon. To clarify this point, let us now turn to Schmitt's *katechon* (from the Greek for 'to hold down'). In *The Nomos of the Earth*, Schmitt (2003) contends that the legacy of Roman law, and temporal political orders established over the centuries, is katechontic: what is the best possible order that prevents decay, the victory of 'evil', and resists the Anti-Christ, the end of finite time? With the katechon, or the 'restrainer', Christianity emerges as an empire whose centre is Rome, and gains a juridical, cultural, and prosecutorial imperial power within history.

The katechon is what transforms eschatological time into the time of Christian Empire, always prepared to act against the apocalypse. Empire, according to Schmitt, 'meant the historical power to restrain the appearance of the Antichrist and the end of the present eon' (2003: 60). The empire becomes the katechon because it delays the fulfilment of history. It sustains, restores the order, and thus fights the absolute state of lawlessness.

The idea of the katechon refers to the second letter of the apostle Paul to the community in Thessalonica, where the apostle Paul is explaining why the Lord has not arrived yet (see Hoelzl 2010: 98). Verses 6–7 constitute the central parts of the letter: 'And you know what is now restraining him, so that he may be revealed when his time comes. For the mystery of lawlessness is already at work, but only until the one who now restrains it is removed'. The passage is a Pauline warning to the primitive community in Thessalonica against the revelation of the lawless activity of 'Satan', of Antichrist, upon whom God sends a 'strong delusion', 'so that all may be condemned who did not believe the truth but had pleasure in unrighteousness' (II.2.11). According to the apostle, the lawless Satan threatens to replace God, the throne of God. We are also told that the Christ will return soon to delay the apocalypse and institute the reign of God. In order for the second coming of the Lord, the lawless

Satan has to be revealed. As such, the lawless Antichrist is already visible but has not been fully revealed yet (Hoelzl 2010: 100). The reason for this, however, is not clear.

The katechon is an appointee of God to overturn the current evil world, to prevent chaos. There is also no dispute about the importance of the katechon in Schmitt's thinking: 'I do not believe that any historical concept other than katechon would have been possible for the original Christian faith' (Schmitt 2003: 60). The concept of the katechon, according to Schmitt, is a 'historical concept', a 'lucid Christian faith in potent historical power' because, as a belief, as a restrainer, what it 'holds back' is nothing other than the eschatological 'end of the world' (Schmitt 2003: 60). For Schmitt, 'chaos' can precede the end of time. The apocalypse is always possible. The katechon, therefore, holds the end at bay and suppresses the power of Satan, the Antichrist. 'Who holds the Anti-Christ at bay?' thus becomes the historical question from which Schmitt's concept of the political derives.

The katechon, according to Schmitt, is a political and existential category to maintain absolute authority within an authoritarian state in order to deal with the political chaos that threatens the Weimar republic. It is a theology in the service of sovereignty, of power, which seeks a theological legitimation of the political. It is a matter of life and death, doing whatever is necessary to maintain order. As Jacob Taubes writes:

> Schmitt's interest was in only one thing: that the party, that the chaos not rise to the top, that the state remain. No matter what the price. This is difficult for theologians and philosophers to follow, but as far as the jurist is concerned, as long as it is possible to find even one juridical form, by whatever hairsplitting ingenuity, this must absolutely be done, for otherwise chaos reigns. This is what he later calls the katechon.
>
> (2004: 103)

The Earth, it seems, has been annihilated on films many times. Sometimes a few heroes save the world from monsters, zombies, or 'enemies'; sometimes the end of the world, the apocalypse is celebrated. Lars Von Trier's *Melancholia* is an example of the latter. The real subject of *Melancholia* is the coming apocalypse and our response to it. What do we do when we know that the world will end soon? The film features two main protagonists, Justine and Claire. Justine 'perceives' the evil, that is, the imminent extinction of the Earth. She knows that the apocalypse is on its way; she has the capacity to see the coming event. Justine, therefore, has a 'werewolf perspective' (Dienstag 2015).

However, she can't make others believe in that bitter truth. After all, possessing the truth does not always make you the sovereign; instead, it can bring with itself a feeling of weakness, an impotence in which you are isolated, withdrawn from the real world. Justine is depressed, but her depression is neither chemical nor psychological; it is ontological and moral. She seems to welcome the end of the world in favour of a new one. This world, she believes, is unnecessary and full of evil. It must go. Hence she declares: 'the Earth is evil. We don't need to grieve for it. Nobody would miss it.' Thus, hers is a revelation, which signifies the event in and through which history's meaning emerges—in a word, the apocalypse. For this reason, the fact that Melancholia will destroy the world does not bother her. Instead, this she finds satisfying because it satisfies her desire to see this evil Earth punished by another planet. Therefore, she prepares for the coming event precisely because it 'reveals the conditions for the beginning of the new, and beyond the possible, the darkness of absolute freedom' (Dienstag 2015: 190). She has a perspective. She thus emerges the only figure 'who is able to propose an appropriate answer to the impending catastrophe, and to the total obliteration of every symbolic frame' (Žižek 2014: 40). Justine's message is thus: sometimes you need an apocalypse to create a new life.

Claire is, however, blind to an evil. Devoid of any meaningful content, she appears to be a woman 'without quality'. As such, she is a control freak and always sides with the given. She 'never ventures beyond the limits of bourgeois common sense' (Shaviro 2012: 36). Hers is, in other words, a post-political world where no questioning or meaningful political action is possible. This is why the moment it becomes evident that Melancholia will in fact hit Earth, she breaks down. Justine is the radical other, whereas Claire is conservative. Justine struggles against social conformity, whereas Claire accepts the existing situation as it is. Justine's acts interrupt the social order, whereas Claire strives to maintain it. Justine's reactions are joyful, whereas Claire is an example of the fearful subject. Justine's is a world in which 'chaos reigns' (Shaviro 2012: 39), whereas Claire lives in a world where order and control is the best policy. In short, Claire opts for the status quo rather than disruption. She fears social change because losing her bourgeoisie life is far more dangerous than the annihilation of the world.

For Justine the earth is finite; she accepts the apocalypse. Rather than fearing radical change, she emerges 'in affirmation of active welcoming of another world' (Evans & Reid 2014: 188). Claire, however, desperately attempts to delay the apocalypse. Her escapist fantasy from the extinction is so absurd that she even proposes to spend their last moments together out on the terrace, with music and wine, but Justine explicitly rejects this idea. In contrast to Justine, who ignores the cheap, ready-made happiness, Claire seems to live entirely 'in the present moment of bourgeois satisfaction, without any further temporal horizon' (Shaviro 2012: 45).

Though the main contrast in *Melancholia* is between Justine and Claire, Claire's husband John is also an interesting figure. Representative of the economic-technical rationality, he is a workaholic and too money-minded. With his expensive telescope he always stares into, he sees the world objectively, 'realistically', repeatedly assuring Justine and Claire that science is the sovereign domain of truth, that Melancholia will miss the world. But when he realises that the scientists got it all wrong, that Melancholia will in fact destroy the world, he commits suicide rather than witness the apocalypse. In other words, it is precisely because of his attachment to techno-scientific capitalism, to the givenness, that John is unable to cope with the destruction of the planet.

The lesson that should be drawn from *Melancholia* is that, whatever you do, you can't prevent the apocalypse. This world is itself already the apocalypse, and it is precisely this point of view that makes modern biopolitics continue out of control. According to the system, though the apocalypse is near, to celebrate this reality is an impossible idea. Though it knows that it is finite, it believes to delay that end. In this sense, modern biopolitics is a preemptive counterrevolutionary tendency that seeks to sustain the existing neoliberal order of things. Thus, rather than welcoming the end of the world as in *Melancholia*, the katechontic modern biopolitics is an active figure, prepared to sacrifice everything to keep the apocalypse at bay. For modern biopolitics, the idea of surrender is an impossible one.

If the sovereign is he who 'decides on the state of exception'; his main task is to restore and maintain the political order, which is threatened by an exceptional event. Whereas revolution seeks to establish a new order, the katechon strives to maintain the existing social, economic, and political order. Revolution attempts to turn over the old order, whereas the katechon tries to appropriate revolutionary ideas by sovereign exceptionalism. Sovereignty (katechon) and revolution are thus intimately connected. The katechon is a biopolitical imaginary of an imperial sovereign who insists that 'time is limited', thereby radicalising modern biopolitics and the politics of security even further.

Acting under the sovereign law, the katechon is a radical reconceptualisation of a biopolitical imaginary, attempting to prevent its own end. It is here that the biopolitical imaginary of the katechon coincides with its central aspect: the state of exception. The time of the biopolitical imaginary is the time of the exception. Thus, confronted with the coming defeat of the existing social, economic, and political order, the state of exception becomes the central aspect to postpone its own end by restraining the powers of revolution. The katechon is haunted by the knowledge that existing orders (empire) are always preceded by the apocalypse. The apocalypse, however, is not to be confused with disaster, catastrophe, or decay. To speak of the apocalypse is very different from ecological or economic crises. Crises are temporary, but the apocalypse has a capacity to overthrow the existing liberal regimes. A crisis, for instance, reveals conditions for the existing order to renew or consolidate itself. The apocalypse is, however, an end that one cannot escape.

The apocalypse has a lengthy history that is intimately connected to the historical development of Christianity (see Evans & Reid 2014: 160). Etymologically, it refers to revelation or discover. Historically speaking, it means an end. In his *Occidental Eschatology*, Jacob Taubes (2009) argues that every apocalypse needs a seer, a visionary. The visionary knows what will happen and how he'll live and die. He sees the evil deeds of the Satan, the Anti-Christ that annihilate him. For this reason, he is engaged in a permanent struggle for survival. If the apocalypse is revolution, the seer is the biopolitics of security. In this sense, the katechontic response is an imperial biopolitical order of securitisation, a political reality, on which the 'new normal' runs. It is the spectre of the event that haunts modern biopolitics. The spectre of the event, revolution, is intimately bound up with security politics and modern biopolitics: without it, they are doomed to fail at their mission to ensure society's well-being through enforcing market relations.

Put simply, the katechontic discourse empowers liberal regimes biopolitically: 'the analytic of which . . . furnishes its governmental technologies and military strategic operational concepts and doctrines, as well as its political rationalities' (Dillon 2011: 783–4). When Foucault theorised biopolitics, he did not explicitly address the transformation of theological reasoning. In this sense, Foucault's genealogy should be extended to take note of how theological reasoning is one of the central characteristics to the development of biopolitics. Schmitt reminds us forcefully that 'in modernity, theology continues to be present and active in an eminent way' (quoted in Agamben 2011: 4). As far as the event is concerned, which aims at bringing about the end to the existing order, theological and political reasoning become increasingly difficult to distinguish. If 'the transformation of political reasoning often finds its expression through the tropes of theological discourse', so, too, 'the transformation of theological reasoning often finds its expression through newly addressing questions of temporal conduct and rule' (Dillon 2011: 785). The task of each reasoning is to organise 'the conduct of conduct' and establish a social regime in changing circumstances.

Eschaton

Every politics of security (and counterrevolutionary strategy) is also a politics of the limit; it is concerned with the limit, and end times, of the existing rule. The political orders of modern finitude know very well that they are finite. This is why the katechontic response becomes an imperative to delay that end. However, in legitimising the politics of security and the war on terror for which it kills, modern biopolitics must also be seen as a political *eschatology*. Thus, following Dillon, for security politics and neoliberal biopolitics, we can diagnose a 'political eschatology', a 'modern eschaton', in which the transcendental finitude of horizon is transposed into a 'factical finitude' and thus becomes an immanent quality (Dillon 2011: 782). Modern biopolitics, in this sense, has secularised eschatology, excluding by appropriating it; that is to say, 'the time of the end is naturalized into little more than a historical process of completion or fulfilment which culminates in . . . neoliberal modernity' (see Bradley & Fletcher 2010: 2). As a secularised eschaton, biopolitics and security politics in general are concerned 'with the end of things', 'the very end of time itself', which has to be delayed through social, political, and economic interventions. As opposed to the transcendental finitude of biopolitics, the modern aspects of the eschaton provide biopolitics with an open horizon of temporal possibility, an open historicity, within the infinite becomings of finite beings, happenings, or events (Dillon 2011: 781). That is to say, the temporal imagination that informs modern biopolitics changes from time as a derivate of eternity to time as a continuous emergence in which life is conceived as an immanent process, a life of becoming (Dillon & Reid 2009: 108). There is no relief, no day of rest for modern biopolitics because, as a modern eschaton, it is defined by continuous processes and patterns of continuous contingent emergence. Taking life as the main focus of inquiry, modern biopolitics is, like liberalism, diverse and heterogeneous. It is based on the regulation of the 'infinity of finite beings'. The temporal limit of modern biopolitics is marked, in other words, an open horizon of finite possibilities, 'an infinity of finite possibilities and becomings'.

In this precise sense, modern biopolitics as a modern eschaton deals with potential events as a matter of managing the infinity of finitudes, without allowing these finitudes to universalise themselves, and thus leading to radical structural change. Doomed to time, modern biopolitics can thus be seen as an extension of Christian eschatology. Securing the liberal order from its ongoing struggle against the event is a task that is shaped by religious traditions. In this sense, biopolitics derives its warrant to secure the neoliberal order from the fear of the event, of revolution, 'eschatologically'. Modern biopolitics is motivated by the fear of the event, which is intimately bound up with the fear of a breakdown of order tout court. As Dillon rightly observes:

> [T]he catastrophic threat-event of the dissolution of the temporal order of things is continuously also interrogated to supply the governing technologies, by which the political order is regulated in peace to be 'fit' for war and is regulated so as to resist the same catastrophic threat-event.
>
> (2011: 782)

Modern biopolitics is, in short, a political eschatology that is 'concerned with the end of things', and this gives rise to an updated understanding of security politics that 'derives from the positive exigencies of government and rule that arise in restricting that end' (2011: 782).

The eschaton remains a source of political as well as 'religious' dissent and resistance today, and it seems that today there are two responses that continuously call the nature of the eschaton into question: the first response is *katechontic*, which legitimises the existing order; the second is *revolutionary*, which seeks a total delegitimisation of that order. The first is to side with neoliberalism and the war on terror, the second with 'divine violence' and revolution. As both katechontic (preventing radical structural change and delaying the coming of end times) and as figured around the eschaton (beliefs, hopes, and expectations concerning the end time), modern biopolitics is a preemptive take on the event/revolution, which legitimises counterrevolution in general and the neoliberal security politics (the war against everything) specifically. As a political eschatology that refers to an open horizon of temporal possibilities, modern biopolitics is also a katechontic response, which attempts to foreclose the reservoir of temporal possibilities so that they cannot become eventual. Where there is a fear of revolution, there is always a counterrevolutionary tendency that defuses that threat. Whereas the eschaton concerns the open finitudinal horizon of the modern account of life, the katechon concerns the preservation of that horizon (2011: 789).

In Hobbes's political eschatology, Leviathan was the main solution that acts with an eye towards the catastrophic end. Thus, Leviathan centralised all individual fears to react to such fears of dangerous events. Consequently, fear became the currency of the political order and the constitutive rule of the sovereign. This eschatology for Hobbes was nonetheless based upon the virtuality of threat and danger. In Schmitt's 'secularised' political eschatology, Hobbes' model of absolute sovereign would be revisited, and the sovereign decision on the exception become a mechanism that could centralise all individual fears so as to ensure control over fear/danger. In Schmitt's political eschatology, the sovereign decision was the katechon that delays the empire's end. Modern biopolitics of security, similarly, emerges as an eschatological, katechontic response, whose mission is to manage life to make life live by preventing the event. It is that katechontic gesture which legitimises perpetual security and perpetual war against the threat that the event (Satan, the Anti-Christ) mobilises against this move. Delaying empire's end, modern biopolitics of security and war thus become empire's katechontic tools, and the same goes for fear. Modern biopolitics' relation to fear is revisited and becomes a new modality of power that is able to preserve or enhance the life efficiency of a given population (see Debrix & Barder 2009: 406). Modern biopolitics turns fear into a dispositif, a katechontic response, geared towards preempting disruptive events and supplying the governing technologies and military apparatuses of security. When we speak of a biopolitical production of fear, what we are really describing is a series of scare tactics that can only produce 'good' social effects by agents/agencies of neoliberal governmentality.

If the event is the problem, then a new productivity of biopolitical fear is the answer. Life, therefore, gets fused with fear. As an eschatological katechontic response, which takes place in life for life, modern biopolitics 'sacralises' the liberal democratic market and understands 'freedom' only in terms of existing neoliberal values. Modern biopolitics only recognises market freedom, that is, the freedom to talk endlessly about consumer products. Other freedoms will invariably follow. As a political katechontic response, modern biopolitics is concerned with the virtuality of what already exists. As an eschatological katechontic response, the rule of truth spoken by biopolitics, in short, is prepared to sacrifice everything to keep 'the threat of revolution' at bay. The revolutionary event of the dissolution of the neoliberal order is continuously also interrogated to renew and modify biopolitics (Dillon 2011). In short, there is always a need for modern biopolitics to think in terms of disruptive events, or to mobilise the spectre of fear and absolute threat in changing circumstances. What modern biopolitics dreads most is the impotence of neoliberal power. Its objective is to neutralise anything that can threaten the existing order. In this sense, modern biopolitics is a preemptive counterrevolutionary tendency that seeks to sustain the existing neoliberal order of things.

Modern biopolitics is a finitudinal form of rule, a privileged form of intervention, whose mission is to secure life with its vital new capacities. In this sense, as Foucault (2008) insists, when one says 'biopolitics', one says 'biopolitics of security'. Or, to paraphrase Foucault, when one says 'biopolitics', one says 'biopolitics of fear'. With the biopolitics of fear, life itself becomes the enemy of life itself because life 'threatens life in its positive procreativity' (Dillon 2011: 788). Thus, rather than only a politics of sovereign exceptionality, modern biopolitics of fear is enacted by way of governmentality that mobilises all sorts of public agents to use the spectre of fear, danger, and threat (see Debrix & Barder 2009: 400), and, crucially, it is the fear/danger/threat of revolution that leads to a biopolitics of fear because it is through the event that fear is rendered productive in order to establish disciplinary control. When biopolitical agents/agencies of fear production become the loci of disciplinary techniques of neoliberalism, the production and the reproduction of fear is no longer the exception but the rule, and this means wondering how the biopolitics of fear takes place and reproduces itself in special sites or exceptional events. In the next section of the chapter, I argue that disciplinary techniques—and the biopolitics of fear—also perform an important segregatory function. They divide society/city into particular groups, such as responsible/reliable individuals and dangerous individuals, and thus serve as significant lines of demarcation that are spatially materialised and spatialised in urban governmental practices. Examples of this are almost too numerous, but a single one will suffice for a bullet point: kettling.

Geographies of Kettling

In November 2010, British students staged a series of demonstrations in several cities of the UK and Northern Ireland. Organised by the National Campaign against Fees and Cuts (NCAFC), thousands marched against spending cuts to further education, and an increase of the cap on tuition fees by the Conservative–Liberal Democrat coalition government. After the 2003 anti-Iraq war protest in London, which attracted almost a million people, the 2010 protests have marked something of a turning point in modern British history: the political protest was back. But if these protests made dissensus visible, and posited it at the heart of British politics, they also gave police an opportunity to widely use a scare tactic, an extrajudicial punishment, ensuring that protest against the status quo is ineffective. The tactic is called 'kettling', which so easily turns a legitimate protest into a 'violent disorder'.

Though kettling may at first seem a tactic within a wider assemblage of 'total policing', it is in fact a more complex spatial strategy. To get closer to an understanding of kettling, we need to unpick its political logic in relation to liberal security dispositifs. I shall argue that kettling aims to achieve two seemingly relational results: to discipline and incite the crowd in order to produce 'good' social effects by agents of neoliberalism, and displace dissent and resistance in order to defuse the fear of the event.

First, kettling aims to encircle protesters and discipline them in a specific site. Police officers with batons, sniffer dogs, and riot shields block the protesters into a specific area for hours. Thus, kettling aims to organise what Steve Herbert has called the 'protest zoning state'; where 'the expression of dissent . . . is controlled with a territorial strategy—it is banned from some areas and confined to others' (2007: 601). The protesters are held in tightly confined spaces without time limit and thus become the subject of police brutality at its most devious: anybody can be crushed by a horse, or hit with batons to the head. Legitimising police violence, kettling is designed to limit the disruption in the interests of 'public safety'. Punishing protesters without charge or trial, kettling is, in other words, designed to silence the crowd in the interest of 'public security'. If the first aim of kettling concerns the specific day where the protest takes place, the long run aim is to dissuade protesters from demonstrating in the future. Kettling acts on the future.

Aiming to discipline the crowd, kettling also attempts to incite the crowd. By seeing and treating the protesters as *adversaries*, the police aims to produce violent reactions from them. By creating difficult and unpleasant conditions (sub-zero or warm temperatures without food, water, toilets, or freedom of movement) and by preventing people from leaving the demonstration, the police aims to provoke the crowd into action. The containment process can last until protesters lose their moral energy. It makes people feel utterly helpless, hopeless, and 'discharge' their anger until it overflows into acts of criminal damage. Schoolchildren, or university students, for instance, join the protest to defend their right to protest, but what they learn from kettling is nothing other than fear: fear of missing lessons and lectures, fear of missing their train back to colleges, universities, and most importantly, fear of being arrested in a 'peaceful protest'. After all, 'managers of the event' know very well that fear and political anger can be easily turned into violence, seeking action above and beyond words. Thus, what appears to be targeted is the possibility of a violent act to the police. The logic which underwrites this is rather simple: by provoking the crowd, violence is inflamed by kettling itself. The exercise of kettling is *incitatory* in that it creates the threat in order to deal with the threat. In colonising the imaginary of the protester, kettling strives to make this imaginary real. Thus, the crowd is addressed affectively as it is rendered controllable and manageable for the stable unity of the order. What is at work here is an intersection of sovereign, disciplinary, and control rationalities in which the affective subject of 'action' is rendered governable and manageable. As a classificatory disciplinary technology, kettling, therefore, 'makes up people' (Hacking 1995).

A crucial ideological operation of kettling in this respect is its repression or the moral castigation of all radicalism as 'bad' or 'violent'. This strategy is based on the assumption that the protesters can be divided into two basic categories: 'peaceful', legitimate protesters and violent, illegitimate 'anarchists', which include radical student groups, left-wing groups, and initiatives like UK Uncut. At this stage, the media play a central role in shaping 'public opinion'. 'Anarchists' are frequently labelled as a 'violent minority' and 'anti-capitalists' by the sympathetic media. For this reason, they must be separated and marginalised from the crowd, for kettling builds upon the distinction between an inside and an outside. Inside the kettle, order reigns. Outside the kettle, disorder lurks around the corner. Managing disorder, the main aim is take robust action against aggressive 'troublemakers' and deal with them as quickly as possible. What becomes vital, therefore, is anticipating the 'crowd effect' to be created in the context of the demonstration as a whole. Discipline and the knowledge of the crowd must be total so that 'a becoming of the crowd' can be controlled. Kettling is, therefore, designed to stop the formation of an alternative political subjectivity. It aims to preempt or prevent 'dangerous multitudes' from forming.

This brings us to the main point in the logic of kettling: to normalise 'social struggles' by disorienting and demoralising the masses. The goal of kettling is to care for a 'liberal life' by neutralising threats to that life through some form of intervention: it is a fight to 'hit' the target before it takes actual shape. Therefore, one should analyse kettling within the framework of neoliberal governance. Kettling holds together as a response to an 'urgent threat': how to govern events in a world where neoliberalism is perpetually on the verge of collapse. In order to guarantee and secure neoliberal capitalism, the exercise of kettling is being done in a way that makes 'total policing' more confrontational or more political. In kettling, the 'politicisation' of the police proceeds in parallel with the 'militarisation' of the police. For the police, or total policing, even a peaceful protest is treated as a problem to be kettled, predetermining the political outcomes. Protest is, in other words, prevented from explaining its purpose to the public. The TUC march on Wednesday, November 30, 2011, in London, where more than two million public-sector workers staged a nationwide strike, is a case in point. The march was subject to extraordinary police control and restriction, including the erection of a preemptive 'ring of steel'.[5] In this sense kettling functions as a preemptive strategy that aims to empty out the emancipatory core of demonstration in advance: anything potentially dangerous must be excluded. Because demonstration is seen as an 'inconsistent' element within the existing neoliberal order, kettling must prevent its massification. Thus, the crowd must be continuously kettled so that its demands cannot reach the public but rather remain regulated and controlled in its own particularity.

In this sense, kettling is the materialisation of neoliberal security practices of the state. If the state of exception is an instance of neoliberalism, kettling is an instance of the state of exception. In neoliberalism, certain social practices are normalised and legitimised (kettling, police brutality), whereas practices that disrupt the neoliberal political-economic configuration are criminalised. Note that kettling protesters, used extensively during the G20 protests in London in 2009, was upheld as 'lawful' in the Court of Appeal. The European Court of Human Rights also ruled on March 15, 2012, that kettling was the 'least intrusive and most effective' tactic available to the police. These rulings show that the exercise of kettling is ideological in that it defends the legal, spatial and juridical, as well as the moral and symbolic forms of neoliberalism. It is another way of suppressing political differences. It is another way of sustaining a liberal way of life.

Neoliberalism is always haunted by the knowledge that it is underwritten by the event. After all, it knows that history is replete with events, revolutions to come. By targeting the affectivity of the individual, neoliberalism is animated by fear and danger. It aims to be purely *preemptive*. After all, every new tactic of power is simply the outcome of a particular power struggle. Its inscription always follows the management of the event. When the UK Court of Appeal ruled on January 19, 2012, that kettling was lawful, it meant that neoliberal capitalist states would be more efficient and effective in response to the contingency of the crisis event than they now are. The war on terror, for instance, has made presidents and their men, including CIA torturers to remote drone pilots, into 'political actors' who aren't interested in law-based governance but instead improvise against the event (disorder) and the courts that would severely limit their abilities. After all, laws cannot be politically neutral. Whatever the jurisdiction, they are enacted in a highly tactical way in response to the fear of potential events. Today, the state of emergency and state terror are normalised in the name of 'public security'. As Neocleous writes, 'The ruling class was never going to be so stupid as to produce a liberal-democratic constitution which does not allow it to exercise power and violence in the name of emergency, and to defend its vision of order' (2008: 71).

Thus, the effective normalisation of a neoliberal politics of fear and violence should be seen as a far more sinister attack on social movements than an attempt to improve the natural foundation of 'civilised' contemporary society. Liberalism is not to be confused with the juridical problem of order. More than that, it is a form of governmentality that operates through complex and overlapping historical social regimes. But if there is one defining singularity to its global strategy of pacification, then it is the biopolitics of fear itself. Today, more than ever before, the politics of fear resides in contemporary society and is woven into the quotidian spaces and circulations of everyday life. It operates within a global imaginary of the event. It establishes the overwhelming fear of revolution as the driving force of general culture.

Each regime (and each legal tactic) and every law (and every decision) responds to the event, for making sense of the event is essential to the operation of neoliberal order. This is because neoliberalism treats 'the social' as problematic (Rose 1996). Rendering the social problematic, in other words, is always a crucial step in turning it into a manageable entity. Not only do law (the state of exception) and scare disciplinary techniques (kettling) permit the reworking of the boundaries of neoliberal existence, but the fluctuating shift from sovereignty to disciplinary normalisation and biopolitical security/fear governance defines the neoliberal encounter. In other words, kettling is intimately bound to the neoliberal politics of fear, just as fear is intimately bound to the active production of political subjectivities. Both set out who we are as people, what we are fighting against (the event, revolution), and define what we are to become (neoliberal subjects as homo economicus). Because what is dangerous today (the event) is seen as productive to the very life processes that sustain neoliberalism, the biopolitics of fear is directly related to the vitality of existence on which the neoliberal order depends. As a consequence, it is the event that appears to become the generative source of neoliberalism. Neoliberalism declares the contingency of the event to be *the* problem to be solved.

As an instance of the state of exception, kettling is a spatial imprint of discipline, a neoliberal order which can face 'terminal decline'. As the threat continues, however, it becomes increasingly violent. When a weak system is threatened and thus 'legitimized by fear', it 'is virtually fit to become terroristic' (Badiou 2008: 13). Given that neoliberalism's struggle for survival knows no boundaries, it is safe to say that it would fight tooth and nail to stop or derail that defeat. In short, this will be a permanent struggle to delay the apocalypse. But let's not assume that liberalism's permanent war completely forecloses the possibility of resistance and change. As Deleuze insists: 'there's no need to fear or hope, but only to look for new weapons' (1995: 178).

Notes

1. Note that Marx and Engels (1970: 122) see Bentham as one of the theoreticians of liberal capitalism, along with James Mill.
2. By disciplinary mechanisms of normalisation I mean social and political processes through which ideas and actions become 'normal' and 'natural' in everyday life.
3. The rule of law (Rechtsstaat) first appeared in political theory and German jurisprudence, at the end of the eighteenth—beginning of the nineteenth century. It 'corresponds to the English 'Rule of Law' but with a special focus—particularly relevant in the XIX century—on the concepts of the State and public administration' (see Mannori & Sordi 2009: 242).
4. I follow Hobbes' conception of the multitude, which refers to the very negation of the sovereign authority with its entailing techniques of normalisation.
5. Note that this was erected on a trade union strike! Coaffee *et al.* argue that the term 'ring of steel' was first used in 1976 'to refer to the amalgamation of the four individual security zones around Belfast city centre into one large security sector ringed between 10–12 foot high, steel gates' (2009: 26–27).

4 Societies of Neoliberal Control

The previous chapter explored the functioning of disciplinary regime in contemporary society. Taking Foucault's analysis as its point of departure, it showed that that the hegemony of discipline coincides with the advent of neoliberalism, whose mission is to pacify life to make life live. We found also that the (re)productive mobilisation of the biopoliticised fear is central to disciplinary neoliberalism, for it is the fear of the event that defines neoliberalism's legitimacy.

This chapter proposes to rethink Deleuze's framework about 'the society of control'. Deleuze proposes a new phase of power that allows us to examine how the Foucauldian disciplinary regime has been reorganised into our present social state. Within this new system of governance a new field of power and domination emerges, which operates through localised and decentred points. In moving beyond Foucault, therefore, Deleuze speaks of a generalised form of 'neoliberal control' which does not destroy but rather sustains and regulates life in its productive new capacities. Neoliberalism constitutes a governance of free-floating control that works in conjunction with disciplinary panopticism. Moreover, it is a mode of governance which is made possible through the expansion of the market, and the shift from industrial to post-industrial modes of production. Thus, control is a social regime in which the truth of neoliberal capitalism is produced. Furthermore, the chapter discusses cynicism as the main affect that pertains to neoliberal capitalism, arguing that cynicism reinforces and (re)produces individuals motivated by self-interest. Then, it discusses debt as a mode of governance, an apparatus of capture, which has become an almost ontological condition of neoliberal capitalism. Last, the chapter conceptualises preemptive biopolitics, which attempts to prevent potential events from occurring. It is toward these Deleuzean considerations for a governmental approach to societies of neoliberal control that I now turn.

The Emergence of Neoliberal Control

> Ceaseless control in open sites.
>
> (Deleuze 1995: 175)

The axiom underlying the disciplinary regime is that circumstances make the subject. Disciplinary panopticism and the formation of 'docile bodies' are based on the subject as a source of knowledge, where the disciplinary sites of enclosure both individualise and normalise identities appropriate to that enclosure. 'There are two images . . . of discipline', Foucault writes. The first one is that of 'the enclosed institution, established on the edges of society, turned inwards towards negative functions' (1977: 209). The other image is that of panopticism which improves 'the exercise of power by making it lighter, more rapid, more effective' (1977: 109). It is the latter image of discipline that enables Deleuze to develop his notion of 'the society of control'. With the emergence of societies of neoliberal control, there is a movement from the strictly ordered spaces of enclosure—hospital, prison, military barracks, factory, school—to a more general dynamic model in which human beings are regulated through digital networks that facilitate free-floating surveillance (see Deleuze 1995: 178). This, however, does not mean that the disciplinary panoptic has vanished. Instead, human beings continue to be identifiable and representable for power and management. Thus, we should not see things as the replacements of societies of discipline with societies of control, but as an alliance between them. Indeed, the disciplinary panoptic is built more firmly into the 'axiomatic' and socialised model of activity that operates according to the logics of circulation, 'the *perpetuum mobile* of circulation' (Marx 1976: 71).

Whereas Foucault introduced discipline (and biopolitics) as an analytics of power that emerged with, and continues to accompany, liberal modernity, Deleuze argues that the society of control is concerned with the transformation of life into value, in the form of commodity and capital, which is directly related to digital computing technology. The control society is about 'surfing' through time; thus one never arrives at any destination. It is a society in which life is lived as a constant flux. Individuals are thus replaced with fluid and endlessly 'divisible', fractal, digital 'dividuals', and 'masses become samples, data, markets, or banks' (Deleuze 1995: 180). To this end, the symptom of control reveals a self that is fragmented and dispersed, resulting in exhaustion rather than satisfaction. The subject of control is always in a hurry to do anything, thereby hungering for more things, more distractions. It experiences a kind of life that is always, for some reason, urgent. For it is pulled apart by quantitative accomplishments and never ending investments. This feeling of dispersion and defeat is what Ulmer and Schwartzburd call 'hurry sickness', meaning that the self has 'severe and chronic feelings of time urgency that have brought about changes affecting personality and lifestyle' (1996: 331). Control is a regime in which nothing is allowed to be original and genuine.

The society of control is concentrated on the management of life and production rather than confinement, as is the case in the disciplinary society. Thus, the transition from the disciplinary to societies of neoliberal control marks a fundamental change in the way the physical production is managed and controlled. Deleuze consistently argues that 'this technological development is more deeply rooted in a mutation of capitalism' (1995: 180). He carefully points out that the transition from discipline to control is organised and governed with the major changes in capitalism that some others have noted: the transition from classical liberalism to neoliberalism; from welfare state to the neoliberal state; from Fordism to post-Fordism, and 'flexible accumulation' (Harvey 1990); from disciplinary panopticism—in which workers are required to obey—to the capitalist free-market—in which workers become adaptable, flexible, and 'entrepreneurial' (Boltanski & Chiapello 2005: 108–21); and from the formal to the real subsumption of labour under capital (Hardt & Negri 2000: 254–56). Though Deleuze does not use the term neoliberalism, he addresses the ways in which neoliberalism seeks to accelerate the shift from discipline to control through the emergence of new communication technologies.

Indeed, neoliberal capitalism operates through 'continuous control and instant communication' through the market (Deleuze 1995: 174). It is based on the continuous process of production; it is a system of 'production for production's sake' (Marx 1976: 742). In this context, one could identify two important characteristics of the capitalist socius. First, it is a continuous process of deterritorialised flows (decoding). Second, and relatedly, the circulation of capital has no necessary external limit; its only barrier is capital itself. Because capital has the ability to constantly renew itself, it undergoes mutations, adjusting its mechanisms to the logic of the neoliberal market in which it is exercised. Capital becomes the new 'body without organs' of the social from which everything else emanates.

Indeed, Deleuze and Guattari argue that capitalism 'has realized immanence' in the 'flows on the full body of capital-money' (1983: 261). Hence, they rejoin Marx in their analysis of capitalism as an immanent system that constantly modifies itself. As Marx and Engels write in *The Communist Manifesto*, referring to the 'immanent barriers' to capitalist development:

> Constant revolutionising of production, uninterrupted disturbance of all social conditions, everlasting uncertainty and agitation distinguish the bourgeois epoch from all earlier ones. All fixed, fast-frozen relations, with their train of ancient and venerable prejudices and opinions, are swept away, all new-formed ones become antiquated before they can ossify. All that is solid melts into air, all that is holy is profaned, and man is at last compelled to face with sober faces his real conditions of life and his relations with his kind.
>
> (1973: 36–7)

What Deleuze and Guattari are particularly concerned with Marx is his analysis on the system of credit in capitalism in *Capital Volume III*. Capitalism is for Deleuze an immanent system that continually overcomes barriers and limitations. Whenever a new market is opened up, it becomes assimilated into the capitalist system itself. Furthermore, as an immanent system neoliberal capitalism values 'equality' insofar as all things are turned into a commodity. In other words, equality makes sense if everything can be bought and sold on the open market. Capitalism is an immanent system because the operation of its monetary system is 'axiomatic' in the sense that flexible decoded flows make no reference to value.

Deleuze and Guattari present three aspects of capitalism's axiomatic: its operationality, its flexibility, and its multiple realisability. First, the capitalist axiomatic is purely operational (Bonta & Protevi 2004: 57). Deleuze and Guattari argue that 'money as a general equivalent' signifies an 'abstract quantity' that generates indifference to flows (1983: 248). Money, in other words, has no truth value, but the equivalence of money itself marks a position of relation that has no necessary external limit. Second, capitalism's axiomatic is always flexible (1983: 248; see also Bonta & Protevi 2004: 57). Money as an abstract quantity cannot be separated from the destruction of all codes that would become concrete. Consisting of abstract quantities and entities, neoliberal capitalism does not operate according to rules of codes. It differs from previous regimes by its capacity to function directly by decoded flows without the insertion of fixed points or rules of codes. The capitalist axiomatic is therefore not a closed totality. Rather, it is independent of the values of buyer and the seller, establishing relations and decoded and flexible flows that are unrelated. Third, as a result of its operationality and flexibility, the capitalist axiomatic is also multiply realisable that 'deals directly with purely functional elements and relations whose nature is not specified, and which are immediately realized in highly varied domains simultaneously' (Deleuze & Guattari 1987: 454). Because the current capitalist model is neoliberal, the attempts to privatise all public assets that are seen as outside the market (e.g. the university, the healthcare system, and so on) demonstrate how neoliberalism attempts to restrict the multiple realisability of capitalism to a single model (Bonta & Protevi 2004: 58). Simply put, the axiomatic method is the key for legitimising neoliberal control, which is thus identified with the capitalist regime of accumulation. Neoliberal capitalism is a hegemonic ideology, presiding over an accumulation regime without growth. Human consciousness, leisure, play, and so on, are all directly covered by this regime of accumulation. The immanent axiomatics of neoliberal capitalism as a regime of accumulation must be understood as a system of money and credit, which opens up a new space where the entire capitalist production and circulation of commodities is regulated by specific financial institutions such as banks, creating a flow of credit-debt. What the regime of indebtedness makes possible, credit makes profitable (see Dienst 2011: 30). The neoliberal capitalism of our present is thus characterised by the widening circulation of credit capital and the regime of indebtedness. Consequently, the flow of credit-debt remains infinite, but it is no longer a debt owed to the sovereign.

The result of the capitalist axiomatic is what Deleuze and Guattari call 'deterritorialisation', a process in which identities, institutions, bodies, and labour power are destabilised and integrated into global circuits of neoliberal capitalism. In this new regime, the productive labour-power has expanded to cover all spheres of society and life such as human DNA, credit card histories, lifestyles, etc.—in short—all aspects of life itself that have become commodified outside of the old-fashioned labour process under neoliberalism. With neoliberal capitalism, capital is no longer limited to the factories or offices, and as 'dividuals', human beings selling their labour-power are no longer necessarily how capitalism gets a hold of the products of their labour-power. Therefore, the entire raison d'être of neoliberal capitalism is that it requires a concomitant transformation of labour-power and value, enabling the maximisation of the body's capacity of labour-power, for biopolitics is now inscribed in the habits and vital practices of bodies. In the capitalist mode of production, labour-power 'does not exist apart from' the worker because his 'specific productive activity . . . is his vitality itself' (Marx 1973: 267). If the specific productive activity of the worker is the vitality itself, then neoliberal capitalism must first of all grasp the importance of labour-power.

Because, with capitalism, economy no longer depends on slavery but on a 'free' deterritorialised subject, the nature of labour is also transformed. As Marx put it, labour-power 'is the use-value which the worker has to offer to the capitalist, which he has to offer to others in general, is not materialized in a product, does not exist apart from him at all, thus exists not really, but only in potentiality, as his capacity' (Marx 1973: 267). In other words, the continuous and unstable process of adaptation as labour-power, according to Marx, is sheer 'potentiality'. However, capitalist biopolitics is not simply the management of labour-power. Rather, as Virno demonstrates, it 'is merely an effect, a reverberation, or, in fact, one articulation of that primary fact . . . which consists of the commerce of potential as potential' (2004: 84). That is to say, capitalist biopolitics is nothing other than the commerce of labour-power, and it exists wherever that potential does appear. This potentiality refers to 'all the different faculties' (speaking, producing, etc.) and potentialities of human beings. And 'where something which exists only as possibility is sold', argues Virno, 'this something is not separable from the living person of the seller' (2004: 82). In contrast, 'the living body of the worker is the substratum of that labor-power which, in itself, has no independent existence.' Life as 'pure and simple bios', Virno continues, 'acquires a specific importance in as much as it is the tabernacle of dynamis, of mere potential' (2004).

Marx had already acknowledged the unique role of 'species-being' of human labour and the way in which capital was in the process of being realised as species-being. Similarly, Foucault argued that biopolitics configures the population as 'species-being'. With neoliberal capitalism, or bios, the body becomes the object of biopolitics as mere potentiality, a commodity, which obtains an empirical manifestation or mode of labour power, which has the capacity of self-actualisation (see Kordela 2011). The object of neoliberal control societies, therefore, is life as an immanent quality, that is, the potentiality of being to actualise itself, which provides biopolitics with an open horizon of temporal possibility in the form of 'labour-power . . . as a capacity of the living individual' (Marx 1976: 274). Life is now widely interpreted by neoliberal capitalism (and thus modern security politics) as a radically contingent force, an open historicity, which takes infinite becomings of finite beings, or 'events', as its focus of inquiry. Put differently, the body's creative capacity is what makes 'the event' possible because it is where creative potentialities take place, especially in relation to every living form's independence with other existing forms. The body produces the event because it is composed of infinite possibilities for new emergent forms of actualisations.

To say that with labour-power, or bios, the body becomes an immanent quality, a sheer potentiality of being to actualise itself, is tantamount to saying that bodies are now conceived as 'eternal' bodies—the species of eternity—and thereby secularising the 'eschaton' of time as a metaphysical category that can be bought and sold from every angle in the market. With the secularised eschaton, the subject's relation to eternity becomes the object of biopolitics, which aims to provide only secured and controlled illusions thereof. In this way, infinity enters the historical realm of neoliberal capitalism under the name of the market in which 'one never finishes anything' (Deleuze 1995: 179). In this process, therefore, continual monitoring, lifelong learning, and constant modulation become an imperative. For this reason, social control is no longer left to ideological state apparatuses such as schools, police forces, and the army but is now a branch of marketing, as even 'elections themselves are conceived along the lines of buying a commodity (power, in this case): they involve a competition between different merchandise-parties, and our votes are like money which buys the government we want' (Žižek 2008b: 284). Thus, contemporary society is a neoliberal control society, which models all sociality according to the logic of businesses. It initiates an 'endless postponement' in the mundane realm of the capitalist market that is never complete (see Deleuze 1995: 179). With the biopolitical production of infinity, 'don't make money, be money' becomes the capitalist dictum, a weightless, infinitely circulating, immortal idea. The biopolitical production of infinity through market means that the potentialities of life itself become subject to the pernicious logics of capitalist accumulation.

All of this brings us to surplus-enjoyment, a concept that lies at the heart of neoliberal capitalism. The extended regime of capitalist accumulation is coterminous with the constant availability of all social relations that create surplus-value. Indeed, surplus-enjoyment is the main target of neoliberal capitalism because it is where the exchange-value and the subject's relation to infinity coincide. In this way, 'the time of capital extends the end of history into the dead eternity of surplus time' (Hamacher 2002: 89). Enjoyment occurs only in the surplus time; it 'is constitutively an excess' because subtracting the surplus in enjoyment means losing 'enjoyment itself' (Žižek 1989: 52).

Human beings usually seek to satisfy life by satisfying the needs of human life. But more importantly, this results from our desire for life. As Aristotle argues, human beings 'are eager for life but not for the good life; so desire for life being unlimited, they desire also an unlimited amount of what enables it to go on' (1992: 84). By misunderstanding the 'unlimited desire for life' with what good things that make life worth living, we are invited to believe that we need an unlimited amount of goods, services, or unlimited wealth, to satisfy the unlimited human wants. Turning morality and value into a source of enjoyment, the unlimited desire for life thus comes to be actualised in 'excess'. Whereas aiming at good life, human beings act and communicate in the pursuit of enjoyment; what they seek is nothing other than enjoyment. For, Aristotle goes on to suggest, 'where enjoyment consists in excess, men look for that skill which produces the excess that is enjoyed' (1992: 85; see also Kordela 2011: 18). Consequently, this excess or enjoyment is never fully achieved in itself; instead what we get here is a distinct mode of enjoyment, a 'surplus enjoyment' (see Zupančič 2003: 47).

'Shopping' is a case in point. Through shopping, we maintain an unwitting relationship with capitalism and the money economy. Shopping embraces the cynical individual, rewarding itself by becoming the sovereign of its own personal space. As such, it embraces consumer capitalism, 'turning endless obligation into fleeting enjoyment' (Dienst 2011: 129). Thus, shopping should be seen as an extension of the regime of indebtedness and the mechanisms of surplus-enjoyment. Shopping goes on ceaselessly because 'surplus-enjoyment enables infinity to conquer lived life in the act of shopping—a central biopolitical frustration machine that sustains (the illusion of) immortality' (Kordela 2011: 19). Shopping must continue for the excess of enjoyment of the individual who really benefits from the cynic participation in the market.

In neoliberal capitalism, enjoyment and (the illusion of) immortality do not require belief in order to function. On the contrary, they operate through perpetually infinite mechanisms of surplus-enjoyment predicated on the figure of homo economicus. If the figure of homo economicus is a 'man without a past or a history', then the key to a metaphysical grasp of surplus-enjoyment and immortality is self-interest. Indeed, self-interest is not empirical, utilitarian, or pragmatic, but metaphysical, and it is here, in that secular eschaton, that neoliberal control coincides with its affective subjectivity 'motivated only by self-interest'. Thus, what is distinctive about the form of cynicism characteristic of and necessary for neoliberal capitalism is that it legitimises and ultimately (re)produces individuals based on market-defined self-interest(s). In what follows, I argue that the cynical individual is able to participate within neoliberal capitalism without internally accepting its truth-value ('I am motivated by self-interest but I still obey'). The cynic perceives the mutability of the rules of the game but plays along anyway.

Neoliberal Capitalism and Cynicism

> From something he clings to something he has come to see through; but he calls it 'faithfulness'.
>
> (Nietzsche 2001: 145)

The logic of operation of capitalism is axiomatic in the sense that it does not create any code. Hence, it is characterised by 'the age of cynicism' (Deleuze & Guattari 1983: 225; see also Žižek 1989). However, it should be emphasised that more than one affect may coexist within neoliberal control society. The reason why cynicism should be considered as the main affect is that it invites us to pay attention to how the capitalist system operates not only through war and violence but also through persuasion and hegemony. In other words, capitalism 'relies on the carrot as well as the stick' (Glaser 2012: 15). In this sense, cynicism is a crucial concept for the examination of the affective politics of neoliberal capitalism. Due to its cynical modus operandi, the essence of capital is indifferent to the intentions of its rulers. The fundamental characteristic of capital is not simply the difference between being ruled by abstractions of market-defined self-interest(s) but that 'being ruled by abstractions' produces its own particular form of subjectivity, namely the cynic (Read 2008: 147). Subjectivity is inseparable from the mode of production that makes it possible.

At this point, Žižek's psychoanalytic interpretation of fantasy I find especially telling because it helps us understand how cynicism reinforces neoliberal capitalism. In *The Sublime Object of Ideology*, Žižek argues that jouissance plays an important role for the hegemony. To be sure, jouissance 'always emerges within a certain phantasmatic field', as Žižek writes, and 'the crucial precondition for breaking the chains of servitude is thus to "traverse the fantasy" which structures our jouissance in a way which keeps us attached to the Master—makes use accept the framework of the social relationship of domination' (1997: 48). For Žižek, what psychoanalysis can do to help is precisely to clarify how the dominant understandings are indeed sustained through the surplus-enjoyment individuals gain from the hegemonic world view. Just as neoliberal capitalism is characterised by atomism and individualism, fantasy is individualistic by nature. The law, on the other hand, is constructed against the particularity of the fantasy, for it regulates individuality and sets collective limits on individual desires. The law is the set of rules, mandates, and norms that creates collective limits for individual desire, whereas fantasy is borne out of respect for the law and yet, at the same time, necessitates a law to be transgressed.

This 'tension' between fantasy and the law is crucial for a proper understanding of cynicism. It is the continued transgression of the law that ensures the continued obedience of the subject. Because transgression becomes a norm, a rule, it ends up affirming the principles of the law. This contradiction is what Žižek, recalling a long line of Freudian and Marxist analysis, calls the 'fetishist disavowal'. Here, the subject recognises the absurdity of failures of the existing system yet nonetheless continues to partake in perpetually infinite mechanisms of that absurdity. In other words, it is the perspective of the obedient cynical individual, who justifies its submissive attitude by internally declaring, 'I know that I am governed by market-defined self-interest(s), but still, I am doing it.' Such an attitude is based on a deep ideological commitment to the necessity of a given order and thus serving as its positive condition of possibility of its effective functioning.

It is this awareness of the distance 'between the ideological mask and the social reality' that explains the actions of the cynic (Žižek 1989: 29–30). What this attitude allows is a subjective distance to the problem of change: in action, one praises passivity; yet, in voice, one calls for action. Even at her most frustrated moments, the cynic remains committed to the necessity of the law, of the socio-symbolic order. In this way the subject transgresses the law yet is subservient to the hegemony, thereby reflecting the affective role of the fetishist disavowal for reproducing the existing power relations/configurations. The cynical individual is able to gain the enjoyment of transgressing the law without engaging in the 'Real' of social conflict and antagonism. When the cynic says 'I know that I am ruled by abstractions of money and labour, but still, I am doing it', what s/he is articulating is the surplus-enjoyment gained through the fetishist disavowal, the calculated distance s/he retains to the actual reality, to the set of ideological relations commanding its actions. In this sense, 'today's post-political silent majority is not stupid, but it is cynical and resigned' (Žižek 2010: 390).

Crucially, therefore, this hegemonic strategy prevents cynical subjects from demanding or even imagining radical social change, that is, the disruptive ('revolutionary') events. In this sense, cynicism is the relief from responsibility because it provides individuals to accept the hegemonic power of neoliberal capitalism even in disagreement, yet still comfortably act as they please. As a result, to radically question hegemonic configurations of power becomes impossible, for it is conceived as a challenge to the entire structures of society. Cynicism enables the disenchanted individual to show internal dissent without confronting the hegemony as a spectacular gestalt totality.

In other words, cynicism is internal dissent at its purest, relieving the subject from the obligation of a political act. It is a rational consent to the absurdity of failures of the existing order. If law, in the Lacanian sense, is irrational, then 'it follows from this continuously senseless character of the Law, that we must obey it not because it is just, good or even beneficial, but simply *because it is the law*' (Žižek 1989: 37). For this reason, cynicism is stronger than the ideological compliance that is based on an unconscious belief. For it differs from unconscious belief in that it requires a self-conscious submission to the irrational symbolic order, or authority. 'The only real obedience', Žižek notes, 'is an "external" one: obedience out of conviction is not real obedience because it is already "mediated" through our subjectivity'. That is to say, 'we are not really obeying the authority,' Žižek maintains, 'but simply following our judgement, which tells us that the authority deserves to be obeyed in so far as it is good, wise, beneficent' (Žižek 1989: 37).

The cynical individual expresses a more complete acceptance of the neoliberal framework, and thereby demonstrates 'real obedience', the belief and desire that are necessary for the capitalist mode of production. Cynicism is an assertion and consolidation of power, capable of cancelling out social solidarity and collective human action. It claims the force of 'special loyalty' to the existing order. And when special loyalty, real obedience is to be dealt with, other considerations must be put aside. The cynic's real obedience comes not out of belief or a rational acceptance of its mandates but out of duty and fidelity to the need for power as such. Paradoxically, therefore, the cynic's real obedience relies on not *believing* but *disbelieving*. Rationally accepting the irrational order, the disbelieving fetishist cynics 'are not dreamers lost in their private worlds, they are thoroughly realists able to accept the things the way they actually are' (Žižek 2001: 14). It is in pragmatic realism of the cynical individual that fantasies remain at their most effective, for pragmatic realism makes the subject cling even more tightly to hegemonic ideology. However, if the ruling ideology seems to be taken seriously, pragmatic realism can disintegrate. This is because the rationalisation of an ideology as a fantasy paves the way for radically questioning its legitimacy. Thus, the cynic registers not only her obedience but also her complicity in upholding the system. And to be complicit is to become bound up in crimes committed by the existing regime in everyday lives. The ruling ideology (and the law) is not an object of belief but a clear means to the end where the subject is aware of his own complicity and continues to act accordingly. It is for this reason that neoliberal capitalism is at its strongest when it contributes to the rise of depoliticising conditions in which passive or cynical compliance becomes habitual and self-enforcing. Cynicism is, in other words, the perceived inability to positively confront hegemonic power. The cynic knows what is right in front of its eyes yet she prefers not to know and doesn't act upon it. This mode of regulation and thinking is by no means apolitical. Instead, it is political: The cynic's principal concern is individual survival and the avoidance of conflict.

Central to cynicism, then, is individual consent that is motivated by self-interest. The reduction of the subject to market-defined self-interest(s) is precisely an example of how human beings become cynics, and economic crisis is not an exception to the cynic's surplus-enjoyment. Even in times of crisis, capital increases its own power and ultimately reproduces cynical individuals burdened by credit cards. This is why consuming should be seen as an extension of surplus or the regime of indebtedness. By consuming during times of crisis, the cynical conformist enters the infinite diachronic temporality of surplus and debt. From a biopolitical perspective, the cynic is one in whom certain amounts of capital will flow through her, extending the regime of indebtedness, and it is this that I shall turn to next.

Debt as a Mode of Governance

> A Man is no longer a man confined, but a man in debt.
> (Deleuze 1995: 181)

Neoliberal capitalism has 'biopolitical' control over life. Hence, Deleuze's previous statement in his text on the societies of control, where the regime of indebtedness is as much about biopolitical control as it is an extension of capital. In primitive society, debt is charged through the primitive inscription, or coding, on the body. Blood-revenge and cruelty address a non-exchangist power. In the despotic society, all debts become infinite debts to the divine ruler. In capitalism, all debts finally break free from the sovereign and become infinite by conjoining flows. With capitalism, debt is continuous and without limit: student debt, credit card debt, mortgage debt, medical debt. What is distinctive about neoliberal capitalism is the privatisation of public goods and services as well as the capitalisation of human potential. Whereas in the primitive system debt is incurred through inscription and, in despotism, exercised by divine law, in capitalism 'the market-eye keeps a watch over everything' (Dienst 2011: 124–5). With neoliberal capitalism, the market-eye becomes the new normal that constitutes a biopolitical control around a weightless, infinitely circulating, immortal debt. We now live in the era of debt in which it is the soul of the individual that is imprisoned.

In what follows, I theorise debt as a mode of governance. Before proceeding, however, it is perfectly helpful to revisit the link between religion and capitalism. Drawing on Benjamin's early sketch 'Capitalism as Religion', I argue that capitalism is a cultic religion that creates society and life in always-already guilty and indebted.

If theology is an active force in the contemporary global economy, money is what establishes the link between capitalism and religion. Today, money embodies a theological-political precision; it easily takes the place of God as the supreme value from which all other values emanate. Because money is produced as debt, it contains an obligation to expand economic activity to repay the debt (Goodchild 2010: 149). Seen in this perspective, credit-based capitalism is not only justified by religion, but it itself becomes a religion (Benjamin 1996). We live in a world in which people can easily imagine the end of the world but not that of capitalism (see Žižek 2009: 78). Thus, Benjamin declares that capitalism should be seen as a 'purely cultic religion' in the sense that it is not expiatory but guilt producing:

> An enormous feeling of guilt not itself knowing how to repent, grasps at the cult, not in order to repent for this guilt, but to make it universal, to hammer it into consciousness and finally and above all to include God himself in this guilt, in order to finally interest him in repentance.
>
> (1996: 259)

If guilt is 'the highest category of world history' (Benjamin, quoted in Hamacher 2002: 82), then our critique must target capitalism as the system of guilt/debt continuum. Capitalism is a 'cult-religion', aiming to organise 'the guilt-and debt-nexus of the living' (Benjamin 1996: 204). Capitalism as a cultic religion refers to a world without values, which is total and allows individuals to access truth and enjoy life through partaking in ritual. As a cult, capitalism is therefore cynic and ritualistic, which operates as a 'spiritualized Urstaat' (Deleuze & Guattari 1983: 225). Thus, it is enacted rather than practiced as faith. It follows that it must operate constantly—its permanent duration: 'Here there is no 'weekday', no day that would not be a holiday in the awful sense of exhibiting all sacred pomp—the extreme exertion of worship' (Benjamin 1996: 259). With capitalism's cult of cynicism transcendence is replaced with immanence, creating the illusion that 'perfection has already been attained in the here and now' (Schulz 2014: 25). It is in this context that 'enjoyment' becomes a duty.

If capitalism is a cultic religion, it is the debt (credit) that functions as a religious ritual. Today it is debt that holds the society together. Under capitalism's cult,

> the permanent re-enactment of guilt (Schuld) is no longer rooted in theological doctrine and ritual. Instead, it crystallizes into the very material organisation of life, where capital circuits must remain dynamic and commodities and value must be kept in constant circulation.

(Schulz 2014: 25)

The time of capital is thus lived as an order of guilt and debt, creating the dead eternity of absolute surplus value. Under capitalism's reign, everyone becomes a debtor, and therefore guilty. Debt and guilt have become part of a normality in contemporary society.

Capitalism is an inhumane economic system where humanity's debt is placed. Under capitalism's reign, humanity's debt becomes larger with capital accumulation. In this process, consuming, buying commodities, etc. play an essential role in expanding capitalism as an accumulation regime—a cultic religion in permanent duration. Through the mechanisms of public debt, the accumulation regime grows and grows, turning money into capital, 'which is to say: into money that realizes itself and multiplies itself, always turning itself into more money—and thus into more money than it actually is' (Hamacher 2002: 91). In other words, money is produced by debt. In the process, value is also transformed into surplus value, a process 'of a god's genesis out of something that is not', the process 'of the generation of God out of nothing' (Hamacher 2002: 92). As a result, money in the form of capital emerges as the new God, which makes the 'monstrous consciousness of guilt' and debt universal.

Significantly, debt represents an unequal relationship inseparable from the production of the debtor subject as a particular form of homo economicus. As argued in the sovereignty chapter, the relationship between the creditor and the debtor involves a power asymmetry (Nietzsche 1996: 45). In contemporary society, in a similar vein, debt operates as the very engine of the politics of neoliberal capitalism, a politics which is fundamentally about power. Today debt 'is a universal power relation, since everyone is included in it' (Lazzarato 2011: 32). It is an instrument to capture and control the debtor, and, as such, it creates a specific 'morality', the morality of the promise (Lazzarato 2011: 30–1). In other words, it is within the domain of debt that society begins to be constituted.

The subsequent moralisation of debt, however, allows guilt to be fully internalised by the debtor rather than the creditor. Student debt is a case in point. As students take on loans in order to fund their studies, their future changes form. They graduate with a large amount of debt, which results in solitude and despair. Debt transforms the educational experience of students, producing desperate individuals who try to match their actions to the laws of the market rather than radically question their place within society (Read 2012). As an exceptionally punishing kind, debt prevents students from engaging in politics that makes them think creatively and critically about society, and ask questions. Thus, it has a profound disciplining effect on them, taylorising their studies and undermining the sociality and politicisation that has traditionally been one of the main benefits of college and university life (Caffentzis 2011: 32). With the internalisation of debt, politics and emancipatory thinking are transformed into a monetary relation, and the subject's individuality and morality become parts of the market by emptying public life of moral argument. Thus, to quote Marx, 'instead of money, or paper, it is one's own personal existence, flesh and blood, social virtue and importance, which constitutes the material, corporeal form of the spirit of money' (1844).

In this sense, student debt produces what Paul Mason (2012) calls 'the graduate without a future'.[1] As individual carriers of unpayable debt, students are simply facing a future without a future because it 'has disappeared, shielded by a wall of debt' (Armstrong 2011: 4). This figuring of debt is a form of violence because it preempts the future by reducing the individual to a kind of 'bare life':

> Money as capital destroys time, and it destroys life . . . by reducing everything to the formula of a flat uniformity, to docility, and the univocity of production. Precarity is the existence and essence of the entrepreneur of the self, who no longer possesses rights, but is rather compelled to constantly act and work in accordance with the ideology of risk and the notion that the self itself is his/her capital ('human capital'). . . . This is indeed both the conclusion and premise of the murderous logic of debt. What becomes a commodity, invested by the power relations of money as debt, is no longer simply a person's labor-power, the time of labor, but all power and all time. It is life itself, which is now indistinguishable from death.
> (Guilli 2013: 54)

Reduced to bare life, the indebted students are thus denied all relief. Furthermore, carrying so much debt on their shoulders, they are forced to accept insecure, part-time, temporary, casual, intern, flexible, project-based, contingent, and adjunct positions, thereby becoming a source of cheap, instructional labour. Viewed in this way, debt perpetuates a subjectivity of desperation whose morality and individuality become enslaved by money. In sum, debts are the means by which hopelessness becomes naturalised. Therefore, with the money economy, there has emerged a new kind of dominion, which has the power to decide what deserves to exist and what deserves to perish (see Dienst 2011: 2).

Debt is also the key to creating a certain form of individual associated with neoliberalism. Neoliberalism entails an 'individualisation' that 'does not aim to insure individuals against risks, but to constitute an economic space in which individuals individually take upon themselves and confront risks' (Lazzarato 2009: 118). This entails a new figure of homo economicus that is required to tackle individually the big, tougher systemic problems. Thus, the subject 'must bear all the costs and risks of social life in the most burdensome way: alone' (Dienst 2014: 5). With debt, therefore, there is only an isolated and fragmented individual who cannot show a collective response. It is told to blame itself, rather than look to the economic and social conditions that have driven individuals into deeper and more unsustainable debt. Indeed, in neoliberal capitalism, debt is normalised as a factor of sociality, a way of life. It has 'come to suffuse and shape even the most intimate aspects of our existence' (Graeber 2011: 15). Debt produces society and is produced by society. As such, it defies a collective response precisely because it is seen less as a regime problem, as part of a capitalist free-market ideology, than as an individual fate. Underemployed and broke, the subject of debt is an atomised but networked individual whose lack of collective response is presented as a kind of autonomy and liberation. All that remains is, therefore, individual responsibility, which is often branded as 'freedom'. Enslaved by its own isolation and anxiety, the subject of debt is rendered governable, dealing with competing interests. Importantly, therefore, debt should not be viewed as an individual fate or bad luck precisely because it operates everywhere as a regime of 'top-down control and network discipline, designed to replace older forms of social negotiation and political autonomy' (Dienst 2011: 100). Debt, therefore, needs to be understood as a mode of neoliberal governance, predetermining political outcomes. It is a future acting, restricting, and curtailing human imagination. Debt creates 'a society without time, without possibility' (Lazzarato 2011: 47).

Saddled with massive debt, the subject of debt cannot act, resist. Unable to collectivise struggles against indebtedness and unemployment, the individual is thus produced and governed by the idea of maximising value and minimising risks where the notion of social solidarity is excluded, in which any connection with other groups in the 'precariat' is avoided. Collective action to remedy these precarious conditions is also foreclosed as the state of exception becomes the rule. After all, the only thing that you can do or share in a capitalist society collectively is its public indebtedness. As Marx observes, 'the only part of the so-called national wealth that actually enters into collective possession of a modern is-their national debt' (1976: 919). Marx clearly wants us to see how debt has become a form of dominion and command as well as a mechanism of exploitation and oppression. Neoliberal capitalism's power depends at every moment upon different relations of force and variable governmentalities that operate between. And when they act, they do so to further control based entirely on individual self-interest, or individual human motives and intentions that are ethically justified in capitalism. They operate between the structures of accumulation and the expansion of the regime of indebtedness.

Locked into isolated and immiserated futures, the subject of debt becomes an investor in its own human capital, in which relations of trust and collective action are replaced by security and biopolitical control that aim at life's global pacification. In the contemporary global economy, debt 'supplements and overtakes enclosure to become the crucial apparatus of control' (Dienst 2011: 121). In this sense the regime of debt not only appears to become a defining characteristic of neoliberal biopolitics but also a precondition of human life in general in which the subject is simultaneously bound to capitalism while potentially cynical to its rule. Debt presupposes a kind of (un)sociality of people who are connected only by self-interest, but not engaged in direct conflict. In other words, debt is, like neoliberal capitalism, indifferent to the idea of sociability and politicality, or, worse still, exploits them. The regime of debt creates 'responsible', insecure, yet cynical individuals aimed at decreasing desires for radical social change. Isolation and insecurity combined with cynicism about the world are the marks of the subject of debt. Here, the subject realises its isolation and disillusion yet refuses or is unable to actualise its dissent. For this reason, debt is a future war on human imagination that disempowers individuals from demanding positive social transformation, or collective action. Perhaps for this reason 'the struggle over debt should be one of the frontline conflicts of our times' (Ross 2014: 187).

To cut a long story short, debt functions as a mode of governance for the subjection of populations to neoliberal control. However, it is not to be seen as the only rationality enabling that subjection.

Preemptive Biopolitics

What characterises neoliberalism today is the proliferation of governmentalities. This is because post-political neoliberalism is hostile to collective action and attempts to own the future. Whereas it works hand in hand with exceptionalism, the neoliberal power does not draw upon threats only in terms of states of exception. Thus, we would caution against the claim that neoliberalism is dependent solely upon 'the state of exception'. Whereas the state of exception is a powerful diagnosis in understanding neoliberalism, it is no longer the single and dominant paradigm for the administration of life. My aim, then, is to disclose multiple governmentalities and techniques in which society is governed today in ways that may coexist with or transform the state of exception. As we have discovered, post-political neoliberalism attempts to colonise the future, for the future has the potential to become disruptive, catastrophic. It is a future not to be lived but to be secured and pacified. It is in this sense that new biopolitical ways of governing have emerged in relation to changes in how life and future events are problematised. Preemption is one of them.

This section is focused on the preemptive side of post-political neoliberalism. When the threat of a coming event becomes the norm, biopolitics becomes preemptive. Biopolitics aims to 'preempt an unfolding and emergent event in relation to an array of possible projected futures' (Amoore 2013: 9). What emerges, in other words, is preemptive biopolitics that perceives the future in a particular format: as a disruptive event.

Event

> [T]here are known knowns; there are things we know we know. We also know there are known unknowns; that is to say we know there are some things we do not know. But there are also unknown unknowns—the ones we don't know we don't know.
>
> (Donald Rumsfeld 2002)

To be sure, many have argued that the events of 9/11 have only strengthened Donald Rumsfeld's remarks that we live in a society of 'unknown unknowns' marked by the radical uncertainty of any subjective position. 'Inescapable dangers' are real and imminent, we are continually told, and they are just beyond our ability to understand and control. In the terms of Rumsfeldian terminology, 'we not only do not know where the tipping point is, we do not even know exactly what we do not know' (Žižek 2010: 429). A certain radical reflexivity becomes the positive condition of contemporary society where life no longer 'goes by itself' but by 'unknown unknowns'—things we do not know we do not know. Unknown unknowns thus reveal the post-political aporia; a condition, a catastrophic imaginary in which 'fighting future events' becomes the sole centre of neoliberalism.

To better understand the actual and the possible future implications of the continued re- working of this framework, we need to look no farther than the advances in complexity thinking, which focus on the mystery of 'emergent properties', on the conditions that constitute unknown yet disruptive future 'events'. Overall, complexity approaches tell us that interdependent emerging properties involve a sense of unpredictable and unstable openness. Through a conversation with complexity sciences the world is rendered open to the future, where unknown unknowns open up the social world to the virtual. The politics of security's principal response to the problem of unknown unknowns is now fully reliant upon the virtual. Thus, it is precisely the virtual that now serves to consolidate the biopolitical imaginary. As Brian Massumi succinctly expresses:

> Viral or environmental . . . these faceless, unseen and unseeable enemies operate on an inhuman scale. The enemy is not simply indefinite (masked or at a hidden location). In the infinity of its here-and-to-come, it is elsewhere, by nature. It is humanly ungraspable. It exists in a different dimension of space from the human, and in a different dimension of time. . . . The pertinent enemy question is not who, where, when, or even what. The enemy is a what not; an unspecifiable may-come-to-pass, in another dimension. In a word, the enemy is virtual.

(1993: 11)

In other words, the enemy has attained a summit of virtualisation, an unknowable futurity, which involves a sense of contingent openness and multiple futures. Central, then, to societies of neoliberal control is the idea of 'event', which makes it possible to restructure the virtual from within the actual. It is the emergent, 'what is to come', which terrifies the neoliberal order. Simply put, events will happen. An event is what calls the future into being. The question is clearly whether the event will take place. But we shall never know. What we have, then, is the real repression of a virtual event. The cost of rendering a future event unproblematic is precisely the focus of neoliberal order. Although future events cannot be known, they can nevertheless be enacted and survived. Through its conversation with complexity sciences, the politics of security concerns how the future events are understood, how the emergent properties are understood, how the virtual potentialities are understood, how the abstractions are understood. To consider security under the heading of virtuality is 'relative to an experimental practice':

> Abstraction is not the product of an 'abstract way of seeing things'. It has nothing psychological or methodological about it. It is relative to the invention of an experimental practice that distinguishes it from one fiction among others while creating a fact that singularizes one class of phenomena among others.
> (Stengers 2000: 86)

In this climate of abstraction and uncertainty, everything truly matters. Nothing exists in vain. Anything moves, anything circulates has the potential to be truly *catastrophic*. Neoliberal control is, therefore, concerned with 'circulation' as the main object shifts from the traditional disciplinary enclosure to life: 'circulation concerns a world understood in terms of the biological structures and functions of species existence together with the relations that obtain between species life and all its contingent local and global correlations' (Dillon 2007: 11). It is also in this context that modern biopolitics is transformed from securing populations to embracing contingency. Modern biopolitics is concerned with contingent life, which is identified as the biopolitical collective that 'unpredictable dangers' emerge from and are sustained by. In other words, life is defined by its 'potentiality of danger' rather than actuality. The potentiality of danger has value because it introduces uncertainty and unpredictability. Thus, the final twist that contingent life adds to the prospect of security politics concerns what moves: problems not solutions.

Therefore, within the language of contemporary neoliberal governance, there is clearly the possibility for a movement towards a more pervasive and sophisticated nature of biopolitical power in which distinctions such as reality/representation, the lawful & unlawful, norm/normality, politics of event/counterpolitics of event, terrorism/war against terrorism tend to disappear today. This power is, I suggest, preemption. Contemporary developments suggest that a reengagement with biopolitics is more pressing than ever. In order to broach such a reengagement it is necessary to focus on the differing biopolitical mechanisms and politics embedded within it. 'If biopolitics is a key term . . . for describing the progressive operations of power which, seeking to strategically battle the forces that threaten our finite existence' (Evans & Reid 2014: 29), preemption is also a key term for biopolitical intervention that privileges the liberal life in all its dimensions against threats. As liberalism knows that it is finite, haunted by the spectre of event, the turn to preemption becomes inevitable. So it is my hope that preemptive biopolitics can augment Foucault's discussion of biopolitics in light of the new cartography of contemporary political sovereignty.

Modern biopolitics is concerned with the 'making live' of the threat. However, it does so at the level of preemption in order to prevent any event whatever from occurring. In other words, preemptive biopolitics signifies a desire to oppose the event, both before and after it takes place. An 'uncertain future' is a key term for preemptive biopolitics. Consuming its own imaginable futurity, preemption involves 'assimilation of powers of existence, at the moment of their emergence' (Massumi 1998: 57). Taking unknown unknowns to be its point of departure, it is concerned with the things that have yet to emerge (the virtual). Taking as its target potential risks, it operates in the present to act upon the future. Within this thread, in which unknowable and uncertain performances hold the potential to be truly 'eventful', what is now rendered terrifying 'is anything which could unsettle the normal Liberal flows of life' (Evans 2010: 11).

Preemption implies a relation to our experience in the present. However, in attempting to prevent future bad occurrences, it also colonises the future (see Aradau & van Munster 2008: 198). Yet, it must be borne in mind that the aim of preemption is not simply the future that needs to be ordered against unpredictability and 'bad occurrences' caused by potential disruptive events and terrorism. Rather, it oscillates in between present and future, to make sure that nothing dangerous really happens, that antagonisms do not occur. For preemption, there are disruptive events that are unexpected, but which, in hindsight, can be anticipated and postponed. As 9/11 (perhaps above all else), and other massacres such as Suruç, Ankara, Beirut, and Paris have illustrated (perhaps above all else), it is now the 'spiteful individual' who holds the potential to tell a micro-apocalyptic tale.

In contemporary society, sovereignty is made up of the use of social and political imaginative techniques. The sovereign order is not only that of 'decision' but also that of preemption. Thus, 'who is to be killed' is supplemented by 'who gets to preempt the future?' In other words, preemptive ontology is not only governed by 'sovereign wills' but also by the 'contingency of the event' (Dillon 2008a: 327–8). Importantly, however, the problem of preemption is not simply that of contingency but that of catastrophic contingency (Aradau & van Munster 2007: 101). What counts therefore is a coherent scenario of catastrophic events and the preemption of the future.

In colonising the future to eliminate the event, preemptive biopolitics also creates an affective logic, which becomes a political operator. In agreeing to eliminate all future events, affective uncertainty introduces potentiality within the realm of preemptive biopolitics. What is crucial in this respect is the centrality of the affective exploitation of the present. In this way, future uncertain events are turned into an investment of possibility and translated into more growth. As such, they help restore subjects to social life. All that remains is for the subject to incorporate and internalise the idea of catastrophe, as it becomes a normalised standard. No culture of catastrophe, no preemptive biopolitics, for catastrophe is politically and financially operative. Politically operative, because the acceptance of catastrophe signals a society in which the political is foreclosed; it culminates in the idea that 'nothing can be done' (Evans 2013). Financially operative, because 'there is profit (monetarily) and epistemologically) to be made out of the encounter with the catastrophic' (Evans & Reid 2014: 66). The threat of a future catastrophe is part of the current (re)producing of the neoliberal market.

Preemptive Biopolitics as Counterrevolution

Preemptive biopolitics is based on order and certainty in the face of continual 'disorder', resistance, and uncertainty. It merely uses the future to secure the system and thereby denies the possibility for any radical structural change. Colonising the future through an orderly process, it de-dramatises social struggles and thus defuses the possibility of an event. The possibility of an event in the future upsets preemptive biopolitics. After all, it knows that history is replete with invocations of revolutions to come, and the next revolution, or the event, can radically disrupt and destroy the 'liberal way of life' (Evans 2010). Put simply, the next revolution is nothing other than the breakdown of order tout court. Hence, the temporal effect of preemptive biopolitics is not simply the future that needs to be rendered palpable and governable against events; rather, it is the event that appears to be the problem to be solved, for it can appear to interrupt the temporality of the neoliberal order.

Because the event is an experimental practice, preemptive biopolitics takes as its target the virtual event. The virtual threat calls for a counter-politics of event. Put simply, a counter-politics of event needs to act against the 'events' to effectively appropriate them. Paradoxically, however, such an understanding of the event has been the very stronghold of both Deleuzian and Badiouian thought, but today the political meaning of this form of event has radically changed. Assimilating and appropriating the concepts and thoughts of radical politics of event, neoliberalism has learned to counter the unknowable, the uncertain, the unseen, and the unexpected. Because the event-based neoliberalism becomes the focus in which power struggles take shape and function, the question then becomes how to think through a counter-politics of event that aims at exploiting differences and antagonisms without allowing them to be eventful. For Deleuze (1994), for instance, the politics of event is a belief in the possibility of radical social change, whereas for preemptive biopolitics it is a catastrophe to be preempted and eliminated by means of event-based neoliberalism. For Deleuze, an event, an act, is a virtual potentiality, as excess, up against the actual, whereas for preemptive biopolitics it is what enables a living life, a 'species-life', to continually renew and generate itself. Whereas for Deleuze 'the event is the immanent consequence of becomings or of life' and, for Badiou, 'the immanent principle of exceptions to becoming, or Truths' (Badiou 2009: 385), for preemptive biopolitics it is opened up to military strategies and tactics which today seek to anticipate and survive future catastrophic events. In this sense the radical politics of event becomes a counter-politics of event, transforming the possibility of social change into a new array of tactics for neoliberal security-risk governance, ensuring that 'disruptive events' do not take place. Because it is precisely the event as problem-formation which now appears to be the problem of neoliberalism, the 'cancelling out of differences' becomes the generative principle of life:

> We see the emergence of a completely different problem that is no longer of fixing and demarcating the territory, but of allowing circulations to take place, of controlling them, sifting the good and the bad, ensuring that things are always in movement, constantly moving around, continually going from one point to another, but in such a way that the inherent dangers of this circulation are cancelled out.
> (Foucault 2003: 65)

However, we know from Deleuze that the 'cancelling out of differences' is a 'nihilistic principle' (1983: 46). For each difference can disrupt the continuity of the existing order. The more you cancel out of differences, the more you will remove the sources of conflict. And the more you exploit antagonisms, the more you will empty out the emancipatory core of social movements in advance. Indeed, the argument here is that, in its range and in its depth, the cancelling out of differences requires a power which acknowledges no immanent limit, which assimilates virtual differences and risks without allowing them to be 'eventful'.

In attempting to create a society without potential events, life in this context becomes the main object of study for preemptive biopolitics. However, preemptive biopolitics is not simply interested in life, but in the political and historical context in which life functions and is consistent with the event-based neoliberalism. The life to be protected is 'privatised' life, life that is assayed, organised, optimised, and pacified through a range of mechanisms. Thus, preemptive biopolitics should be understood as a form of governance that orders society and life. It is a way in which we can become clear on the truth of post-political neoliberalism such that it becomes available for contestation.

Absorbing and thus emptying out the emancipatory core of differences and antagonisms and egalitarian movements in advance, the challenge is not to solve a problem, but manage a panoply of risks at every level, from that of society to the state. Preemptive biopolitics always compromises with what exists and thus sustains the functioning of the existing order. In short, the defence of the neoliberal order is fundamental to preemptive biopolitics. Like all counterrevolutionary thoughts, doctrines, and governmentalities, preemptive biopolitics accepts the existing situation as it is, while, at the same time, depicts it as a fragile order in the face of potential upheavals and revolts. Revolution, therefore, is an unthinkable idea because preemptive biopolitics can only think from the perspective of the given. As can be seen in every counterrevolutionary thought, preemptive biopolitics is a principled reaction that keeps the emergence of future events at bay.

Insofar as the event transcends the given by opening up new realms for experimental thought, preemptive biopolitics seeks to delimit those realms by (re)defining what is acceptable and unacceptable. Therefore, the centre of gravity is always what exists, but it also revises, rather than simply opposes, new possibilities. In this sense, the preemption I am referring to constitutes a strategic field of appropriation, in which the struggle revolves around revising and accommodating revolutionary ideas and progressive principles. In this, freedom and revolt are possible as long as they do not challenge the given. Preemptive biopolitics understands freedom only in terms of existing values.

Because the goal of preemptive biopolitics is to care for a 'liberal life' by neutralising threats to that life through some form of intervention, it always evidences war and violence. After all, to intervene into life 'is to violate the body of the living in one way or another' (Evans & Reid 2014: 48). Preemption, therefore, does not accept life as it is. It signifies the end of the event, not necessarily the end of war and violence. Hence, in pursuing the 'liberal flows of life', it can wage war on whatever threatens it. With preemptive biopolitics, war becomes a permanent condition 'with no beginning or end, no front and rear . . . life itself is war' (Agre 2001).

Preemptive biopolitics and war are two sides of the same experiential coin. They are inseparable.

Under the signifier of the event, revolution, the virtual threat implies action, the action that is war. It is total war insofar as there is no 'outside' of preemptive biopolitics, that the politics of preemption should extend to all domains of everyday life. It is total war insofar as it uses surveillance, total control, and information culture to effectively counter the event. Preemptive biopolitics is a total war on human imagination: a virtual threat legitimates all kinds of preemptive security measures and war and violence. Because total war is seen as a natural phenomenon, preemptive biopolitics should be understood not purely as a form of social control, but as a form of counterrevolution that aims to extend the power of securitisation, and thus manage all forms of virtual threats. Its vocation is to be the anti-event.

Here, preemptive biopolitics defines a space in which 'the liberal way of war' meets the necessities of securitisation and violence, extending the circulations of capital even during times of crisis. Making threat its business and identifying the threats which do not simply challenge the capitalist flows of life, preemptive biopolitics requires 'the regulation of each and every type of circulation which propagates either a "good" or "bad" way of life' (Bell & Evans 2010: 383). Even though there are certain threats and abnormalities that currently exist outside of this regulation, they must be somehow incorporated into society and the capitalist economic activity. Circulation is both threat and an opportunity in a 'reflexive' world in which life is suspended between 'freedom' and 'danger'. Unlike the standard security/biopolitics, the threat in preemptive biopolitics is essential to the management of society. Preemptive biopolitics would not succeed without the event. Thus, unlike classic accounts of biopolitics, the preemptive threat must be enabled to survive so that it does have a continued presence in the collective social consciousness. More sinisterly and expectedly, it prevents individuals from demanding radical social change so that they end up imagining alternatives within the boundaries of the neoliberal order.

Hobbes's Leviathan was a response to the English Civil War, legitimating a strong state with exceptional powers to prevent chaos and civil disorder. Foucault argued for a biopolitics that is concerned with the biological species of the population that acts in relation to war and security. Preemptive biopolitics is an updated formulation of Foucault's biopolitics, a condition in which immanent biological species and preemptive security measures are inextricably intertwined in a set of practices. Preemptive biopolitics is the nexus of the species of eternity and war and security that aims at a total pacification of life and society, for order and public security can only be improved through the condition of permanent exception (pacification), that security can only be improved by continually targeting life as vulnerable.

For preemptive biopolitics, the permanent biopolitical state of emergency is maintained by constantly producing virtual threats. Here, the act of preemption folds into a single problem: how to identify virtual threats to the life of the biological species, such that preemption and biopolitics will coincide perfectly. The threat to eternal bodies based on market freedom is also a threat to society, and thus the threat to 'market freedom' is also considered a threat to life itself. In the context of preemption the biopolitical concern over biological species is thus transposed into a call for a politics of life itself because the common threat to biological species is life itself. By definition, the war against everything is without end, precisely because life itself constantly threatens to end life itself. As a foundation upon which the politics of life is constituted, preemptive biopolitics, therefore, aims to own a future. Its aim is to erase the event, revolution.

The Body Politic of Societies of Neoliberal Control

When Deleuze (1992: 255) argues that Spinoza's claim 'we do not know what a body can do' is practically a war cry, his aim was to define a new concept of philosophy and subjectivity, a battle against the transcendental philosophy. For preemptive neoliberalism, in a similar vein, 'what a body can do' functions as a war cry because the body is conceived of as an organ capable of everything. Preemption is a methodical response to the question 'What is a body?' Thus any(body) and every(body) truly matters. What a body is capable of becoming is fundamental to preemptive biopolitics because the body is what threatens to unleash catastrophe (see Dillon & Reid 2009: 108).

In the society of neoliberal control, the body is digitalised. Digital networks have become the new base structuring of body, society, and life. The global control of bodies via technologies deriving from digital networks, the targeting of individual bodies through advanced surveillance technologies such as biometrics, interface life into new complex digital arrangements which are manipulative by 'codes' and 'passwords'. Neoliberal control works by new biopolitical strategies that constitute bodies in relation to populations. The body and life in passwords mean that populations are now considered to be databanks of digital networks.

In contemporary society, the body becomes a property of the state, functioning as an instrument of domination, or better yet, as a dispositif against the event. Catastrophe is always incubating. The body may be on the verge of becoming catastrophic. The body threatens to produce catastrophe because it is where individuation takes place, especially in relation to every living form's independence with other existing forms. Because the body is perfectly aligned between finitude and immortality, it is both thing and the possibility together. Precisely because the body necessarily belongs to infinity, it is conceived of as an element of mass materiality—as an 'eternal' body. The body is *this* world itself, it is the source from which immanent life and perception unfold. And yet, the body is also flesh. It exists in the world, it wants what it lacks, it knows what it wants and strives after what it values. In short, the body is an organism that strives to enhance its life conditions.

Neoliberalism knows very well that the body has a freedom that lodges itself in a realm of historical possibilities. It is not somehow devoid of context, society, history, economy and so on. And it exerts its presence from this historical realm beyond phenomena. The body has its own voice that speaks from the flesh. In other words, the body's own voice can exceed the experience of the body itself. The body is a limit, a border, against which the self is both subjectified and objectified. Thus, the body implicates the subject and the object at the same time. The body either brings the self into life, or prevents the self from life. The body thinks, for itself; it goes on.

Displacing any absolute normative thinking, the body is indefinite and immanent to living. The body threatens to create the event because it has a creative capacity, a 'vital' power through which being becomes. Thus every body bears a biopolitical significance because it is where an irreducible multiplicity unfolds. The body creates the event because it is where the event takes place. Or, to say this differently, the body is the set of everything that the 'eventful individual' mobilises. This is nowhere better illustrated than by the events of 9/11, when the potential of the event changes the way we think and act. Because the event is catastrophic, neoliberalism cannot but counter/preempt the event before it is visited upon it.

This notion of the body is crucial. The body is emergent. The body is contingent. In short, the becoming of the body matters. It matters most, however, when it becomes eventual. In this sense preemptive neoliberalism expresses a fantasised dominance over the movement of 'bad' bodies, protecting the security of the threatened 'good' bodies. In brief, the circulation of bad bodies has to be distinguished from the circulation of good bodies. What has changed under the regime of neoliberal control is the geography of 'body' security, for in an age of global capitalism it is not enough to protect borders. Thus, 'the fight must be taken 'over there', before it reaches here' (Bruce 2007: 22). With preemptive biopolitics, it is necessary to have an 'ontological premise' that 'what is dangerous is precisely that which has yet to be formed, what has *not yet even emerged*' (Massumi 2007). Thus, any virtual challenge before it can take actual root should be eradicated. For preemptive biopolitics, not all bodies are subjected to emergency in the same way and emergency is rarely arbitrary as Agamben seems to imply. What we should abandon therefore is merely the classic narrative of the state of exception, which negates the possibility of considering modern biopolitics as a differential and universal regime. What needs emphasis today is how circulation is fundamental to the effective functioning of neoliberal capitalism, for, in the society of control, capitalism thrives on 'circuits of movement and mixture' (Hardt & Negri 2000: 198).

Because preemptive neoliberalism deals with future as a virtual indeterminacy, then its neutrality and declared indifference becomes a source of an affect, provoking the potential/virtual to become an actual event it can respond to. Post-political neoliberalism is therefore *incitatory* in that it allows the subject no freedom to be, but summons it to reveal itself just as it *is*. After all, 'the most effective way to fight an unspecified threat is to actively contribute to *producing* it' (Massumi 2007). Indeed, the more capable you are of revealing, producing, creating, provoking, mimicking, supporting, and ultimately proliferating your enemy, the better. For it allows the enemy to reveal herself and press the button. Post-political neoliberalism, in this sense, actively provokes a 'fatal' threat to emerge, bringing with itself a unique logic of (self)destruction, spite. Now the 'cheap happiness' is gone. All that is left is spite, and the only glorious ending the subject can imagine is pure destruction. Spite is a stochastic principle in that anyone can become a potential 'hostage' (Baudrillard 1990: 34–5).

Note

1. 'The graduate without a future' refers to an indebted student who is 'part of a wider precariat, poorer and with less life chances than previous generations. The affluence and welfare state that benefited cohorts post-1945 is being replaced by unemployment and the reduction and marketisation of public services' (Martell 2011: para. 1).

5 Age of Spite

In the preceding chapter, I argued that societies of neoliberal control manage and regulate life in its vital new capacities. Drawing on Deleuze's 'Postscript on the Societies of Control', I suggested the regime of control is directly related to neoliberal capitalism, which cannot be thought of without its associated affect, cynicism. Furthermore, I claimed that neoliberal control goes hand in hand with preemptive biopolitics, which attempts to create a society without all possible eventualities.

This chapter aims at theorising a new affect, spite, which may be defined as a willingness to cause harm for harm's sake. With spite, everything is pushed to its boundaries; everything is taken to the extreme, to its outermost limit. The chapter contends that spite has become one of the major affective dimensions of post-politics. The question is, however, what corresponding social regime would produce the distinctive affective modality of 'spite'. I contend that spite corresponds to a fourth, paradoxical social 'regime': terrorism. In the aftermath of 9/11, I argue, terrorism is no longer merely an 'exceptional' event but seems to have become part of the everyday political lexicon.

Spite is the antithesis of one of the most cherished of aims commonly espoused by 'progressive ideologies'. Indeed, 'enlightenment' ideologies such as liberalism have had a longstanding interest in the value of reason because it enables people to become 'rational' and 'controllable'. Progressive ideologies, in other words, have been always aiming to produce rational individuals who are abstracted from their passions and thereby become harmless and faithful to the existing order, and the same goes for neoliberalism. As a 'progressive' ideology, neoliberalism asserts rationality and reason as the proper bases for nature and society. It desires self-interested human beings who act rationally so that they become less of a threat to themselves as well as to the existing order.

In short, neoliberalism, with the utilitarian, competitive individuals 'motivated only by self-interest' at its heart, takes it as given that human beings act 'rationally' and that they want to act rationally. However, as I noted in the previous chapters, the forms of freedom and rationality fostered by neoliberalism are regulated and subject to forms of coercion.

The concept of freedom and rationality make sense only as far as they facilitate the consumer choice-making process. Neoliberalism is underpinned by the idea that human beings are governed by reason, science, and self-interest in their activities.

However, a growing body of scholarship has called into question the liberal democratic assumptions about rationality and the consequences of reason. Ranging from Marxists, poststructuralists to postcolonialists and postmodernists, such critiques have explored the importance of affects and emotions, arguing that reason cannot be thought of independently of affect (see, for example, Ahmed 2004; Boltanski 1999; Borch-Jacobsen 1988, 1993; Damasio 1999, 2003; Furedi 2005; Goodchild 1996; Massumi 1993, 2002; Ngai 2005; Sedgwick 2003; Thrift 2007). And so this chapter aims to show the limits of reason and neoliberalism, arguing that today the 'social' is closely related to spite understood as a total (self) destruction. As such, spite offers an invaluable opportunity for diagnostic social and spatial theory to study terrorism, which has legitimated as a social regime in contemporary society.

Islamic Terrorism

They came from all around Turkey to attend a leftist rally in the capital Ankara on October 10, 2015, which was labelled 'Labour, Peace, Democracy'. Among the participants were socialists, trade unionists, feminists, gays and lesbians, Alawites, Kurds, and Turks. Some were singing peace songs while others were holding placards reading 'Stop the war!' Then came two jihadist suicide bombings in rapid succession, killing more than 100 people in the deadliest terror attack in Turkey's modern history. Bits of dead bodies were scattered all over the pavement. The scenes in Ankara were of a war zone.

The suicide attacks were apparently carried out by the Islamic State terrorists. In July 2015, the jihadists also specifically targeted a cultural centre in Suruç near the Syrian border and killed 33 people from the Federation of Socialist Youth Association who had been planning to visit the Syrian Kurdish bastion of Kobani. The young members had been planning to assist in rebuilding Kobani, which became as a symbol of fierce Kurdish resistance against Isis.

After Taliban in 1990, and Al Qaeda in 2000s, we now have a new religious fascism, which is embodied in Isis. But what does Islamic terrorism really want? To understand the ideology that animates Islamic terrorism, we need to inspect its political context more closely.

Isis, like all such groups, uses violence intentionally, and the recent massacre in Paris—which has left nearly 130 people dead—confirms that it 'has gone global' (Burke 2015). With its sheer fanaticism, unbridled spite, barbaric executions and message of violent retribution against those who do not share its ideological outlook—only puritanical Sunnis fit this ideology—Isis has become the new 'terrifying threat' in contemporary society. Portraying Syria as the central battlefield in the final struggle between jihad and its enemies, Isis has been able terrorise its enemies, mobilise its sympathisers, and, more importantly, attract thousands of radical or sympathetic young Muslims both from the Middle East and the West. Exhibiting a campaign of 'shock and horror', the group is said to draw on 'apocalyptic' ideas in Islamic culture and thought. After all, apocalyptic ideas under a powerful leadership have always polarised communities and appealed to people in the Middle East, who are searching for some meaning in life. The jihadists see themselves as appointees of God, pursuing a divine mission. They are so sure that they are acting in the name of God in order to restore Islam to its lost power and glory and refound the caliphate.

In a society which seeks to maximise utility and minimise harm through self-interested, choosing competitive individuals in the pursuit of enjoyment, suicide is a toxic act. Now the toxicity has spread. Islamic terrorism uses spite as a strategy, the spectacle of death against 'the pacified life' on offer in post-politics. Contrary to neoliberalism that wants a 'ready-made' happiness, separated from action and reduced to passivity, the spiteful terrorist lives suffering as a state of (self)punishment. Neoliberalism is an inability to accept pain, conflict, and antagonism, whereas terrorism is an internal condition of neoliberalism which insists that pain/suffering, conflict and antagonism are necessary in order to construct a subjectivity. Neoliberalism is content with the actual world; it opts for a decaffeinated reality by directing desires, emotions into surplus value and security/militarism, whereas terrorism primarily seeks to negate the value of such ready-made decaffeinated reality for the sake of passions and values, including suffering.

Post-politics, as we have seen, attempts to create a reactive life in which 'happiness' is reduced to consumerism, politics to a depoliticised expert administration, to something that 'appears essentially as narcotic, anesthetic, calm, peace . . . in short, *passively*' (Nietzsche 1996: 23–4). The mission of post-politics is, in short, to pacify life by turning passions and affects into the language of market freedom and 'neoliberal harmony'. However, in a society of the spectacle, in a neoliberal age that fails to provide many of its members with the basic necessities of life, that constantly produces 'radical losers' (Enzensberger 2005), some of them are not resigned to their fate, waiting for their 'moment' to come. Thus, their spite turns against the happy-indifferent centre of society as well as the whole system. Touching the void, the 'nothing', becomes the truth of the spiteful individual. The person who pays back is the one with the 'lasting will' (Nietzsche 1996). Once this subject is constituted, spite can last for long periods of time.

In the age of the spectacle, the radical other goes by the name of terrorism, which is frequently associated with religious spiteful fundamentalism:

'Know also that we will cut off your head in the White House, and transform America into a Muslim Province', declared Isis (Weaver & Siddique 2014). Isis sees itself as warriors defending the Islamic world against crusaders from the West. In this context, it signifies 'holy war' with religious belief and holds itself accountable only to God (Hoffman 1995: 273). An Islamic terrorist is convinced that her narrative is the only true one; she is certain that she is the elect of God. Hence, she pledges her submission to God and meditates on the blood to come (DeLillo 2001). In appealing to the divine world, she builds a plot around spite and eliminates all contradictions in order to serve God's purpose on Earth. Taking the scriptures and commandments and prophecies literally, Islamic terrorism 'liberates the true believer from secular morals, from obligations to tolerance and other norms of the Enlightenment and allows him—even demands of him—to dehumanise the "others"' (Hess 2003: 348–9). Thus, anything can be justified by an appeal to God and judiciously selected passages from the holy books, such as Koran. The realisation of God's will on earth is the prototype for all Islamic terrorists; they are certain that they represent God's will and see themselves merely as the servants of God. For extremists who see themselves as instruments of God's will, everything is allowed. To paraphrase Augustine, 'Love God, and then everything is permitted.'

Because of the abstract, monological character of religious fundamentalism, there can be no commerce with it, no mediation; in short, there is nothing to discuss, nothing to compromise, nothing to sort out. When spite and destruction become sole principles, the idea of freedom becomes an abstract idea, something that *is felt* or perceived in consciousness, and here the claim is that 'freedom' is only so felt or perceived through acts of spiteful destruction. The spiteful terrorist is convinced that hers is the only truth, for her the truth lies in complete annihilation and destruction.

An overall religious devaluation of existence thus becomes exploited and expressed in spite, where it does not matter who dies, self or other. Religion is capable of offering its followers a clear, aggressive, and grandiosely theatrical 'worldview' that rests on a clear differentiation of friend and enemy (Sloterdijk 2010: 220). Fuelling future cycles of spite and violence, such a discourse evil is apocalyptic, evoking a permanent war with 'enemies'. When a binary logic of 'us' and 'them' is invoked, terror could happen anywhere, anyplace, anytime. The spiteful terrorist knows where it wants to hit. It enters society 'like the bullet enters the battle' (Sloterdijk 2010: 10). Thus, he dares to face the abyss of the real, in the form of suicide, martyrdom, as a terrorising *jouissance*. Being indifferent to the choice of targets, fundamentalist terrorists have an active desire for the spectacular acts of destruction: they are skilled at dying.

In this regard, fundamentalist terrorism articulates a symbolic sacrifice of life which is 'alien' to post-political neoliberalism; it is deeply shocking to neoliberalism governed by the principle of the preservation of life and the careful, methodical, and administrative functioning of the established social and biopolitical regimes. In other words, what is truly 'shocking' about Islamic terrorism is that we are witnessing a religious dimension, an 'apocalyptic' tradition, that is entirely alien to neoliberalism, which assumes human beings are 'good' and when governed by reason and self-interest in their activities, they can become harmless to the existing order, and that spite is an impossible affect in a 'rational' and 'enlightened' society. Islamic terrorism, therefore, seems to share the foundation of the eschatological tradition as it declares that one should always 'act' in order to destroy the given. Whereas Islamic terrorism is the ideology of believing 'too much', neoliberalism is the ideology of believing 'too little' (Eagleton 2014).

As a result, earthly ends are devalued, even as they are pursued. The Islamic terrorist realises that her values and goals cannot find a place in this world. She is present in this world while she mentally belongs to another. Beyond *this* world, there is *that* other world, which promises 'emancipation' (Taubes 2009: 27). In this sense, the spiteful personality of the terrorist brings to mind Nietzsche's radical (or 'suicidal') nihilist, whose will becomes a will to nothingness, to annihilation. Nietzsche argues that the ascetic ideal is ultimately a failure, an illusion. When the illusion disappears, this is followed by the emergence of radical and passive nihilisms. A radical nihilist is one 'who judges of the world as it is that it ought not to be' (Nietzsche 1967a: 318). In other words, a radical nihilist wants to destroy all values, including those that are attached to 'this' world. Passive nihilism, on the other hand, is a sign of weakness: 'the strength of the spirit can be tired, exhausted, so that the previous goals and values are insufficient and no longer inspire belief' (Nietzsche 1967a: 23). Passive nihilism emerges when the man of ressentiment turns 'his ressentiment against God', when he puts 'himself in the place of the God he has killed' (Deleuze 1983: 155). In this sense it refers to 'a depreciated life . . . a world without values, stripped of meaning and purpose' (Deleuze 1983: 148). If the passive nihilist seeks to deny the virtual, the radical nihilist seeks to deny and destroy actual existence for the sake of realising her values. Because freedom from the existing world is her goal, the radical nihilist comes to realise that she has values and goals, but they are not realisable in this (actual) world. Hence, she hopes for another, transcendent or 'true' world, and her world tends to lose its virtual dimension. It is precisely for this reason that this world must be annihilated for the world to come.

Such a comparison between the terrorist and the radical nihilist is of crucial importance, for it serves to strengthen the view that spite is an active feeling that results from passive nihilism (Nietzsche 1996: 67, 119). Seen in this perspective, the relationship between passive and radical nihilism can be described as a non-dialectical, complementary synthesis in which will is oscillated between spite and passivity. Spite, that is to say, has become legitimated as a technique of governance because it justifies itself with reference to and thus mirrors passivity and slavish comforts imposed by neoliberalism. Whereas the passive nihilist, or neoliberal society is obsessed with fear/security, the radical nihilist is addicted to danger. Whereas post-political neoliberalism opts for a pseudo-freedom devoid of passions and instincts, the radical nihilist is ready to destroy the 'society' for his passionate attachment. Thus spite has become the only object of 'fascination' for human beings who destroy the actual in the name of the virtual. As a false, mystifying reaction, spite, therefore, becomes a radical nihilist strategy which does not mirror the level of antagonism and conflict but the level of comfort and security. Spite, which is generated by the system, is thus normalised as a factor of sociality.

As argued in the discipline chapter, today there are two responses that endlessly call the nature of the eschatological tradition into question: the first response is *katechontic*, which sides with the given, the second is *revolutionary*, which seeks a total deligitimisation of the given. At first glance, Islamic terrorism looks like a continuation of the eschatological tradition, but a closer look reveals that it is not radical enough to be seen as an example of 'real apocalypticism'. Real apocalypticism not only draws a distinction between this and that world but also employs a dialectical thinking, which puts the actual and the virtual, or history and what is to come into interaction (see Diken 2012: 117). In Islamic terrorism, on the other hand, the gap between divine liberation and earthly realms is no longer mediated but cancelled, for it believes that it has direct access to willing God and is appointed by God. In other words, the dialectic between the actual and the virtual, the earth and heaven, is not preserved; divine justice is found in *that* other world. Thus, everything is permitted, at whatever cost, to eliminate 'evil' or 'kaffir', from the earth. Precisely in this sense, Islamic terrorism cannot be seen as revolutionary. Real apocalypticism seeks to combine violence with a transvaluation. And this is what is missing in Islamic terrorism. Whereas real apocalypticism targets the given framework of sensibility, Islamic terrorism plays a given game, using spite against neoliberal capitalism. In this sense Islamic terrorism is marked by a lack of promise, of emancipation.

What defines fundamentalist terrorism is a depoliticised gesture, that is, the nihilistic quality of violence that leads to a state of disengagement from politics as purposive, collective action. Islamic terrorism is not acting without purpose; rather, its actions consist only of 'reactions' because it justifies itself with reference to and thus mirrors the preemptive war against terror. Islamic terrorism is thus post-political in the sense that it is 'the product of listless and indifferent forces' (Baudrillard 1993: 76) rather than social and political conflicts and antagonisms, and this also explains why we are witnessing the rise of Islamic terrorism today. Precisely because ours is a post-political society in which the politics is reactive, and conflict/antagonism is eliminated. Precisely because post-politics proposes that change is no longer desirable or possible, and that there is no alternative. Precisely because post-politics is an inability to act politically. Weakened by preemptive biopolitics, hedonism, and consumerism accompanying neoliberal capitalism, we, 'the Westerners', cannot find a worthy cause to fight for (see Žižek 2002: 40–1). For the dead men, on the other hand, there is always 'something' for which the 'fight' takes place.

It is true that Islamic terrorism has social origins in the global neoliberal order, in social, political, and economic forces that attempt to create homogenous global networks. However, it is also equally true that, today, terrorism produces contemporary society. Terrorism is the state's pronouncedly evil changeling, its perfect friend and enemy, whose existence prefigures and summons forth the (re)production of the social by the global security state as our saviour and redeemer. In the aftermath of 9/11, terrorism (and the war against terrorism) has become a social regime, a factor of sociality, which sustains, rather than disrupts the consensual neoliberal order.

It would seem that in an age where the concept of death has vanished from the register of politics and contemporary society, it has returned as a spectacle itself—the spectacle of Islamic terrorism paralyses our gaze. Islamic terrorism attaches itself to the spectacle horror, producing political infantilism and regressive morality. However, I argue that the spectacle of terrorism is inseparable from the spectacle of security. The spectacle of security, conjured by the established social regimes and counterrevolutionary principles, must produce the state's most necessary social and political enemy, terrorism. In other words, terrorism has become a generative principle of formation for the consensual neoliberal order. The social regime of terrorism does not only mean the global security state that is now embodied in the war against terrorism, it also demonstrates how post-political neoliberalism is now also governed by multiple affects, such as a widespread fear of terroristic events or spiteful fundamentalism. It locates those affects in the way that the global security state has made 'contingency' as a generative principle of formation for rule (Dillon 2007; see also Aradau & van Munster 2007; Dillon & Lobo-Guerrero 2008). Contingency therefore is the very operational practice of neoliberal security politics (Dillon 2007: 9).

When fear escapes state control and instead is disseminated by the 'dangerous multitudes', absolute terrorism and the spectre of security can easily return. Such a fear of terrorism should not only be understood as a fear of spiteful destruction, though. This fear (or a biopolitics of fear) is also crucial to the administration and pacification of society and life, for it follows those who mobilise its spectre periodically to renew and modify the neoliberal order that is distributed among political rationalities and counterrevolutionary technologies that have accompanied the development of the global security state. This also means that the global security state is tempted to create policies for the management of fear.

Fear, then, becomes part of the military industrial-surveillance complex through which the neoliberal security state sustains and extends its activities. If fear becomes a generative principle in post-political neoliberalism, it can no longer be to prevent a transgression of the existing order maintained by the security state (Debrix & Barder 2009: 406). Rather, it can also help produce, create, proliferate spiteful terrorism with the established social regimes and security technologies. Thus, the biopolitics of fear and terrorism seem to accompany the deployment of political technologies and governmental rationalities, as much as it precipitated by a contingent possibility of a terroristic event (Dillon 2007: 8). In the context of neoliberalism, the biopolitical (re)production of fear is the result of a series of scare tactics, political rationalities, or terrorism regimes that can only produce 'good' social and political effects by agents of government. For this reason, terrorism has both a philosophical and political logic, and on the other an affective logic.

The primary purpose of the war against terrorism is to bring terrorism with the established social regimes and the corresponding characteristics of the neoliberal security state with the aim of destroying it, or preempting it. The aim is to eliminate terrorism through the massive global security effort, or make terrorism at least manageable through preemptive risk-security measures (Aradau & van Munster 2012; Dillon 2007). This radical ambiguity—to govern terrorism in order to bring terrorism within the orbit of the established social regimes and security technologies—bears within it an essential risk: 'a state which has security as its sole task and source of legitimacy is a fragile organism; it can always be provoked by terrorism to become itself terroristic' (Agamben 2001: para. 1).

If a contingent catastrophic event is the problem, and if the biopolitics of fear and the social regime of terrorism is the answer, governmental technologies and political rationalities must ensure that the conduct responsible for 'unknown threats' is done away with (before they shape and become eventful). But, more importantly, these terrorism regimes upon which the political rationalities and governing technologies of post-politics rely must also make certain that human beings are not only to become mobilised and adaptively govern themselves. Rather, the self-rationalising, self-governable individuals that act, react, and interact in coordination with governmental technologies and the established social regimes of post-political neoliberalism that are found at the heart of fear and terrorism production are more likely to represent what Michael Dillon has called 'emergent life' (2007).

Dillon argues that emergent life in societies 'governed by terror' can be understood 'as a constant potential for adaptation in biopolitical terror apparatuses' (2007: 8). As he notes, 'emergent means that they [human beings] are capable of moving out of phase with themselves and becoming other than what they were' (2007: 14). The 'living things' that are governed 'by a widespread fear of terror' have no choice but to rely on the very contingency of terrorism and terrorism of contingency. This means that they have to redefine themselves constantly inside the established social regimes and governmental technologies. Yet, because the social regime of terrorism and biopoliticised fear, and security technologies create conditions that allow it to thrive, emergent life undergoes constant change and transformation but always remains on the look-out (Debrix & Barder 2009). And, as discussed throughout the book, it is a life that endlessly needs to regulate and monitor itself so that it can fear today what can be tomorrow's terrorism. Thus, unlike the standard security/biopolitics in which individuals are rendered inert, emergent human beings actively and energetically partake of the biopolitical (re)production of fear, terrorism, and, ultimately, neoliberal capitalism. Today there are no 'passive' subjects, only actively driven subjects of the liberal struggle and war.

There is an important caveat to address here. Emergent life should not be understood as 'a becoming that is politically different'. Nor is it to be understood as 'the embrace of positivist ontology' (Evans 2013: 74–5). What emergent life and emergent human beings (re)produce through their constant 'events watch' is nothing else than the perpetuation of the biopolitical regimes of terrorism. As Dillon pithily put it, 'the more effort that is put into governing terror, the more terror comes to govern the governors' (2007: 8). Emergent life in today's neoliberal society, guided by the established social regimes, governing technologies of security and the affective politics, ensures that terrorism (no matter which enemy or dangerous situations such as 'chaos', 'disorder', 'revolution' are targeted) will not be completely eliminated but, instead, will remain as one of the main generative principle of formation, of government. Terrorism, in other words, has become normalised as a social regime on account of how it functions to 'make life live' for the neoliberal order. Or, to say this differently, post-political neoliberalism needs terrorism in order to depoliticise politics, to recast 'political and economic choices as military necessities' (Bauman 2008: 246–7).

Sovereignty operates through cruel and contingent acts, transforming the state of exception into a form of sociality. The always present possibility of war and of violence is what defines state sovereignty's legitimacy. As such, cruel and contingent acts are mobilised alongside other techniques of governance (the war on terror) to avoid future terrorist threats within life. Established as a social regime based upon war, violence, and permanent states of exception, sovereign political power reconstitutes itself in the form of an endless terrorisation of life's 'radical undecidability' (Reid 2005). Life's radical contingency, however, initiates a politics of security. Moreover, what we see in the politics of security's response to terrorism is nothing other than sovereign vengeance, which disguises this violence and cruelty through a terrorism of its own. The desire to continually justify state terrorism is more than a mere feature of the war against terrorism being waged by the contemporary neoliberal state. That is to say, if we are to understand terrorism as a social regime of violence, it is difficult to distinguish it from the violence that is carried out by the sovereign power of the state. The social regime of terrorism has the effect of unmasking the intimate relationship between law, war, and violence at the heart of sovereign political power. In this sense, the concept of terrorism is internal to state sovereignty, or the politics of security in contemporary society. Hence, the emergence and development of liberalism conditioned by what Foucault called as 'strategies of security' (2008: 65). And strategies of security, as we have discovered, generate more terrorism.

In contrast to discipline and control, which operate through confinement and decoded and flexible flows, terrorism functions through fear, insecurity, and uncertainty. Thus, the fantasy generated by insecurity is terrorism, which allows the neoliberal state to extend its power and makes the state of exception permanent. Indeed, post 9/11, the global security state increasingly needs to generate and intensify the evil of terrorism as a 'fact' of contemporary society. Its 'evildoers', ultimately, needs a materialised enemy. For the spectacle of security, our life and labour-power supply the global neoliberal state with the innumerable and multiple manifestations of its perfect enemy and friend. The global security state operates through both the capitalist market and the established social regimes that legitimise and protect it, but also through the spectacle of terrorism that (re)produces an alienated everyday life.

False 'Clash'

Significantly, in this context, both spiteful terrorism and the war against terrorism have convergences and divergences, differences and similarities, without, of course, being the same. The forces of terrorism and the war against terrorism function with equal strength in opposite directions: the former driven by religious spiteful fundamentalism, the latter by the market ideology, the nihilism of capital. Whereas terror negates this world for the freedom in the other world, the war against terror seeks to sustain this world, recognising it only in a conservative manner, specifically as neoliberal market. If the first perceives terrorism as a means of destruction to open up a space for a God to come, the latter turns (state) terror into a form of governmentality, aiming to counter preempting eventualities.

Yet, there are also significant convergences between Islamic terrorism and the war against terror. In both the dominant discourse is fundamentally religious and Manichean, introducing a binary opposition between good and evil, us and them. Whereas, for instance, the religious emphasis of Islamic terrorism lies on absolute values such as jihad, the religious emphasis of the war against terrorism lies on capitalism and neoliberal democracy. The war against terrorism sacralises capitalism and the liberal democratic market as unquestionable, naturalised backgrounds, and understands 'freedom' only in terms of existing neoliberal values. Just as the war against terrorism needs the figure of Islamic terrorism as a 'radical evil', so religious fundamentalism needs the figure of 'evil empire'. Whereas Islamic terrorism is seen as 'a cancer' (Obama 2014), the war against terrorism is understood as a 'battle for civilisation' (Glasman 2014). Thus, both justify their actions, attacks with reference to hostility and spite.

In other words, both speak in absolutes of the ideologies, the one driven by religious fundamentalism, the other by universalising capitalist markets. And finally, both are convinced that their narrative is the only 'true' one, that they possess the truth (religious orthodoxy, and capitalism as a new religion). In this sense, the 'clash' between spiteful terrorism and post-political neoliberalism is a false clash—'a vicious cycle of two poles generating and presupposing each other' (Žižek 2015b). In such a space, the only form protest can take is meaningless spiteful violence.

By turning security into an internal perversion, and with its neutrality and indifference to social and political reality, neoliberalism provokes lethality and radicality, a 'fatal' violence to emerge. Affirming the 'good' and getting rid of the 'bad', it actively incites an abstraction, a terrorism to itself to emerge. It brings everything into the open. Post-political neoliberalism is being reproduced by terrorism, just as terrorism is being actualised through 'a terror based on 'law and order measures', that is, 'a security terror' (Baudrillard 2003: 32). Neoliberalism, in short, 'needs the otherness of the terrorist in order to legitimate itself affectively and in order to self-actuate' (Massumi 2007). It tames terrorism, turning its radical potentiality into a counterrevolutionary justification of the system. Because neoliberalism is an open ontogenetic governance productive of otherness, it should be seen as a heterogeneous 'consensual' order rather than a stable order, strictly speaking. It always brings with it a violence of a system based on a consensual preemptive and post-political order by transforming antagonisms into harmony, by excluding those who understand themselves as increasingly alienated and abandoned by neoliberal forms of power and rationality.

The nightmare of neoliberal capitalism is that of living in an eternal present while prey to a preemptive order based on certainty in the face of continual 'event', a life governed by an infinite extension of the market ideology, the nihilism of money. A world devoid of all passion, commitment, and meaning. In short: a world constructed with the sole intent of surplus with regard to capital accumulation and the commodification of human relations and life. The violence involved in such a situation is relative to neutralisation, that is, the violence of consensus, which forces the 'enemy' to reveal itself in a violent manner, without bringing real political change. To put it bluntly, capital's indifference to social and political reality is the source of a complex, systemic violence that cannot be attributed to concrete individuals and their intentions.

Most importantly, neoliberalism cannot attain the post-political consensual unity other than through war and violence. And this is what is missing in Wendy Brown's analysis of neoliberalism 'as a political rationality'. Her new book, *Undoing the Demos: Neoliberalism's Stealth Revolution,* is an excellent account of how neoliberalism operates as a political rationality 'through which capitalism finally swallows humanity' (2015: 44). Inspired by Foucault, Brown prefers to examine neoliberalism as a 'normative order of reason', the 'conduct of conduct', a 'regime of truth' (2015: 9, 21, 115). However, neoliberalism is not only a rationality but also an ideology that operates through war and violence. In other words, violence and war are modalities of neoliberalism. Post-political neoliberalism is a complex of enforcements and exclusions, devoted to the suppression of all radicalisms and their energies, with the demonisation and the victimisation of those energies being only one (among many) of its apparatuses. Consensual neoliberal order, that is to say, is deeply (constantly) a form of violence, a deliberate action against political possibilities that can lead to an event. In fact, violence and war have not been 'others', or optional, means of neoliberalism. They have been what neoliberalism most fully and essentially is. War, for instance, not only creates the society but also subsumes the political imagination of the future by closing down alternative possibilities (Neocleous 2014: 203). What's more, it is necessary to the symbiosis of the market and state, stimulating the economy in difficult times (see Stallbrass 2006: 88). Colonising social life by capital and neutralising antagonisms and conflicts, neoliberalism is 'the submission of more and more facets of human sociability . . . to the deadly solicitations of the market' (Retort 2005: 19). It produces opportunities for endless accumulation and inures the population 'to the spectacle of their armed forces punishing some recalcitrant state by killing and maiming its citizens' (Stallbrass 2006: 88).

Today wars are conducted in the name of 'peace'. We live in a society where the old Orwellian motto 'war is peace' has become a reality (Žižek 2002: 93–4). Thus, Foucault was no doubt right to say that 'peace itself is a coded war' (2003: 50). However, and contra to Foucault, law is also pacification because liberalism manages and governs society through law. The 'liberal peace' is nothing other than peace as *permanent pacification*, and it is achieved through pacification and elimination of the spiteful individual, and also of all non-liberal elements. Neoliberalism is the nexus of war and violence that aims at a total pacification of nature and society. Violence as peace, peace as permanent pacification.

Through an endless biopolitical war and violence against the forces of dissent, neoliberalism would fight tooth and nail to maintain the current order to the end. Because 'factical finitude' conditions the problematisation of politics, neoliberalism and rule in the modern age (Dillon 2011), war and violence are normalised biopolitical conditions, for they produce and reproduce all aspects of social life (Hardt & Negri 2004: 31). The exercise of post-political neoliberalism is thus incitatory in that it seeks to actively produce (hence profit from) spiteful terrorism. Neoliberalism informs and enforces spite. Mostly, that fact is hidden. Neoliberalism *is* that hiding. And the endless (re)production of spiteful terrorism, to whatever immediate end, serves also to normalise and *keep neoliberalism running*.

Thus, in contrast to political violence, which is based on the internal contradictions of the system, spite only reflects the level of neoliberal consensus. Rather than a political act, the fantasy of a salvation through the suffering of violence, through spite, should be seen as, to borrow Žižek's term (1997: 61), 'a trancelike subjective experience' in which the traditional political subject ceases to exist. Being reactionary, spite, like an 'antibody', turns against the system that creates it. This lethality does not have the capacity to create new, immanent values. It ends up reproducing the militarism of post-political neoliberalism which it originated. It is just as clearly complicit with the very political, economic, and technological processes of neoliberal capitalism that it seeks to destroy. It is both resistant to the system and contaminated by it, or better still, its so-called resistance *takes the form of a* contamination (see Bradley 2010: 176), which is why it is doomed to fail. for sheer spiteful destruction is merely the reverse side of creation and radical social change.

Let us put it succinctly: One cannot destroy post-political neoliberalism by producing the same spite and indifference. Politics proper cannot occur within the bounds of spiteful terrorism. Because the post-political nature of neoliberalism is intimately linked to war and violence, anything else that goes by the same name is simply a reproduction of the system. Seen in this perspective, spiteful fundamentalism and neoliberalism become two aspects of the same cycle of bare repetition, that is, repetition without real political change. The farcical character of the post-political neoliberalism and spiteful terrorism derives from the fact they both produce non-events within the confines of the given; they are both characterised by the absence of revolutionary events. In the end, therefore, they do not provide an altogether different perspective on social change, and everybody returns to the same position as in the beginning. Neoliberalism versus terror: such is the wager, because no other exists. Although they are opposed, both spiteful terrorism and neoliberalism are Siamese twins of sorts, as they both agree 'on the meaninglessness of reality, or rather its essential unreality, which inspires either passive withdrawal or violent destruction' (Critchley 2007: 6).

Consequences

In this book I theorised the post-political nature of neoliberalism, and through it I addressed key debates on governmental social regimes and affective structures. In so doing, I offered an original topological analysis that makes the following critical interventions: an exploration of how the much-discussed social regimes of sovereignty, discipline, and control relate to each other in the production of post-political neoliberalism; an analysis of the affective logic each regime entails and how they interrelate; a proposal for a fourth regime, 'terrorism', and a theorisation of its associated affect, 'spite'. Through my empirical discussions I put social and cultural theory in conversation with Friedrich Nietzsche, Gilles Deleuze, Michel Foucault, and Walter Benjamin, all of whom I contextualise as crucial to understanding contemporary neoliberal governance and radical politics.

And so we have moved from post-political neoliberalism to radical politics. So what is the role of radical critique in neoliberal society? Before suggesting an answer to this question, let us, at this point, summarise the relationship between four social regimes and their affective logics. As I argued throughout the book, post-political neoliberalism is a moving target. And the same goes for social regimes and their associated affects. The established social regimes and the corresponding affects are means to, and methods of, the post-political nature of neoliberalism. This line of thinking enables us to question and interpret the dynamics of social regimes and their relation to neoliberalism mentioned so far. So the aim is to discuss concepts from the point of view of the book, focusing on tendencies and affects each regime produces. Any social regime, any sociality, contains within itself all the four social regimes, just as it contains within itself all the four affects. In other words, the aim is to construct a perspective on the social by illustrating a dynamic field of forces between social regimes and the corresponding characteristics.

Modernity has traditionally understood the social as an 'ordered' and 'stable' process. Deleuze, however, views the social as a contingent process, incorporating hybridity and ambivalence into modernity itself. If modernity seeks to purify the social, Deleuze seeks to impurify it. Whereas modernity emphasises the ordered aspects of a differentiated sociality, Deleuze moves beyond differentiation and depicts the social from the point of view of de-differentiation.

'Sovereignty', for instance, implies a process, a radical contingency rather than a state of being without dependence on territory. Sovereignty is a social regime, a set of contingent governmental practices and rationalities, where cruel acts of the modern state manifest itself. As such, it endlessly attempts to 'appropriate', or 'capture', countermovements and utilise them for its own purposes. In doing so, it employs a 'regime of violence' which creates its counter-affect, ressentiment. Sovereignty signifies an eternal vengeance, whereas ressentiment refers to a passive, powerless emotion. However, ressentiment also gains an astonishing potential for unproductive violence when it encounters sovereign vengeance. The victims of sovereignty do not, cannot forget. After all, what defines objects of ressentiment is their weakness, their technique 'for remembering things' (Nietzsche 1996: 42).

We are witnessing in sovereignty also the revival of violent apparatuses, such as torture, by depoliticising conflicts via permanent states of exception. In this sense torture and the state of exception are inextricably connected. Intimately connected to the liberal way of war, torture is not only the most privileged actualisation of sovereign political power but also a form of state terror. Cruel and contingent practices and the state of exception are thus fundamental to the operation of political sovereign power in particular and post-political neoliberalism in general.

However, sovereignty is not simply the only social regime that constitutes post-politics. 'Discipline' is our second social regime where neoliberal governmentality is born and takes shape. The birth of neoliberalism goes hand in hand with the market, with its competition between self-governing subjects in which everything can be bought and sold. This, however, does not mean that we have left behind state sovereignty. Rather, disciplinary neoliberalism is a social regime in which sovereign political power is still present. Whereas sovereignty puts cruel manifestations into play, neoliberal governmentality emphasises the individual as a homo economicus that is motivated by self-interest. Whereas sovereignty declares the state of exception, discipline is based on high levels of normalisation upon life so that the neoliberal order is maintained and thus remains intact. Discipline is a social regime constructed to make individuals internalise the sovereign gaze, creating docile, yet free, bodies that are governed by an intensified competition in which the strong extinguish the weak. The primary goal of disciplinary neoliberalism is, therefore, the extension of free-market policies to all aspects of society. Neoliberalism necessitates free trade and competition that adopts individual freedom understood as 'economic freedom' from a *given* menu.

Moreover, sovereignty puts death into play, addressing bodies from the angle of fear and danger. With neoliberal governance fear becomes an organising force that secures and pacifies a life to make life live; it becomes a productive aspect of everyday life, individually and collectively. For it is essential for defusing disruptive events. In this way, a biopolitics of fear becomes essential for producing docile-species bodies as well as preventing future events from occurring. The biopolitics of fear is a necessary condition of neoliberalism because it converts fearful bodies of the sovereign into productive subjects of the system. However, modern biopolitics should also be viewed as a political eschatological katechontic response whose aim is to defuse the idea of the event. Thus, when we analyse biopolitics, we should also pay attention to its theological reasoning, because how to delay radical structural change is motivated by 'secularised theological concepts'. As an eschatological katechontic response, modern biopolitics is a preemptive counterrevolutionary principle whose mission is to keep 'the threat of the event' at bay.

'Control', our third social regime, is a heterogeneous order that incorporates hybridity, flexibility, and an axiomatic of decoded flows into the heart of the social. Neoliberal control is discipline without walls, regulating subjects and objects on the move. In the process, 'freedom of movement' (along the regulation of each and every type of circulation which is 'good' or 'bad' to the liberal way of life) coexists with disciplinary surveillance and the mechanisms of normalisation. Neoliberal control works by codifying the flows, again, arguably, targets bodies, but in a very different way: it reduces them to codes and passwords. With the control society, the individual is dispersed among a set of possibilities, governed through multiple systemic codes and inscriptions. Furthermore, the main affect that pertains to neoliberal capitalism is cynicism, which continuously reinforces and (re)produces perpetually infinite mechanisms of surplus-enjoyment based on the figure of homo economicus. Whereas disciplinary neoliberalism works through instruments of correction and normalisation, neoliberal control works through preemption, a contemporary biopolitical mechanism, whose aim is to prevent any disruptive event whatever from occurring. Disciplinary panoptic sustains the political economy of neoliberalism, whereas the society of control produces hybrid and reflexive subjectivities that are governed through free-floating surveillance as is the case with preemptive risk management in relation to digital 'networks'. Whereas disciplinary neoliberalism manages and regulates individuals qua homo economicus, neoliberal control targets the conduct of bodies and 'mobile' subjects (Bauman 1998: 51–2), accommodating them for its own purposes.

Moving from disciplinary panoptic to 'generalised surveillance' (Foucault 1977: 209), the regime of control extends the power of neoliberalism. With preemptive risk and security mechanisms and circulation which have direct access to life, neoliberal control 'knows no outside' (Hardt & Negri 2000: 413). Whereas disciplinary neoliberalism is about constituting a differentiation between an inside and outside, neoliberal control focuses on the conditions that constitute unknown unknowns. Thus, it is precisely the virtual that now serves to consolidate the neoliberal control society. Because unknown disruptive events are the problem, the becoming of the body becomes one of the organising principles of control societies to wage war on whatever threatens the neoliberal capitalist order.

And finally, there is 'spite', which is associated with a fourth social regime: 'terrorism'. Neoliberalism has its own discontents, bringing with it a new form of repression with a vengeance: that of terrorism. With sovereignty, post-political neoliberalism governs the population through cruel manifestations of the state within spaces of exception. Within disciplinary panoptic, neoliberal governmentality produces docile and obedient subjects through agents/agencies of fear and market mechanisms that facilitate competition. With neoliberal control (the global capitalist market), multiple governmental rationalities monitor the mobile individuals through generalised biopolitical surveillance. Yet, this creates immanent problems, bringing forth a suicidal line of flight that is indifferent to neoliberalism. When the political is foreclosed through the very proliferation of neutrality and cynicism, this provokes a 'fatal' violence to emerge, expressing a radical nihilist passion that can find truth only in nothingness, in spiteful terrorism. In today's society terrorism has become normalised as a fourth social regime which sustains, rather than challenges, 'business as usual'. Thus, what previously appeared exceptional has become the rule in everyday life. Neoliberalism finds a perfect enemy in terrorism, where political problems are presented as military necessities. Post-political neoliberalism and spiteful terrorism are thus the twin faces of contemporary society, embodying a non-dialectical, complementary synthesis, a synthesis between passive and radical nihilism. In other words, cynicism and spite together form a vicious cycle, a synthesis, in which post-political neoliberalism generates the violent *passage à l'acte* and thus mimics the very force it tries to ward off, spiteful fundamentalism. Rather than a political act, the fantasy of a salvation through terrorism should thus be seen as bare repetition, that is, repetition without difference or real events. Spiteful terrorism is 'pure chaos' that does not produce anything.

Sovereign political power produces subjects of *ressentiment* that are rendered reactive and obedient through cruel acts and practices. The subject produced by disciplinary neoliberalism is that of the *fearful* subject, who is not a passive subject but an active one, continuously reproduced through competition and free-market regulation. With societies of neoliberal control we have the *cynical* subject, governed through digital technologies as well as the infinite diachronic temporality of debt and surplus-enjoyment. The figure of the subject produced by terrorism is that of the *spiteful* subject, who destroys the existing, sensual world in the name of a true, other world. When the difference between terrorism and state terrorism disappears, they start to mimic each other, without bringing radical political change. In other words, they do not seek to find political solutions to political problems. Therefore, the key to understand both neoliberalism and spiteful terrorism is bare repetition, that is, an inability to create immanent values, a new way of life.

Post-political neoliberalism, then, is a dynamic field of forces, which consists of differentiation and de-differentiation, hybrid networks as well as lines of death. It is not an ontological term but an expression of changing and contingent social regimes, rationalities, and affects that are historical and political in formation. What is at issue here is how these four social regimes and associated affects interact with and differ from each other. In brief, sovereignty, discipline, control, and terrorism do not merely follow a chronological order. What is interesting is how sovereign political power opens the space for disciplinary neoliberalism, disciplinary neoliberalism for neoliberal control, neoliberal control for spiteful terrorism and spiteful terrorism for state terrorism, or the politics of security. In order to continually justify itself, neoliberalism accommodates spiteful terrorism, transforming it into a public spectacle.

But, to reiterate, none of these social regimes and the corresponding characteristics exist in a pure form; each type simply seeks to mark out the consistency of a concept and is valid only to the degree that it provides a critical tool for analysing concrete dispositifs and modes of existence, which are by definition mixed states requiring a 'microanalysis' of the characteristics they have and lines they actualise (see Deleuze 1995: 86). In this sense, each social regime can be taken up into another social regime, like, for example, the return of sovereignty in the neoliberal control society. Within one social regime we can always find a coextensive functioning of different social regimes and their associated affects.

To sum up, within discipline, tendencies towards neoliberal control constantly coexist, just as within control, tendencies towards sovereignty and discipline operate together. Thus, one no longer has to follow the succession of sovereignty, discipline, control, and terrorism; they develop alongside of it throughout post-political neoliberalism. Any social regime contains within itself all the four characteristics and corresponding affects that are actualised in varying degrees. However, the regimes and affects characterising post-political neoliberalism do not mean the end of politics, only its reconfiguration. The central question, then, is how we can theorise the intimate relationship between critique and social change in contemporary neoliberal society. This is examined in the last chapter.

6 Post-Politics to Political Spirituality

In the previous chapter, I theorised spite as a fourth affect. I suggested that today spite plays a major role in relation to the 'social'. I found also that spite corresponds to a fourth social 'regime', terrorism, which uses pain/suffering against passivity and cynicism offered by neoliberal governance. Furthermore, I argued that spite is not to be seen as a political act, for it refers to a will to nothingness that no longer creates new values.

This chapter aims to radicalise critique in contemporary neoliberal society. What gives rise to post-political neoliberalism is also what gives rise to alternative social and political imaginaries for radical politics. The possibility of radical politics exists within neoliberalism. For Foucault, critique is the 'will not to be governed as such'. This will is, however, formed in resistance and contestation with governmental regimes (see Foucault 1997a: 72). This will now requires a critique of post-politics. Insofar as the contemporary regime of governmentality is post-political, post-politics constitutes the problematic of critique today. As such, the critique of post-politics is part and parcel of a wider critique of neoliberal power.

And so this chapter is an attempt to retain the belief in two interrelated ideas: critique and spirituality. It argues that critique and spirituality are commonly associated, aiming at social and self-transformation. The chapter is in two parts. It first explores the development and meaning of critique through the concept of parrhesia. It argues that critique as parrhesia is always in relation to spirituality. Second, it explores the consequences of adopting this critical approach for spirituality in the constitution of subjectivity. However, in order to explore this relationship, one must first understand what critique means in neoliberal times.

Groundhog Day

Twenty-three years after its release, *Groundhog Day*, a film by Harold Ramis, still has a crucial resonance. At its best, it poses philosophical questions regarding the role of critique and change in contemporary society. The movie tells the story of a cynical weatherman, Phil Connors, who is sent to a small American town called Punxsutawney to cover the annual February 2nd festivities. Referring to himself as 'the talent', Phil doesn't like anybody, and nobody likes him. Thus, he is inattentive, almost blind, towards others, and has no meaningful insight into the world outside; he is completely detached from the existing world. But things get worse for this cynical and selfish man when he is stuck in a time loop that makes him relive the same day over and over again. Hence, he turns suicidal, but even suicide can't get him out of the same emotional prison. For him it is always February 2nd.

Phil then figures out how to get out of the cycle; he begins to confront and learn. This allows him to go beyond good and evil, that is, to accept that this world is his fate. It is precisely then that he escapes from the cycle; he is liberated from the time loop. In the end, he learns from his mistakes and becomes a good man whom everybody likes and admires. Indeed, the greatest strength of the movie lies in showing us that change can arise from repetition. Life actually repeats itself, everything that has happened in the past will happen again. What we should do is desire for things that are different in nature. In a world in which bare repetition is the rule, a single day can make a real difference. So it is the 'return' of the different rather than the return of the identical that matters. As Deleuze writes, 'the eternal return is linked, not to a repetition of the same, but on the contrary, to a transmutation. It is the moment or the eternity of becoming which eliminates all that resists it. It releases, indeed, it creates, the purely active and pure affirmation' (1983: x).

Contemporary critique is, however, functions as an impotent and 'disengaged' gesture, which consolidates, rather than disrupts, the existing order. Today, critique is locked into a post-political paradigm in which everything is constantly criticised and assessed, but nothing really changes radically. Thus, contra to *Groundhog Day*, critique cannot arrest the cycle; it generates the same detachment over and over again. It has become exquisitely incorporated—and depoliticised in 'the new spirit of capitalism' (Boltanski & Chiapello 2005).

With the new spirit of capitalism, critique is stuck into a paradox. On the one hand, we are witnessing an 'immense and proliferating criticizability of things, institutions, practices, and discourses' (Foucault 2003: 6). In this era of 'unprecedented freedom', we all, to a greater or lesser extent, sometimes more and sometimes less, find ourselves in an endless critique. This is the objective irony of neoliberal society: nothing sells better than critique. On the other hand, the foundations, instruments and aims of contemporary critique turn out to be, to borrow Zygmunt Bauman's (2000: 23) felicitous term, 'toothless'; they support, rather than subvert, the neoliberal order. Thus, today everything can be politicised and discussed, debate is open and encouraged, but in a reserved way, in so far as our critique remains within the bounds of neoliberal dialogue. Consensus, not antagonism, is the essence of contemporary critique. In this sense contemporary critique does not seek to transcend but to transform neoliberalism as neoliberalism. Contemporary critique is uncritical.

Indeed, in neoliberal times critique no longer refers to radical structural change. It is unable to accede to a true creation that would disrupt the existing social order and constitute a new political scene. Contemporary critique becomes fundamentally outmoded, which no longer supplements the given situation with an 'event', with a subject that can create a new present beyond the temporality of post-political neoliberalism. Contemporary critique is, therefore, locked into an 'atonic reality', for it is aligned with the meaninglessness of the present, with the resigned acceptance of 'anything goes'. Thus, a depoliticised radical politics, a *softened* Marxism, and a Marx without revolution are no longer exceptional but part of a normality in contemporary society. Marx is acceptable only in so far as 'the revolt, which initially inspired uprising, indignation, insurrection, revolutionary momentum, does not come back' (Derrida 1994: 38). Differently put, Marx, Marxism, the revolt, uprising, and revolutionary momentum can reappear as long as they speak the language of power and sustain the belief that it is possible to achieve real change within the boundaries of neoliberal capitalism. We have a *decaffeinated* Marx and Marxism that no longer refer to revolutionary events.

Is critique useless then? What might constitute a form of critique that is antithetical to post-political neoliberalism? I contend that a *revisionist critique* leaves nothing but to rethink the idea of social change. Insofar as the neoliberal order is characterised as 'business as usual', critique is a break with the given. Critique is an answer to the problem of neoliberalism. Thus the post-political nature of neoliberalism and the established social regimes—their penetration through one another, their assimilation of counter spaces—must be critiqued, as an immediate task. This requires that one cannot accept the existing order *as it is*, including the reformist sides of neoliberal post-political promises. Because the neoliberal order is presented as the 'end of history', it relies on the denial of a radical, utopian dimension to politics and depicts the given reality as the only reality. Whereas it sacralises the neoliberal market as an unquestionable, naturalised background, it also builds a moat around revolutionary possibilities so that they become redundant. What needs to be recovered, then, is the promise of emancipation.

Parrhesia and Spirituality

If neoliberal capitalism is shaped by a life of fundamental meaninglessness governed by an infinite extension of the market ideology, critique makes sense if it is critical of its own historical present, the given order of the sensible, and it can do so relating itself to another time. Thus, critique 'only exists in relation to something other than itself' (Foucault 1997a: 25). In this sense it is marked by something that has not yet existed: a future to come. This also involves problematising our relationship to the present, inviting others 'to share an experience of what we are, not only of our past but of our present' (Foucault 1991b: 33–4), an ethos which continues to link us with the Enlightenment. For it is not an accomplishment, but a project in the making. In this context the project of critique is a never-ending task, a 'permanent critique of ourselves' in our autonomy (1997b: 313).

If critique as 'ethos' is a 'permanent creation of ourselves', then the subject also refuses to be captured by governmental regimes that determine us. Critique therefore is marked by a refusal of what we are, a refusal of being governed by power. The question is to liberate ourselves from the state and its apparatuses and the type of subjectivation they produce. Liberation therefore should start with the relation through which we constitute ourselves. It is the relation to ourselves that is important. 'Perhaps the target nowadays is not to discover what we are but to refuse what we are' (Foucault 1982: 785). But refusal in the name of what? Foucault calls this 'political spirituality' to indicate forms of transformation and change. Importantly, however, the 'spirituality' at issue here is not to be confused with its Christian or religious associations. Rather, it 'entails faith in Enlightenment' (Foucault 1997a: 319) rather than denying it.

Referring to a set of exercises, practices, and experiences, political spirituality is 'what enables the subject to have access to the truth' (Foucault 1991b: 14), to refuse to being ruled by power—and become something that it is not. In this sense political spirituality is intimately connected to truth telling—*parrhesia* as an agonistic activity, 'as a role'. Parrhesia is thus defined as follows: *fearlessly* speaking the truth as a means for criticising public politics and as a means for self-care. The parrhesiast develops itself not through its ability to 'dare to know' but as one who dares 'to act'. For Foucault, critique is 'the movement by which the subject gives himself the right to question truth on its effects of power and question power on its discourses of truth' (1997a: 32). Speaking the truth is 'never given to the subject by right' (Foucault 1991b: 17), but only when the subject takes a risk. To speak the truth, to criticise involves a certain risk: the risk of falling outside the policed partition of the sensible. The activity of truth telling, parrhesia, then, 'is linked to courage in the face of danger: it demands the courage to speak the truth in spite of some danger' (Foucault 2001: 18). Seen in this light, truth telling contributes to the creation of new subjectivities 'acceding to a certain mode of being and to the transformations' (Foucault 1991b: 14). That is, a political subject defined through acts and practices sustained by a simultaneous relationship to itself and to others. In other words, in the activity of truth telling the subject is constantly 'changed, shifted', opening up the politics for debate and continual transformation.

Critique and Subjectivity

Parrhesia is a 'spiritual exercise' (Foucault 2001: 165), an event that not only 'alters the rules of the game' but also shapes the critical relation between the subject and the society, between the self and truth. Parrhesia is as much about a public activity—a permanent critique of public institutions and politics—as it is a transformation in the subject's relation to truth and style of life. It is as much about a permanent critique of an external order or governance as it is about a creative constitution of the self. In this sense spirituality is an ability to link together the moment of parrhesia and care of the self. This is what Greeks called 'the kairos', the appropriate time to act or to make political interventions. For this reason, what defines political spirituality is the kairos, 'the decisive or crucial moment or opportunity' (Foucault 2001: 110), which is not only a question of 'perceiving' but also of 'seizing' the moment (Dillon 2008b). Thus, in the first place, kairos signifies a decision to seize the moment of becoming, which can be grasped by a strategic decision. However, referring to the temporal dimension of the event, kairos is not only about a strategic, rational act. 'While one seizes the moment, one must also be seized by the moment' (Diken 2012: 35–6). That is to say, an 'intoxicating' component that results from being 'seized' by the moment lives in every moment of revolutionary subject. Kairos is a revolutionary moment in which the rational subject meets the intoxicated subject. Intoxication and strategy are thus inextricably linked. In this sense kairos is a revolutionary time which creates one's ethos, the revolutionary ethos: being in the moment, one is created by the moment. What matters in kairos, therefore, is an interactive surface between 'seizing' and 'being seized'. Kairos is as much about the intoxicated subject as it is about a strategic, rational act; it is as much about the virtual as it is about the actual. Kairos is what mediates strategy with intoxication, the actual with the virtual.

The concept of kairos is opposed to a linear, determinist notion of time; it cannot be reduced to actual social space and chronological time. In every instance of a revolution, there emerges an element that is profoundly spiritual that cannot be reduced to the existing order, and which has no raison d'etre other than conflicts, confrontations, efforts at pure refusal. For the subject of revolution sees struggle and parrhesia—critique as truth telling—as duty. The practices of parrhesia thus offer an alternative manner of subject-formation without reference to any external order (such as the state, religion etc.). From parrhesia emerges a subject able to question its 'own ontological status' (Butler 2005: 23). From parrhesia emerges a subject as a relation to oneself, to becoming. Rather than a fixed object of study, subjectivity is, in other words, a process of becoming where being *old* oneself simply doesn't make any sense. When something new occurs, 'the self that awaited it is already dead, or the one that would await it has not yet arrived' (Deleuze & Guattari 1987: 199). In this sense political spirituality itself is to be considered as a state of becoming other than the present self. The intensive capacity of being seized by the moment and seizing the moment, is part of the dynamic subject's formation. The politics of subjectivity, when understood as a process of becoming, is close to the 'art of oneself that's the exact opposite of oneself' (Deleuze 1995: 115). It becomes manifest in one's ability to express oneself passionately and freely (see Semetsky 2003: 215). In this way, subjectivation brings something new to life, frees life 'from where it's trapped', creates 'lines of flight' (Semetsky 2003: 141). It creates a space, and thus a struggle with power, within which it is possible to make oneself thinkable in a different way—to become other than what you are. It breaks through the limits of the existing world and 'turns it back against himself so as to summon forth a new earth, a new people' (Deleuze & Guattari 1994: 99).

Perceiving truth telling as duty, subjectivity creates and invents alternative new possibilities and forms of life that are not reducible to the existing order. It is a rupture with the given order that leads to practices of emancipation. It is related to the future constellations of an event, to values to come. It is able to avoid being trapped in a vicious circle because it is free to break 'things open' (Deleuze 1995: 86). In short, it is through political spirituality that a subjectivity introduces himself into history and creates lines of flight, to carry out the necessary transformations on himself (Foucault 2005: 15). But spirituality here should be understood as a 'profane' concept, which contains within itself the possibility of its own self-critique. So, to reiterate, spirituality is not necessarily a religious experience according to which truth is opaque, but a 'profane illumination' (Benjamin 1979: 236)—that is, a kind of materialist epiphany irreducible to religious domain. Spirituality engages with intoxication and faith in a dialectical way.

To be sure, this understanding of spirituality, intersecting the care of the self with parrhesia, a self in a continuous practice of introspection with the courage of truth, is alien to neoliberal governance. For it reduces life to 'the spectral resilience of the living dead' (Dillon 2013: 129). For it is marked by non-events in which neutrality, ignorance, and institutionalised indifference are continuously (re)produced. In short, it is about the disappearance of the spiritual with respect to event. What makes political spirituality significant is not only its actualised forms and structures but also an infinite series of incorporeal events and singular expressions of force that have never been present (see Diken 2015a: 33–4), not only its actuality but also its potentiality at the level of singularities (Deleuze 1990: 19, 187). This is a point at which something new and different constantly emerges, as distinct from ordinary points. And crucially, this affirmation of the potentiality of transformation also entails the recognition of the virtual aspect of spirituality. The virtual aspect of spirituality, however, can never be fully actualised because it nurtures in its heart an 'irreducible' element (Foucault 2005: 264). Political spirituality is irreducible because it is an ever-present possibility.

In short, spirituality refers to a virtual dimension, or an infinite serious of singular potentialities, that cannot be reduced to the actually existing state of affairs. In this sense, the virtual side of political spirituality includes all potential worlds and their every potential to differ that coexists with the actual (Deleuze 1994: 81–2). After all, there is always a virtual potentiality which 'preserves itself as such in actuality' (Agamben 1999: 183). Political spirituality is valuable only insofar as its virtual aspect is not exhausted in existence, insofar as it remains 'inactual'. For 'inactuality' or the virtuality of spirituality is as real as its actuality.

But there is another dimension to political spirituality. Though political spirituality persists in the virtual, it nevertheless 'happens' within the actual existing world (Deleuze 1990: 24). Political spirituality can be a virtual potentiality but its varieties are also actualised in concrete historical situations. Political spirituality is the virtual because it refers to 'unknown' possibilities and subjectivities, while at the same time the actual because it also expresses itself in 'known', existing situations. Political spirituality is transcendent because it contains within itself virtual potentialities for change, but at the same time immanent because it has an actual existence. In short, spirituality can be thought of as a 'unity of multiplicities in which different conceptions signify actual diversification' (Diken 2012: 8). Political spirituality can thus be approached as the interaction between the virtual possibility of a new world and the concrete subjectivity and consequences of *this* world. It combines the reality of the existing order and unknown potentialities of challenges into the present. What matters, therefore, is the mediation between its virtual and actual components, which is precisely what gets lost in spiteful terrorism. Only on this basis can we able to invent new ways of conceiving time and temporality and create new perspectives on life and being, leading to revolutionary events.

Afterword
'There Is Another Turkey Out There': On the Gezi Revolt

Recall the moments in İstanbul, where a Turkish riot policeman attacked protesters with tear gas in an attempt to prevent them from gathering at Gezi Park, the last green area in Taksim Square. The police officer's rage was understandable, for in Taksim Gezi Park, we witnessed angry protesters who have turned Turkey upside down. What the Gezi revolt suggests is that the people of Turkey are no longer determined by the climate of fear and relations of power but determine the conditions that determine them. Thus Gezi Park signals the arrival of an era in which the politics of hope extinguishes the politics of fear.

Taksim Square, the heart of İstanbul's entertainment district known for its restaurants, shops and cafes, made a powerful setting for protesters' struggle. But in Taksim Gezi Park no one looked entertained. Rather the conservative/Islamist imperative to 'obey' ceased to exist and was replaced by genuinely angry and determined human beings who did not protest just against the cutting down of trees in Taksim Gezi Park and its redevelopment into a shopping mall, or the imposition of religious-conservative values such as restrictions on the sale and consumption of alcohol, the morning-after pill and abortion, or Erdoğan's religion/sectarian-based foreign policy, or the killing of 34 innocent Kurdish civilians in Roboski after a Turkish military air strike, but against Erdoğan himself. They put the authoritarianism of Erdoğan in the dock. As Gezi revolt has made clear, authoritarian neoliberal and Islamist policies and a fear of police state are insufficient answers to the question of how to govern a pluralistic society such as Turkey.

Specifically, what made Gezi revolt unexpected is the fact that it occurred at the hands of the people, who demanded freedom and justice. What we could and should learn from the revolt is that the people aren't powerless, indifferent, depotentialised; they have a choice. Insofar as there is inequality and repression, people have a right to revolt. Thus political spirituality is not far away. In this sense Gezi revolt is an example of political spirituality, an attempt at linking truth telling and subjectivity, a link which makes it possible for the participants to experience the actual reality in a transcendental perspective. The demonstrating masses acted within the perspective of virtual potentialities and at the same time created spaces (Gezi Park) that actualise these virtual possibilities. Refusing neoliberal Islam, which is embodied in the AKP, the revolt was political in the sense that it redefined the framework of politics rather than being content with the AKP's neoliberal and post-political interest negotiation—counterrevolution as bare repetition which produces the same non-events within a given framework.

Through the desire for refusal of consensus, of Islamic governance and its economic-governmental social regimes, a collective subject emerged, which articulated a set of 'practices of liberty' that constitute a 'way out' of the existing framework of post-political politics. The political subjects of Gezi did not want consensus; 'truth' mattered more. When they made themselves visible and audible to Erdoğan, and reminded him that it is his dividing and marginalising neoliberal-Islamic regime that *is* the problem, they spoke boldly the language of truth, articulated a sense of refusal of who it is that they do not want to be. Thus, they took a risk. Theirs was a struggle over and against what it is they have become, what it is that they do not want to be. In this sense, the demonstrating masses have changed the 'normal course' of the present, of time, with a view to bringing forth 'a new people', a new Turkey. The revolt occurred between the people of Turkey, who have been silent for a long time—'people, who are present in the world but absent from its meaning and decisions about its future' (Badiou 2012: 56).

Along the same lines, the temporality of Gezi was kairos, a 'seized' chronos, an undetermined period of time, the moment at which unthinkable becomes thinkable, impossible becomes possible. The revolt, above all, offered the people of Turkey a moment of decision, a choice: the revolt events or the status quo represented by the AKP. The occupying crowds seized the moment and were seized by the moment; they formed the moment and were formed by the moment. What we have witnessed is a resurgence of political will—a kind of revolutionary spirituality which is inextricably connected to the actual conditions as well as the virtual possibilities. As such, spaces such as Gezi Park were an indicator that the place of political spirituality is not reducible to the empirical space, for it mediates the actual conditions with the virtual world of potentialities. For this reason, one should never underestimate the political power of place, for it can become a space of critique, dissensus, and collective resistance to build new, potential worlds. The Gezi revolt has demonstrated that people can clearly use places to house political energy. Whereas the free movement of capital exists as an invisible abstraction, occupying a place is exceedingly concrete, a visible presence at 'the spaces of hope'. Instead of the market, or competition, the protesters depend upon cooperation; instead of reckless individuality, they rely upon collective solidarity. In this sense, Gezi revolt is an indication of how places are common grounds; they haunt the imaginations of people who can build a consciousness towards existence. The place is intimately connected to political spirituality. What's more, it is intimately connected to truth telling, where the people find the courage to refuse authority, seeing and speaking with regard to truth in the face of risk or danger. Parrhesia is what the demonstrating masses practised in the Gezi revolt. They fearlessly spoke the language of truth, and most importantly, they risked their life:

> When you accept the parrhesiastic game in which your own life is exposed, you are taking up a specific relationship to yourself: you risk death to tell the truth instead of reposing in the security of a life where the truth goes unspoken.
>
> (Foucault 2011: 17)

As such, parrhesia materialised in the demonstrating masses' will not to be ruled as such. Converting fear into courage, the occupying crowds 'undertook a passionate, even mad act, which also, as a disruptive force, enabled them to redefine themselves as citizens' (Diken 2015b: 96). In their parrhesiastic act, time was experienced intensively: in the tent city some kind of elemental process took place where the living fabric of life was transformed into the experimental commune. The Gezi revolt has transformed the place into a virtual centre in which new potentialities emerged. It was in the 'Gezi commune' that another world and the ideals of an emancipated Turkey were realised. And it was this commune which posed a real threat to the AKP. Erdoğan's authoritarian rule and police brutality against protesters in Gezi Park united many factions of Turkey—socialists, communists, Alevis, unions, Kemalists, Kurds, and members of the gay and transgender communities despite political, sectarian, ethnic, and social differences. There was incessant political debate. Gezi Park created an immense impetus for the intentional acting of a political subjectivity. Everything was shared, from space to beds and food. Developing a culture of dissent and confrontation, the protesters shared ideas/thoughts, avidly discussing them, mobilising a life around an idea. As a result, Gezi Park became an eventual space, microcosm of debate, a profusion of ideas, a site of encounters, which enabled the occupiers to organise a life around an idea in the service of a moment of awakening. Hence, their truth telling was an agonistic practice, a praxis, not a normative one.

What we've learned from the Gezi revolt is that the repressive neoliberal and Islamic regime of the AKP is not the only alternative—in short, the realisation that there is an alternative. Before Gezi, one couldn't even imagine an alternative to Erdoğan and the hegemony of the AKP. This appeared to represent the restriction and curtailment of human consciousness and political imagination implied by Fukuyama's 'end of history'. As a result, Turkey has become a country in which people can easily imagine the end of the world but not that of the AKP. But the Gezi revolt has shown that we can now at least imagine new political possibilities. That is to say, the revolt has finally managed to break the 13-year stronghold of the AKP's authoritarian/Islamist neoliberalism that has been placed on the people's thoughts and imagination. In this sense, the Gezi revolt possesses a gleam of hope for the people of Turkey who have been living in a generalised counterrevolution since the 1980 military coup. This is what makes the Gezi revolt a revolutionary becoming.

The Gezi revolt and the alternative political possibilities it has revealed may yet prove to be a catalyst for radical structural change. That is not the point. The Gezi revolt is a turning point in modern Turkish history, not because it succeeded in putting the AKP's neoliberal and Islamic regime at the centre of debate, which so recently seemed the only game in town, but also because it has illustrated how political engagement with the actual conditions can create new possibilities, the event.

The Gezi revolt caused the people of Turkey to think change might be possible. That realisation should deepen and enrich them. Thus, we should begin to imagine and experiment with what is possible. After all, freedom is valuable insofar as it can mean experimenting with the link between what exists and what happens. In this sense, Gezi must not be reduced to its consequences, allowing its virtual aspects to disappear into actual conditions. After all, the virtual aspect of the event bears no relationship with the existing order. The Gezi revolt materialises the becoming of a people without prophets, connected up to a people to come.

References

Agamben, G. (1998) *Homo Sacer: Sovereign Power and Bare Life*, Stanford, CA: Stanford University Press.
Agamben, G. (1999) *Potentialities: Collected Essays in Philosophy*, Stanford, CA: Stanford University Press.
Agamben, G. (2001) 'Security and Terror', *Theory & Event* 5(4), The Johns Hopkins University Press. Retrieved November 29, 2015, from Project MUSE database.
Agamben, G. (2005) *State of Exception*, Chicago: University of Chicago Press.
Agamben, G. (2011) *The Kingdom and the Glory*, Stanford, CA: Stanford University Press.
Agnew, J. (1994) 'The Territorial Trap: The Geographical Assumptions of International Relations Theory', *Review of International Political Economy* 1: 53–80.
Agnew, J. (2005) 'Sovereignty Regimes', *Annals of the Association of American Geographers* 95(2): 437–461.
Agnew, J. and Corbridge, S. (1995) *Mastering Space: Hegemony, Territory and International Political Economy*, London: Routledge.
Agre, P. (2001) 'Imagining the Next War: Infrastructural Warfare and the Conditions of Democracy', *Radical Urban Theory*, http://polaris.gseis.ucla.edu/pagre/war.html
Ahmed, S. (2004) *Cultural Politics of Emotion*, Edinburgh: Edinburgh University Press.
Amin, A., Massey, D. and Thrift, N.J. (2000) *Cities for All the People Not the Few*, Bristol: Policy Press.
Amoore, L. (2006) 'Biometric Borders: Governing Mobilities in the War on Terror', *Political Geography* 25: 336–351.
Amoore, L. (2013) *The Politics of Possibility: Risk and Security Beyond Probability*, Durham: Duke University Press.
Appadurai, A. (1996) *Modernity At Large: Cultural Dimensions of Globalization*, Minneapolis: University of Minnesota Press.
Aradau, C. and van Munster, R. (2007) 'Governing Terrorism through Risk: Taking Precautions, (un)Knowing the Future', *European Journal of International Relations* 13(1): 89–115.
Aradau, C., Lobo-Guerrero, L. and van Munster, R. (2008) 'Security, Technologies of Risk, and the Political: Guest Editors' Introduction', *Security Dialogue* 39(2–3): 147–154.

Aradau, C. and van Munster, R. (2008) 'Insuring Terrorism, Assuring Subjects, Ensuring Normality: The Politics of Risk After 9/11', *Alternatives* 33: 191–210.
Aradau, C. and van Munster, R. (2012) 'The Securitization of Catastrophic Events: Trauma, Enactment and Preparedness Exercises', *Alternatives: Global, Local, Political* 37(3): 227–239.
Aristotle. (1992) *The Politics*, London: Penguin Books.
Armstrong, A. (2011) 'Insolvent Futures / Bonds of Struggle', *Reclamations Journal* 4: 4–7.
Badiou, A. (2008) *The Meaning of Sarkozy*, London: Verso.
Badiou, A. (2009) *Logics of Worlds: Being and Event 2*, London: Continuum.
Badiou, A. (2012) *The Rebirth of History*, London: Verso.
Barber, B. (1984) *Strong Democracy: Participatory Politics for a New Age*, Los Angeles, CA: University of California Press.
Baudrillard, J. (1990) *Fatal Strategies*, Paris: Semiotext(e)/Pluto.
Baudrillard, J. (1993) *The Transparency of Evil*, London: Verso.
Baudrillard, J. (2003) *The Spirit of Terrorism*, London: Verso.
Bauman, Z. (1998) *Globalization: The Human Consequences*, New York: Columbia University Press.
Bauman, Z. (2000) *Liquid Modernity*, London: Polity.
Bauman, Z. (2004) *Wasted Lives: Modernity and Its Outcasts*, Cambridge: Polity Press.
Bauman, Z. (2008) *Does Ethics Have a Chance in a World of Consumers?*, Cambridge, MA: Harvard University Press.
Bauman, Z. (2010) 'Communism: A Postmortem? Two Decades On, Another Anniversary', *Thesis Eleven* 100: 128–140.
Bauman, Z. (2012) 'Fuels, Sparks and Fires: On Taking to the Streets', *Thesis Eleven* 109(1): 11–16.
BAVO. (2007) 'Introduction: Who's Afraid of Urban Politics', in BAVO (ed), *Urban Politics Now: Re-imagining Democracy in the Neoliberal City*, Rotterdam, London: NAi Publishers, pp. 6–11.
Bell, C. and Evans, B. (2010) 'Terrorism to Insurgency: Mapping the Post-Intervention Security Terrain', *Journal of Intervention and Statebuilding* 4(4): 371–390.
Benjamin, W. (1969) *Illuminations*, New York: Schonken Books.
Benjamin, W. (1979) *One-way Street and Other Writings*, London: Verso.
Benjamin, W. (1996) 'Capitalism as Religion', in M. Bullock and M.W. Jennings (eds), *Selected Writings Vol. 1 1913–1926*, Cambridge, MA: Harvard University Press, pp. 288–291.
Benjamin, W. (1999a) 'Critique of Violence', in M. Bullock and M.W. Jennings (eds), *Selected Writings Vol. 1 1913–1926*, Cambridge, MA: The Belknap Press of Harvard University Press, pp. 277–300.
Benjamin, W. (1999b) *[1927–1940] The Arcades Project*, Cambridge, MA: Belknap Press.
Benjamin, W. (2003) *Selected Writings Vol. 4 1938–1940*, Cambridge, MA: Harvard University Press.
Bentham, J. (1995) *The Panopticon Writings*, London: Verso.
Bigo, D. (2006) 'Protection: Security, Territory and Population', in J. Huymans, A. Dobson and R. Prokhovnik (eds), *The Politics of Protection: Sites of Insecurity and Political Agency*, London: Routledge, pp. 84–100.

Bigo, D. and Tsoukala, A. (2008) *Terror, Insecurity and Liberty: Illiberal Practices of Liberal Regimes After 9/11*, London: Routledge.
Bloch, E. (1988) *The Utopian Function of Art and Literature*, Cambridge, MA: The MIT Press.
Boltanski, L. (1999) *Distant Suffering: Morality, Media and Politics*, Cambridge: Cambridge University Press.
Boltanski, L. and Chiapello, E. (2005) *The New Spirit of Capitalism*, London: Verso.
Bonditti, P., Neal, A., Opitz, S. and Zebrowski, C. (2014) 'Genealogy', in C. Aradau, J. Huysmans, Andrew Neal and N. Voelkner (eds), *Critical Security Methods: New Frameworks for Analysis*, London: Routledge, pp. 159–188.
Bonta, M. and Protevi, J. (2004) *Deleuze and Geophilosophy: A Guide and Glossary*, Edinburgh: Edinburgh University Press.
Borch-Jacobsen, M. (1988) *The Freudian Subject*, Stanford: Stanford University Press.
Borch-Jacobsen, M. (1993) *The Emotional Tie: Psychoanalysis, Mimesis and Affect*, Stanford: Stanford University Press.
Bradley, A. (2010) 'The Theocracy to Come: Deconstruction, Auto-Immunity, Islam. In A. Bradley and P. Fletcher (eds), *The Politics to Come*, New York: Continuum, pp. 174–90.
Bradley, A. and Fletcher, P. (2010) 'The Politics to Come: A History of Futurity', in A. Bradley and P. Fletcher (eds), *The Politics to Come*, New York: Continuum, pp. 1–12.
Brenner, N. (2004) *New State Spaces: Urban Governance and the Rescaling of Statehood*, Oxford: Oxford University Press.
Brenner, N. and Elden, S. (2009) 'Henri Lefebvre on State, Space, Territory', *International Political Sociology* 3: 353–377.
Brighenti, A.M. (2010) 'On Territorology: Towards a General Science of Territory', *Theory, Culture & Society* 27(1): 52–72.
Brown, W. (2015) *Undoing the Demos: Neoliberalism's Stealth Revolution*, New York: Zone Books.
Bruce, B. (2007) 'Biopolitics and the Molecularization of Life', *Cultural Geographies* 14: 6–28.
Buchanan, I. (2008) 'Power, Theory and Praxis', in I. Buchanan and N. Thoburn (eds), *Deleuze and Politics*, Edinburgh: Edinburgh University Press, pp. 1–24.
Burke, J. (2015) 'Islamic State "Goes Global" with Paris Attacks', *The Guardian*, 14 November.
Butler, J. (2004) *Precarious Life: The Powers of Mourning and Violence*, London: Verso.
Butler, J. (2005) *Giving an Account of Oneself*, New York: Fordham University Press.
Caffentzis, G. (2011) 'The Student Loan Debt Abolition Movement in the U.S.', *Reclamations Journal* 4: 31–44.
Carver, T. (2002) 'Imagery/Writing, Imagination/Politics: Reading Marx through the Eighteenth Brumaire', in M. Cowling and J. Martin (eds), *Marx's Eighteenth Brumaire: (Post)modern Interpretations*, London: Pluto Press, pp. 113–128.
Chiesa, L. (2007) 'Pasolini and the Ugliness of Bodies', in L. Polezzi and C. Ross (eds), *In Corpore: Bodies in Post-unification Italy*, Madison and Teaneck: Fairleigh Dickinson University Press, pp. 208–227.

References

Clausewitz, K.V. (1993) *On War*, London: Everyman.
Coaffee, J., Wood, D.M. and Rogers, P. (2009) *The Everyday Resilience of the City*, London: Palgrave Macmillan.
Coats, F. (2015) 'Austerity: A Very Neoliberal Coup', http://leftproject.scot/2015/austerity-a-very-neoliberal-coup/
Collier, J.S. (2009) 'Topologies of Power: Foucault's Analysis of Political Government Beyond Governmentality', *Theory, Culture & Society* 26(6): 78–108.
Comaroff, J. (2007) 'Terror and Territory: Guantanamo and the Space of Contradiction', *Public Culture* 19(2): 581–405.
Connolly, W. (2002) *Identity/Difference: Democratic Negotiations of Political Paradox*, Minneapolis: University of Minnesota Press.
Connolly, W. (2005) *Pluralism*, Durham: Duke University Press.
Cowling, M. and Martin, J. (eds) (2002) *Marx's Eighteenth Brumaire: (Post) modern Interpretations*, London, Pluto Press.
Cox, K. (1991) 'Redefining "Territory"', *Political Geography Quarterly* 10: 5–7.
Critchley, S. (2007) *Infinitely Demanding: Ethics of Commitment, Politics of Resistance*, London: Verso.
Crouch, C. (2004) *Post-Democracy*, Cambridge: Polity.
Damasio, A. (1999) *The Feeling of What Happens: Body and Emotion in the Making of Consciousness*, New York: Harcourt Brace.
Damasio, A. (2003) *Looking for Spinoza: Joy, Sorrow and the Feeling Brain*, Orlando: Harcourt Inc.
Dardot, P. and Laval, C. (2013) *The New Way of the World: On Neoliberal Society*, London: Verso.
Davies, W. (2014) *The Limits of Neoliberalism: Authority, Sovereignty and the Logic of Competition*, London: Sage.
Dean, J. (2006) *Žižek's Politics*, New York: Routledge.
Dean, J. (2009) 'Politics without Politics', *Parallax* 15(3): 20–36.
Dean, J. (2010) 'Drive as the Structure of Biopolitics: Economy, Sovereignty, and Capture', *Krisis: A Journal for Contemporary Philosophy* 2: 2–15.
Dean, M. (1999) *Governmentality: Power and Rule in Modern Society*, London: Sage.
Debrix, F. (2015) 'Topologies of Vulnerability and the Proliferation of Camp Life', *Environment and Planning D: Society and Space* 33: 444–459, doi:10.1068/d13089p.
Debrix, F. and Barder, A.D. (2009) 'Nothing to Fear But Fear: Governmentality and the Biopolitical Production of Terror', *International Political Sociology* 3: 398–413.
Deleuze, G. (1983) *Nietzsche & Philosophy*, New York: Columbia University Press.
Deleuze, G. (1990) *Logic of Sense*, New York: Columbia University Press.
Deleuze, G. (1992) *Expressionism in Philosophy: Spinoza*, New York: Zone.
Deleuze, G. (1994) *Difference & Repetition*, London: The Athlone Press.
Deleuze, G. (1995) *Negotiations*, New York: Columbia University Press.
Deleuze, G. (2006) *Two Regimes of Madness. Texts and Interviews 1975–1995*, New York: Semiotex(e).
Deleuze, G. and Guattari, F. (1983) *Anti-Oedipus: Capitalism and Schizophrenia*, Minneapolis: University of Minnesota Press.

Deleuze, G. and Guattari, F. (1987) *A Thousand Plateaus: Capitalism and Schizophrenia II*, Minneapolis: University of Minnesota Press.
Deleuze, G. and Guattari, F. (1994) *What Is Philosophy?*, London: Verso.
DeLillo, D. (2001) 'In the Ruins of the Future', *The Guardian*, 22 December.
Derrida, J. (1994) *Specters of Marx: The States of the Debt, the Work of Mourning and the New International*, London: Routledge.
Dershowitz, A. (2002) *Why Terrorism Works: Understanding the Threat, Responding to the Challenge*, New Haven: Yale University Press.
Dienst, R. (2011) *The Bonds of Debt*, London: Verso.
Dienst, R. (2014) 'Where Are You When You Are in Debt?', *The New Reader*, 1(1): 1–13.
Dienstag, J.F. (2015) 'Evils of Representation: Werewolves, Pessimism, and Realism in Europa and Melancholia', *Theory & Event* 18(2), The Johns Hopkins University Press. Retrieved November 30, 2015, from Project MUSE database.
Dikeç, M. (2007) *Badlands of the Republic: Space, Politics and French Urban Policy*, Oxford: Blackwell.
Diken, B. (2009) *Nihilism*, London: Routledge.
Diken, B. (2012) *Revolt, Revolution, Critique: The Paradox of Society*, London: Routledge.
Diken, B. (2015a) 'Political Spirituality: The Devils, Possession, and Truth-Telling', *Cultural Politics* 11(1): 18–35.
Diken, B. (2015b) *God, Politics, Economy: Social Theory and the Paradoxes of Religion*, London: Routledge.
Diken, B. and Laustsen, C.B. (2005) *The Culture of Exception: Sociology Facing the Camp*, London: Routledge.
Dillon, M. (1996) *Politics of Security*, London: Routledge.
Dillon, M. (2002) 'Network Society, Network Centric Warfare and the State of Emergency', *Theory, Culture & Society* 19(4): 71–79.
Dillon, M. (2007) 'Governing Terror: The State of Emergency of Biopolitical Emergence', *International Political Sociology* 1(1): 7–28.
Dillon, M. (2008a) 'Underwriting Security', *Security Dialogue* 39(2–3): 309–332.
Dillon, M. (2008b) 'Lethal Freedom: Divine Violence and the Machiavellian Moment', *Theory & Event* 11(2), The Johns Hopkins University Press. Retrieved November 30, 2015, from Project MUSE database.
Dillon, M. (2011) 'Specters of Biopolitics: Finitude, Eschaton, and Katechon', *The South Atlantic Quarterly* 110(3): 780–792.
Dillon, M. (2013) 'Afterlife: Living Death to Political Spirituality', *Millennium - Journal of International Studies* 42(1): 114–134.
Dillon, M. and Lobo-Guerrero, L. (2008) 'Biopolitics of Security in the 21st Century: An Introduction', *Review of International Studies* 34(2): 265–292.
Dillon, M. and Reid, J. (2001) 'Global Liberal Governance: Biopolitics, Security and War', *Millennium - Journal of International Studies* 30(1): 41–66.
Dillon, M. and Reid, J. (2009) *The Liberal Way of War: Killing to Make Life Live*, London: Routledge.
Dreyfus, H.L. and Rabinow, P. (1982) *Michel Foucault: Beyond Structuralism and Hermeneutics*, Chicago: University of Chicago Press.
Duffield, M. (2011) 'Total War as Environmental Terror: Linking Liberalism, Resilience, and the Bunker', *The South Atlantic Quarterly* 110(3): 757–769.

Eagleton, T. (2012) 'Religion for Atheists by Alain de Botton', *Guardian Review*, 14 January.
Eagleton, T. (2014) 'Terry Eagleton Reviews Trouble in Paradise and Absolute Recoil by Slavoj Žižek', *The Guardian*, 12 November.
Elden, S. (2007) 'Terror and Territory', *Antipode* 39: 821–845.
Elden, S. (2009) *Terror and Territory: The Spatial Extent of Sovereignty*, Minneapolis: University of Minnesota Press.
Elden, S. (2010) 'Land, Terrain, Territory', *Progress in Human Geography* 34(6): 799–817.
Elden, S. (2013) *The Birth of Territory*, Chicago: University of Chicago Press.
Enzensberger, H.M. (2005) 'The Radical Loser', www.signandsight.com/features/493.html
Evans, B. (2010) 'Terror in All Eventuality', *Theory & Event* 13(3), The Johns Hopkins University Press. Retrieved November 29, 2015, from Project MUSE database.
Evans, B. (2013) *Liberal Terror*, Cambridge: Polity.
Evans, B. & Hardt, M. (2010) 'Barbarians to Savages: Liberal War Inside and Out', *Theory & Event* 13(3), The Johns Hopkins University Press. Retrieved November 29, 2015, from Project MUSE database.
Evans, B. and Reid, J. (2014) *Resilient Life: The Art of Living Dangerously*, Cambridge: Polity.
Foucault, M. (1977) *Discipline and Punish: The Birth of the Prison*, London: Penguin.
Foucault, M. (1980) 'The Confession of the Flesh', in C. Gordon (ed), *Power/Knowledge: Selected Interviews and Other Writings 1972–1977*, New York: Pantheon Books, pp. 194–228.
Foucault, M. (1982) 'The Subject and Power', *Critical Inquiry* 8(4): 777–795.
Foucault, M. (1984) 'Nietzsche, Genealogy, History', in P. Rabinow (ed), *The Foucault Reader*, London: Penguin, pp. 76–100.
Foucault, M. (1991a) 'Governmentality', in G. Burchell, C. Gordon and P. Miller (eds), *The Foucault Effect*, Chicago: University of Chicago Press, pp. 87–104.
Foucault, M. (1991b) *Remarks on Marx*, New York, Semiotex(e).
Foucault, M. (1997a) 'What Is Enlightenment?' in P. Rabinow (ed), *Ethics: Subjectivity and Truth*, London: Penguin, pp. 303–319.
Foucault, M. (1997b) 'What Is Critique?', in S. Lotringer and L. Hochroth (eds), *The Politics of Truth*, New York: Semiotex(e), pp. 41–81.
Foucault, M. (1998) *The History of Sexuality Vol. 1: The Will to Knowledge*, London: Penguin Books.
Foucault, M. (2001) *Fearless Speech*, Los Angeles, CA: Semiotex(e).
Foucault, M. (2003) *Society Must Be Defended*, London: Penguin.
Foucault, M. (2005) 'Is It Useless to Revolt?', in J. Afary and K.B. Anderson (eds), *Foucault and the Iranian Revolution*, Chicago: University of Chicago Press, pp. 263–267.
Foucault, M. (2007) *Security, Territory, Population: Lectures at the Collège de France, 1977–1978*, New York: Palgrave Macmillan.
Foucault, M. (2008) *The Birth of Biopolitics: Lectures at the Collège de France, 1978–1979*, New York: Palgrave Macmillan.
Foucault, M. (2011) *The Courage of Truth: Lectures at the Collège De France 1983–43*, London: Macmillan.

Fukuyama, F. (1992) *The End of History and the Last Man*, New York: Free Press.
Fumagalli, A. and Lucarelli, S. (2015) 'Finance, Austerity and Commonfare', *Theory, Culture & Society* 32: 51–65, doi:10.1177/0263276415597771.
Furedi, F. (2005) *Politics of Fear, Beyond Left and Right*, London: Continuum.
Gill, S. (1995) 'The Global Panopticon? The Neoliberal State, Economic Life, and Democratic Surveillance', *Alternatives: Global, Local, Political* 20(1): 1–49.
Glaser, E. (2012) 'Eliane Glaser on Why People Act Against their Best Interests', *G2*, 31 March.
Glasman, M. (2014) 'This Is a Battle for Civilisation. . . the UK Cannot Remain Neutral', www.dailymail.co.uk/debate/article-2720948/MAURICE-GLASMAN-This-battle-civilisation-UK-remain-neutral.html
Goodchild, P. (1996) *Deleuze & Guattari: An Introduction to the Politics of Desire*, London: Sage.
Goodchild, P. (2010) 'Economics of Promise: On Casear and Christ', in A. Bradley and P. Fletcher (eds), *The Politics to Come*, New York: Continuum, pp. 141–160.
Graeber, D. (2011) *Debt: The First 5,000 Years*, Brooklyn, NY: Melville House.
Graham, S. (2010) *Cities Under Siege: The New Military Urbanism*, London: Verso.
Graham, S. (2012) 'When Life Itself Is War: On the Urbanization of Military and Security Doctrine', *International Journal of Urban and Regional Research* 36(1): 136–155.
Graham, S. (ed) (2004) *Cities, War and Terrorism*, Malden, MA: Blackwell.
Graham, S. and Marvin, S. (2001) *Splintering Urbanism: Networked Infrastructures, Technological Mobility and the Urban Condition*, London: Routledge.
Gregory, D. (2006) 'The Black Flag: Guantanamo Bay and the Space of Exception', *Geografiska Annaler: Series B, Human Geography* 88(4): 405–427.
Guardian Editorial. (2011) 'Europe: The Rise of the Technocracy', *The Guardian*, 14 November.
Guilli, B. (2013) 'A Second Innocence: Deactivating the Debt Machine', *Reviews in Cultural Theory*, 4(2): 51–55, www.reviewsinculture.com/?r=121
Habermas, J. (1996) *Between Facts and Norms: Contributions to a Discourse Theory of Law and Democracy*, Cambridge, MA: The MIT Press.
Hacking, I. (1995) *Rewriting the Soul: Multiple Personality and the Sciences of Memory*, Princeton: Princeton University Press.
Hamacher, W. (2002) 'Guilt History: Benjamin's Sketch "Capitalism as Religion"', *Diacritics* 32(3–4): 81–106.
Hardt, M. and Negri, A. (2000) *Empire*, Cambridge: Harvard University Press.
Hardt, M. and Negri, A. (2004) *Multitude*, London: Hamish Hamilton.
Harvey, D. (1990) *The Condition of Postmodernity: An Enquiry into the Origins of Cultural Change*, London: Blackwell.
Harvey, D. (2003) *The New Imperialism*, Oxford: Oxford University Press.
Harvey, D. (2005) *A Brief History of Neoliberalism*, Oxford: Oxford University Press.
Herbert, S. (2007) '"The Battle of Seattle" Revisited: Or, Seven Views of a Protest Zoning State', *Political Geography* 26(5): 601–619.
Hess, H. (2003) 'Like Zealots and Romans: Terrorism and Empire in the 21st Century', *Crime, Law & Social Change* 39: 339–357.

Hoelzl, M. (2010) 'Before the Anti-Christ Is Revealed: On the Katechontic Structure of Messianic Time', in A. Bradley and P. Fletcher (eds), *The Politics to Come*, New York: Continuum, pp. 98–110.
Hoffman, B. (1995) '"Holy Terror": The Implications of Terrorism Motivated by a Religious Imperative', *Studies in Conflict and Terrorism* 18(4): 271–284.
Honig, B. (1994) *Political Theory and the Displacement of Politics*, Ithaca, NY: Cornell University.
Human Rights Watch. (1997) 'Torture and Mistreatment in Pre-Trial Detention by Anti-Terror Police', www.unhcr.org/refworld/publisher,HRW,,TUR, 3ae6a7dd4,0.html
Isin, E. (2004) 'The Neurotic Citizen', *Citizenship Studies* 8(3): 217–235.
Jameson, F. (2003) 'Future City', *New Left Review* 21: 65–79.
Jessop, B. (2002) 'The Political Scene and the Politics of Representation: Periodizing Class Struggle and the State in The Eighteenth Brumaire', in M. Cowling and J. Martin (eds), *Marx's Eighteenth Brumaire: (Post)modern Interpretations*, London: Pluto Press, pp. 179–194.
Jones, C. (2015) 'Lawfare and the Juridification of Late Modern War', *Progress in Human Geography* 1–19. doi:10.1177/0309132515572270.
Jones, J. (2005) 'The Pasolini Code', *G2*, 24 November.
Kelly, T. (2009) 'The UN Committee Against Torture: Human Rights Monitoring and the Legal Recognition of Torture', *Human Rights Quarterly* 31(3): 777–800.
Kelly, T. (2011) 'The Cause of Human Rights: Doubts about Torture, Law and Ethics at the United Nations', *Journal of the Royal Anthropological Institute* 17(4): 728–744.
Kordela, A.K. (2011) '(Psychoanalytic) Biopolitics and BioRacism', *Umbra (a): A Journal of the Unconscious*: 11–24.
Krugman, P. (2015) 'Disaster in Europe', *New York Times*, 12 July.
Laclau, E. and Mouffe, C. (1985) *Hegemony and Socialist Strategy*, London: Verso.
Langbein, J.H. (2006) *Torture and the Law of Proof: Europe and England in the Ancien Regime*, Chicago: University of Chicago Press.
Lavin, C. (2005) 'Postliberal Agency in Marx's Brumaire', *Rethinking Marxism* 17(3): 439–454.
Lazzarato, M. (2009) 'Neoliberalism in Action Inequality, Insecurity and the Reconstitution of the Social', *Theory, Culture & Society* 26(6): 109–113.
Lazzarato, M. (2011) *The Making of the Indebted Man*, Cambridge: Semiotex(e).
Lefebvre, H. (1976) 'Reflections on the Politics of Space', *Antipode* 8: 30–37.
Lefebvre, H. (1991) *The Production of Space*, Malden, MA: Blackwell.
Luban, D. (2005) 'Liberalism, Torture, and the Ticking Bomb', *Virginia Law Review* 91: 1425–1461.
Lyon, D. (2001) *Surveillance Society: Monitoring Everyday Life*, Buckingham: Open University Press.
Lyon, D. (2003) *Surveillance After September 11*, Cambridge: Polity Press.
Mannori, L. and Sordi, B. (2009) 'Science of Administration and Administrative Law', in H. Hofmann, P. Grossi and D. Canale (eds), *A Treatise of Legal Philosophy and General Jurisprudence*, New York: Springer, pp. 225–261.
Mansbridge, J., Bohman, J., Chambers, S., Estlund, D., Føllesdal, A., Fung, A. Lafont, C., Manin, B. and Martí, J.L. (2010) 'The Place of Self-Interest and the Role of Power in Deliberative Democracy', *Journal of Political Philosophy* 18: 64–100.

Margulies, J. (2004) 'A Prison Beyond the Law', *Virginia Quarterly Review* 80(4): 37–55.
Martell, L. (2011) 'A Future for the Graduate without a Future', http://brightgreen.org/2012/08/11/a-future-for-the-graduate-without-a-future/
Martin, J. (2002) 'Performing Politics: Class, Ideology and Discourse', in M. Cowling and J. Martin (eds), *Marx's Eighteenth Brumaire: (Post)modern Interpretations*, London, Pluto Press, pp 129–142.
Marx, K. (1844) 'Comments on James Mill', www.marxists.org/archive/marx/works/1844/james-mill/
Marx, K. (1850) 'The Class Struggles in France, 1840 to 1850', in *Marx-Engels Collected Works 10*, London: Lawrence & Wishart, www.marxists.org/archive/marx/works/download/pdf/Class_Struggles_in_France.pdf.
Marx, K. (1970) *Economic and Philosophic Manuscripts of 1844*, London: Lawrence & Wishart.
Marx, K. (1973) *Grundrisse*, Harmondsworth: Penguin.
Marx, K. (1976) *Capital: Vol. 1*, Harmondsworth: Penguin.
Marx, K. (1986) 'The Rule of the Pretorians', in *Marx-Engels Collected Works Vol. 15*, New York: International Publishers, pp. 464–467.
Marx, K. (1852/2002) *The Eighteenth Brumaire of Louis Bonaparte*, London: Pluto Press.
Marx, K. and Engels, F. (1970) *The German Ideology*, New York: International Publishers.
Mason, P. (2012) 'The Graduates of 2012 Will Survive Only in the Cracks of Our Economy', *The Guardian*, 2 July.
Massumi, B. (1993) *The Politics of Everyday Fear*, Minneapolis: University of Minnesota Press.
Massumi, B. (1998) 'Requiem for Our Prospective Dead: Toward a Participatory Critique of Capitalist Power', in E. Kaufman and K.J. Heller (eds), *Deleuze and Guattari: New Mappings in Politics, Philosophy*, Minneapolis: University of Minnesota Press, pp. 40–64.
Massumi, B. (2002) *Parables for the Virtual: Movement, Affect and Sensation*, Durham, NC: Duke University Press.
Massumi, B. (2005) 'The Future Birth of an Affective Fact. Conference Proceedings: Genealogies of Biopolitics', http://browse.reticular.info/text/collected/massumi.pdf
Massumi, B. (2007) 'Potential Politics and the Primacy of Preemption', *Theory & Event* 10(2), The Johns Hopkins University Press. Retrieved November 30, 2015, from Project MUSE database.
Massumi, B. (2011) 'The Half-Life of Disaster', *The Guardian*, 15 April.
Mbembe, A. (2001) *On the Postcolony*, Berkeley: University of California Press.
McGreal, C. (2010) 'Bush on Torture: Waterboarding Helped Prevent Attacks on London', *The Guardian*, 9 November.
Mellor, P.A. and Shilling, C. (1997) *Re-forming the Body: Religion, Community and Modernity*, London: Sage.
Miller, J.A. (1987) 'Jeremy Bentham's Panoptic Device', *October* 41: 3–29.
Misselwitz, P. and Weizman, E. (2003) 'Military Operations as Urban Planning', in A. Franke (ed) *Territories*, Berlin: KW Institute for Contemporary Art, pp. 272–275.
Mouffe, C. (1996) 'Democracy, Power, and the Political', in S. Benhabib (ed), *Democracy and Difference: Contesting the Boundaries of the Political*, Princeton: Princeton University Press, pp. 245–256.

Mouffe, C. (2000) *The Democratic Paradox*, London: Verso.
Mouffe, C. (2005) *On the Political*, London: Routledge.
Neocleous, M. (2008) *Critique of Security*, Edinburgh: Edinburgh University Press.
Neocleous, M. (2014) *War Power, Police Power*, Edinburgh: Edinburgh University Press.
Netz, R. (2004) *Barbed Wire: An Ecology of Modernity*, Middletown: Wesleyan University Press.
Ngai, S. (2005) *Ugly Feelings*, Cambridge, MA: Harvard University Press.
Nietzsche, F. (1954) 'Homer's Contest', in W. Kauffman (ed), *The Portable Nietzsche*, New York: The Viking Press, pp. 32–39.
Nietzsche, F. (1961) *Thus Spoke Zarathustra*, Penguin: London.
Nietzsche, F. (1967a) *The Will to Power*, New York: Vintage.
Nietzsche, F. (1967b) *The Birth of Tragedy*, New York: Random House.
Nietzsche, F. (1986) *Human, All Too Human*, Cambridge: Cambridge University Press.
Nietzsche, F. (1990) *Beyond Good and Evil*, London: Penguin.
Nietzsche, F. (1991) 'On the Uses and Disadvantages of History for Life', in D. Breazeale (ed), *Untimely Meditations*, Cambridge: Cambridge University Press, pp. 59–123.
Nietzsche, F. (1996) *On the Genealogy of Morals*, London: Oxford University Press.
Nietzsche, F. (2001) *The Gay Science*, Cambridge: Cambridge University Press.
Nietzsche, F. (2005) *The Anti-Christ, Ecce Homo, Twilight of the Idols, and Other Writings*, Cambridge: Cambridge University Press.
Nietzsche, N. (1989) *On the Genealogy of Morals and Ecce Homo*, New York: Vintage Books.
Obama, B. (2014) 'ISIS Has No Place in the 21st Century', *National Journal*, August 20.
Patton, P. (2000) *Deleuze and the Political*, London: Routledge.
Pugliese, J. (2013) *State Violence and the Execution of Law*, London: Routledge.
Rancière, J. (1999) *Disagreement: Politics and Philosophy*, Minneapolis: University of Minnesota Press.
Rancière, J. (2001) 'Ten Theses on Politics', *Theory and Event* 5(3): 1–21.
Rancière, J. (2004) *The Philosopher and His Poor*, Durham: Duke University Press.
Rancière, J. (2007) *On the Shores of Politics*, London: Verso.
Rancière, J. (2010) *Dissensus*, New York: Continuum.
Rawls, J. (1996) *Political Liberalism*, Columbia: Columbia University Press.
Read, J. (2008) 'The Age of Cynicism: Deleuze and Guattari on the Production of Subjectivity in Capitalism', in I. Buchanan and N. Thoburn (eds), *Deleuze and Politics*, Edinburgh: Edinburgh University Press, pp. 139–159.
Read, J. (2012) 'Starting from Year Zero: Occupy Wall Street and the Transformations of the Socio-Political', www.unemployednegativity.com/2012/02/starting-from-year-zero-occupy-wall.html
Reginster, B. (1997) 'Nietzsche on Ressentiment and Valuation', *Philosophy and Phenomenological Research* 57(2): 281–305.
Reid-Henry, S. (2007) 'Exceptional Sovereignty? Guantanamo Bay and the Re-Colonial Present' *Antipode* 39(4): 627–648.

Reid, J. (2003) 'Foucault on Clausewitz: Conceptualizing the Relationship between War and Power', *Alternatives: Global, Local, Political* 28: 1–28.
Reid, J. (2005) 'Immanent War, Immaterial Terror', http://multitudes.samizdat.net/Immanent-war-immaterial-terror
Reid, J. (2010a) 'Of Nomadic Unities: Gilles Deleuze on the Nature of Sovereignty', *Journal of International Relations and Development* 13: 405–428.
Reid, J. (2010b) 'The Biopoliticization of Humanitarianism: From Saving Bare Life to Securing the Biohuman in Post-Interventionary Societies', *Journal of Intervention and Statebuilding* 4(4): 391–411.
Reid, J. (2012) 'The Disastrous and Politically Debased Subject of Resilience', *Development Dialogue* 58: 67–79.
Retort. (2005) *Afflicted Powers: Capital and Spectacle in a New Age of War*, London: Verso.
Riquelme, J.P. (1980) 'The Eighteenth Brumaire of Karl Marx as Symbolic Action', *History and Theory* 19(1): 58–72.
Rose, N. (1996) 'Governing "Advanced" Liberal Democracies', in A. Barry, T. Osborne and N. Rose (eds), *Foucault and Political Reason*, London: UCL Press, pp. 37–64.
Rose, N. (1999) *Powers of Freedom: Reframing Political Thought*, Cambridge: Cambridge University Press.
Rose, N. (2007) *The Politics of Life Itself*, Princeton: Princeton University Press.
Ross, A. (2014) 'You Are Not a Loan: A Debtors Movement', *Culture Unbound: Journal of Current Cultural Research* 6(1): 179–188.
Rumsfeld, D. (2002) 'DoD News Briefing – Secretary Rumsfeld and Gen. Myers', U.S. Department of Defense, www.defense.gov/transcripts/transcript.aspx?transcriptid=2636
Sassen, S. (1996) *Losing Control? Sovereignty in an Age of Globalization*, New York: Columbia University Press.
Schmitt, C. (1985) *Political Theology: Four Chapters on the Concept of Sovereignty*, Cambridge, MA: The MIT Press.
Schmitt, C. (2003) *The Nomos of the Earth in the International Law of Jus Publicum Europaeum*, New York: Telos.
Schulz, B. (2014) 'The Guilt Cult of Capitalism Versus the Debt of the Living: Walter Benjamin on Schuld and Redemption', *Studies in Social & Political Thought* 23: 24–31.
Scott, C. (2009) *The Art of Not Being Governed: An Anarchist History of Upland Southeast Asia*, New Haven, London: Yale University Press.
Sedgwick, E. (2003) *Touching Feeling: Affect, Pedagogy, Performativity*, Durham: Duke University Press.
Semetsky, I. (2003) 'The Problematics of Human Subjectivity: Gilles Deleuze and the Deweyan Legacy', *Studies in Philosophy and Education* 22(3): 211–225.
Shaviro, S. (2012) 'Melancholia, or, The Romantic Anti-Sublime', *Sequence*, 1.1, http://reframe.sussex.ac.uk/sequence/files/2012/12/MELANCHOLIA-or-The-Romantic-Anti-Sublime-SEQUENCE-1.1-2012-Steven-Shaviro.pdf
Sloterdijk, P. (2010) *Rage and Time: A Psychopolitical Investigation*, New York: Columbia University Press.
Soja, E.W. (1989) *Postmodern Geographies: The Reassertion of Space in Critical Social Theory*, London: Verso.

Sparke, M. (2005) *In the Space of Theory: Postfoundational Geographies of the Nation-State*, Minneapolis: University of Minnesota Press.
Springer, S. (2015) *Violent Neoliberalism*, New York: Palgrave Macmillan.
Stallbrass, J. (2006) 'Spectacle and Terror', *New Left Review* 37: 87–106.
Stavrakakis, Y. (2007) 'Antinomies of Space: From the Representation of Politics to a Topology of the Political', in Bavo (ed), *Urban Politics Now: Re-imagining Democracy in the Neoliberal City*, Rotterdam, London: NAi Publishers, pp. 142–161.
Stengers, I. (2000) *The Invention of Modern Science, Theory Out of Bounds, Vol. 19*, Minneapolis: University of Minnesota Press.
Swyngedouw, E. (2009a) 'The Antinomies of the Postpolitical City: In Search of a Democratic Politics of Environmental Production', *International Journal of Urban and Regional Research* 33(3): 601–620.
Swyngedouw, E. (2009b) 'The Zero-Ground of Politics: Musings on the Postpolitical City', *NewGeographies* 1(1): 52–61.
Taşkale, A.R. (2011) 'Margins of Nihilism/Nihilisms of the Margin: Social Theory Facing Nihilism', *Theory, Culture & Society* 28(2): 152–161.
Taubes, J. (2004) *The Political Theology of Paul*, Stanford, CA: Stanford University Press.
Taubes, J. (2009) *Occidental Eschatology*, Stanford, CA: Stanford University Press.
Taylor, F.W. (1947) *Scientific Management, Comprising Shop Management: The Principles of Scientific Management Testimony before the Special House Committee*, New York: Harper.
Thiele, L.P. (1990) 'The Agony of Politics: The Nietzschean Roots of Foucault's Thought', *The American Political Science Review* 84(3): 907–925.
Thoburn, N. (2003) *Deleuze, Marx, and Politics*, London: Routledge.
Thrift, N. (2007) *Non-Representational Theory: Space, Politics, Affect*, London: Routledge.
Tiedemann, R. (1983) 'Historical Materialism or Political Messianism? An Interpretation of the Theses "On the Concept of History"', *The Philosophical Forum* XV: 71–104.
Todorov, T. (2009) *Torture and the War on Terror*, London: Seagull Books.
Ulmer, D.K. and Schwartzburd, L. (1996) *Heart and Mind: The Practice of Cardiac Psychology*, Washington, DC: American Psychological Association.
Vatter, M. (2014) 'Foucault and Hayek: Republican Law and Civil Society', in V. Lemm and M. Vatter (eds), *The Government of Life: Foucault, Biopolitics, and Neoliberalism*, New York: Fordham University Press, pp. 163–186.
Virilio, P. (2002) *Ground Zero*, London: Verso.
Virno, P. (2004) *A Grammar of the Multitude: For an Analysis of Contemporary Forms of Life*, Cambridge, MA: Semiotext(e).
Warren, R. (2002) 'Situating the City and September 11th: Military Urban Doctrine, "Pop-Up" Armies and Spatial Chess', *International Journal of Urban and Regional Research* 26(3): 614–619.
Weaver, M. and Siddique, H. (2014) 'Outrage Over ISIS Beheading of US Journalist James Foley', *The Guardian*, 20 August.
Webster, F. and Robins, K. (1993) '"I'll Be Watching You": Comment on Sewell and Wilkinson', *Sociology* 27(2): 243–252.
Wilson, J. and Swyngedouw, E. (2014) *The Post-Political and Its Discontents: Spaces of Depoliticisation, Spectres of Radical Politics*, Edinburgh: Edinburgh University Press.

Younge, G. (2010) 'The Republicans Are Like Frat Boys in Animal House', *The Guardian*, 12 April.
Žižek, S. (1989) *The Sublime Object of Ideology*, London: Verso.
Žižek, S. (1997) *The Plague of Fantasies*, London: Verso.
Žižek, S. (1999) 'Carl Schmitt in the Age of Post-Politics', in C. Mouffe (ed), *The Challenge of Carl Schmitt*, London: Verso, pp. 18–37.
Žižek, S. (2001) *On Belief*, London: Routledge.
Žižek, S. (2002) *Welcome to the Desert of the Real*, London: Verso.
Žižek, S. (2006) *The Parallax View*, Cambridge, MA: The MIT Press.
Žižek, S. (2008a) *Violence*, London: Profile Books.
Žižek, S. (2008b) *In Defense of Lost Causes*, London: Verso.
Žižek, S. (2009) *First as Tragedy, then as Farce*, London: Verso.
Žižek, S. (2010) *Living in the End Times*, London: Verso.
Žižek, S. (2011) 'Shoplifters of the World Unite', *London Review of Books*, www.lrb.co.uk/2011/08/19/slavoj-zizek/shoplifters-of-the-world-unite
Žižek, S. (2012) *The Year of Dreaming Dangerously*, London: Verso.
Žižek, S. (2014) *Event: Philosophy in Transit*, London: Penguin.
Žižek, S. (2015a) 'This Is a Chance for Europe to Awaken', *New Statesman*, 6 July.
Žižek, S. (2015b) 'Are the Worst Really Full of Passionate Intensity?', *New Statesman*, 10 January.
Zupančič, A. (2003) *The Shortest Shadow: Nietzsche's Philosophy of the Two*, Cambridge, MA: The MIT Press.

Filmography

Pasolini, P.P. (1975) *Salò*, United Artists Corporation and Water Beaver Films.
Ramis, H. (1993) *Groundhog Day*, Columbia Pictures Corporation.

Index

9/11 28, 35, 42, 59, 110, 112, 118, 120, 126, 129, 150–1

Abu Ghraib 61–4
actual 5, 9, 14–16, 18, 20–1, 26, 39, 46, 52, 55, 60–1, 69, 73, 77, 90, 99–100, 102–3, 106, 108–11, 114, 118–19, 122, 124–5, 130, 134, 137, 139, 142–6, 148
actuality 16, 20, 69, 111, 143–4
affective logics 1, 8–9, 11–12, 33, 35, 37–9, 133
Agamben, Giorgio 29, 37, 42–4, 50, 56, 58, 62, 85, 118, 127, 144, 149
Agnew, John 49–50, 149
agon 3–6, 15, 160
agonism 3–4, 6–7, 15, 20, 31
Ankara 112, 121
antagonism 2–3, 7–10, 16, 25–6, 30–3, 39, 44–5, 81, 102, 112, 114–15, 122, 125, 130–1, 139
Anti-Christ 82, 156, 158
apocalypse 81–5, 93
Aradau, Claudia 29, 71, 112–13, 126–7, 149–51
Aristotle 100, 150
austerity 39–41, 152, 155

Badiou, Alain 1, 29, 35, 93, 114, 146, 150
bare life 62–3, 107, 149, 159
bare repetition 16, 19, 27–8, 33, 36, 44, 132, 136, 139, 146
Baudrillard, Jean 119, 125, 130, 150
Bauman, Zygmunt 1, 63, 78, 128, 135, 139, 150
becoming 13, 55, 65–6, 86, 90, 99–100, 107, 114, 117–18, 127–8, 135, 139, 142–3, 148

Benjamin, Walter 2, 13, 15–17, 21–2, 26–7, 30, 46, 81, 105, 133, 143, 150, 155, 159
Bentham, Jeremy 18, 70–2, 93, 150, 157
body without organs 53, 56, 65, 96
Boltanski & Chiapello 96, 139
Bonaparte, Louis 17, 21–7, 44, 157
Bonaparte, Napoléon 21, 25, 27
Bonapartism 17, 25, 30, 42, 44
Brown, Wendy 1, 75–6, 131, 151
Butler, Judith 61, 142, 151

capitalism as religion 105, 150, 155
capitalist accumulation 19, 100
capitalist axiomatic 97–8
catastrophe 22, 43, 83–4, 113–14, 117
catastrophic events 113–14, 150
circulation 29, 32, 38, 43, 49–50, 53, 66, 92, 95–8, 105, 111, 114, 116, 118, 135
Claire *(Melancholia)* 82–4
class struggle 26–7, 32–3, 156–7
Clausewitz 43, 152, 157
Collier, J. Collier 11–12, 79, 152
competition 18, 30, 42, 72–7, 99, 134–6, 146, 152
Connolly, William 3–4, 6–7, 152
contingency 49–52, 61–3, 67, 91–2, 111, 113, 126, 128, 133
counterrevolution 2, 7, 9–10, 15–17, 21–2, 26–8, 30, 33–4, 44, 46–7, 81, 84–5, 87–8, 113, 115–16, 126, 130, 134, 146, 148
cynical individual, the 19, 100–3
cynicism 10–11, 19–20, 29, 39, 94, 101–5, 109, 120, 135–6, 138, 158

Dardot & Laval 73, 77
Davies, Will 1, 10, 30, 74, 152

Index

Dean, Jodi 17, 34–9, 152
Dean, Mitchell 10, 152
Deleuze, Gilles 1, 8–9, 11–17, 19, 48, 50–8, 66, 93–9, 101, 104–5, 114, 117, 120, 124, 133, 137, 139, 143–4, 151–3, 155, 157–60
Deleuze & Guattari 14, 48, 50, 52–56, 66, 97, 101, 105, 143, 155
depoliticisation 33–4, 44, 161
Derrida, Jacques 140, 153
deterritorialisation 51, 53, 61, 98
dialectical perspective 15–16, 27
Dikeç, Mustafa 1, 153
Diken, Bülent 1, 11, 17, 27–9, 31, 125, 142–4, 147, 153
Dillon, Michael 10, 28–9, 43, 60, 68, 71, 76–8, 85–6, 88, 111, 113, 117, 126–8, 131, 142–3, 153
Dillon & Reid 10, 28–9, 43, 60, 71, 78, 86, 117
Discipline and Punish 11, 18, 67, 154
distribution of the sensible 32–3
'dividuals' 95, 98
drive 8, 25, 28, 36–8, 40, 78, 108, 128–30, 152

Eagleton, Terry 4, 124, 154
economics 1–2, 10, 18, 40, 155
Eighteenth Brumaire of Louis Bonaparte, The 17, 21–2, 26, 157
Elden, Stuart 29, 49–50, 63, 68, 151, 154
emergent life 127–8
enlightenment 120, 123, 141, 154
eschatological 67, 81–2, 86–8, 124–5, 134
eschaton 18, 85–7, 99, 101, 153
Euro crisis 39
European Union 39–40
Evans, Brad 10, 28–9, 37, 83, 85, 112–13, 115–16, 128, 150, 154
Evans & Reid 10, 28, 37, 83, 85, 112–13, 115
'event, the' 9–10, 12, 14, 29, 31, 67, 74, 80–92, 94, 99, 110–18, 134, 148

faith 6, 71, 77, 82, 101, 105, 120, 141, 143
farce 17, 22, 27–8, 30, 33–4, 36, 44, 46, 48, 161
fascism 2, 16, 59, 121
fearful subject 78–9, 83, 136
financialisation 41
finitude 19, 68, 85–6, 117, 131, 153

foreclosure 13, 32
Foucault, Michel 1, 9–11, 13–15, 17–18, 38, 43, 49–51, 56–7, 59, 67–71, 73–7, 80–1, 85, 88, 94–5, 99, 112, 114, 116, 129, 131, 133, 135, 138–44, 147, 152–5, 159–60
France 21–3, 26–7, 34, 154–5, 157
fundamentalism 122–3, 126, 129–30, 132, 136

genealogy 14, 58, 85, 151, 154, 158
Gezi Park 145–7
Gezi revolt 145–8
Graeber, David 30, 108, 155
Graham, Stephen 29, 42–3, 155
Greece 39–41
Groundhog Day 19, 138–9, 161
Guantánamo Bay 61, 155, 159
Guattari, Felix 14, 48, 50–7, 66, 96–8, 101, 105, 143, 152–3, 155, 157–8
guilt 16, 24, 40, 53, 56, 59, 105–6, 155, 159

Habermas, Jürgen 3, 155
Hardt, Michael 28–9, 61, 96, 119, 131, 135, 154–5
Hardt & Negri 28, 61, 96, 119, 131, 135
Harold, Ramis 19, 138
Harvey, David 1, 63, 96, 155
Hobbes 64, 74, 87, 93, 116
homo economicus 75–7, 79, 92, 101, 106–7, 134–5
homo sacer 149

immanence 43, 78, 96, 105
indifference 97, 119, 130, 132, 143
International Relations i, 12–13
intoxicated subject 142
intoxication 5–6, 142–3
Isis 121–3, 158, 161
Islam 19–20, 36, 121–6, 129–30, 145–8, 151
Islamic terrorism 19–20, 121–6, 129–30
Italy 41, 59, 151

Jameson, Fredric 28, 156
jihad 121–2, 129
jouissance 101, 123
Justine *(Melancholia)* 82–4

kairos 142, 146
katechon 18, 67, 81–2, 84–5, 87–8, 125, 134, 153, 156

katechontic 18, 67, 81, 84–5, 87–8, 125, 134, 156
kettling 18, 88–92

labour-power 98–9, 129
Lacan, Jacques 37, 41, 103
Laclau, Ernesto 3, 20, 156
Lazzarato, Maurizio 106–8, 156
Lefebvre, Henri 50, 63, 151, 156
Leviathan 74, 87, 116
'liberal peace' 131
liberal way of war 43, 60–1, 65, 116, 134, 153

Marx 1, 15–17, 21–7, 29–30, 44–6, 48, 54–5, 69, 77, 93, 95–9, 102, 107–8, 121, 140, 151–7
Marx and Engels 93, 96
Marxism 16, 140, 156
Massumi, Brian 78–9, 110, 112, 118–19, 121, 130, 157
Melancholia 82–4, 160
militarisation 1, 7, 22, 26, 29–30, 37–8, 42–4, 47, 79, 91
military urbanism 42, 155
moment of danger 16, 21, 27
money 84, 96–7, 99–100, 102, 105–7, 130
Mouffe, Chantal 1, 3, 20, 31–4, 156, 158, 161
multitude 68, 74, 78, 90, 93, 126, 155, 159–60

Negri, Antonio 28, 61, 96, 119, 131, 135, 155
Neocleous, Mark 60–1, 92, 131, 158
neoliberal control 94–7, 99, 101, 109, 111, 117–18, 120, 135–7
neoliberal governmentality 18, 67, 72, 78, 88, 134–5
neoliberalisation 7, 26
neoliberal Islam 146
Nietzsche 3–7, 13, 15, 17, 48, 53–4, 58, 101, 106, 122, 124, 133, 152, 154, 158–61
nihilism 59, 124, 129–30, 136, 153, 160
nomadism 52

Overman 4–5

panopticon 70–3, 77, 150, 155
Paris 17, 26, 53, 112, 121, 124, 150–1
parrhesia 20, 138, 140–3, 147

Party of Order 22, 34
Pasolini, Pier Paolo 18, 59, 62–5, 151, 156, 161
passive nihilism 124
peace 5, 45, 50, 60, 86, 90–1, 121–2, 131
police order 32–3, 45
political spirituality 20, 138–47, 153
post-democracy 32, 152
potentiality 7, 69–70, 81, 98–9, 111–14, 130, 143–4
pre-emption 80, 109, 112–13, 115–17, 135, 157
preemptive biopolitics 94, 109–10, 112–18, 120, 126
primitive society, the 53–4, 56–7
productive repetition 17, 27, 33, 36

radical critique 19, 133
radical nihilism 124, 136
radical politics 3, 7–8, 17, 33, 48, 52, 114, 133, 138, 140, 161
Rancière, Jacques 1, 25, 31–4, 158
Rechtsstaat 18, 73, 93
redemption 15–16, 56, 159
Reid, Julian 10, 14, 28–9, 37, 39, 43, 52, 54, 60–1, 71, 78, 83, 85–6, 112–13, 115, 117, 128, 153–4
religion 23, 104–6, 123, 130, 142, 145, 150, 153–5, 157
repetition 16–17, 19, 25, 27–8, 33, 36–7, 44, 132, 136, 139, 146, 152
Republic of Salò 59, 62–4
resilience 37, 143, 152, 154, 159
ressentiment 10–11, 16, 18, 35, 39, 48, 52, 54, 57–8, 62, 67, 78, 124, 133, 136, 159
reterritorialisation 51, 61
Rose, Nikolas 10, 29, 71, 80, 92, 159
rule of law 18, 24, 63, 73–5, 93

Salò 18, 59, 62–5, 161
Schmitt, Carl 44, 64, 74, 80–2, 85, 87, 159, 161
Shaviro, Steven 83, 160
Sloterdijk, Peter 123, 160
spite 1, 10–11, 19–20, 39, 62, 112, 119–27, 129–38, 141, 144, 147
spiteful terrorism 127, 129–30, 132, 136–7, 144
surplus-enjoyment 100–2, 104, 135–6
Suruç 112, 121
surveillance 29, 35–6, 71–2, 95, 116–17, 127, 135, 155–6

Index

Swyngedouw, Erik 11, 29, 31, 33, 45, 160–1
Syriza 39–40

Taşkale, Ali Rıza xiii–xiv, 29
Taubes, Jacob 82, 85, 124, 160
Taylor 71, 106, 160
territory 4, 18, 48–51, 61, 63, 67, 114, 133, 149–52, 154
theology 80, 82, 85, 105, 159–60
topologies of power 11–13, 152
topology 11–12, 39, 160
torture 18, 28–9, 56, 59–65, 68, 91, 134, 156–7, 160
tragedy 22, 27, 33, 44, 158, 161
Troika 39–40
truth telling 20, 141–3, 145, 147, 153
Turkey 65, 121, 145–8

unknown unknowns 110, 112, 135
untimely 13, 27, 158

Virilio, Paul 43, 160
Virno, Paolo 74, 98–9, 160
virtual 2, 13–14, 20, 29, 39, 54–5, 87–8, 92, 110–19, 124–5, 135, 142–4, 146–8, 157
virtuality 13, 20, 55, 87–8, 111, 144
Von Trier, Lars 82

war against terror 28, 63, 112, 125–7, 129–30
will to power 5–7, 15, 58, 158
Wilson & Swyngedouw 11, 31

Žižek, Slavoj 1, 16, 24, 27, 29, 31–5, 40, 42, 44–5, 83, 99–103, 105, 110, 126, 130–2, 152, 154, 161